DARE TO CHANGE:
How to Program Yourself for Success

by

Joe Alexander

A SIGNET BOOK

NEW AMERICAN LIBRARY

AUTHOR'S NOTE

The case histories in this book are real, but names and situations have been altered to protect the privacy of the persons concerned. Where surnames have been used, permission has been granted by the persons mentioned.

SIGNET TRADEMARK REG. U.S. PAT. OFF. AND FOREIGN COUNTRIES.
REGISTERED TRADEMARK—MARCA REGISTRADA
HECHO EN CHICAGO, U.S.A.

SIGNET, SIGNET CLASSIC, MENTOR, PLUME,
MERIDIAN AND NAL BOOKS
are published by New American Library,
1633 Broadway, New York, New York 10019

First Signet Printing, April, 1985

1 2 3 4 5 6 7 8 9

PRINTED IN THE UNITED STATES OF AMERICA

WIN THE GAME OF LIFE

—Rechannel your energies from what you think you should be to what you want to be.
—Manage stress and make it work for you.
—Discover how to overcome negative childhood conditioning.
—Stop procrastinating.
—Train yourself to ask the right questions.
—Be your own boss and set your own goals.
—Find out what you really want out of life and get it.

DARE TO CHANGE

JOE ALEXANDER changed his life at age fifty when he returned to college for a master's degree in interpersonal communications and trained for four years in group psychotherapy. He is the author of *A Winner's Workbook*, *Transactional Analysis for Executives*, and *Pathways to Successful Living* (a Success Motivation Institute cassette).

Self-Help Books from SIGNET and MENTOR

To Rowena . . .

*whose presence has been the "more" in my
life reaching back over forty-eight years*

Recent studies of the "fear of success," a fairly common syndrome, reveal that its likeliest cause is the parent's communication of fear that the child will not be able to master the tasks at hand. The child realizes simultaneously that (1) the task is considered important by the parent, and (2) the parent doubts that the child can do it unassisted. That individual establishes a life-long pattern of sabotaging his own successes whenever he is on the verge of real mastery.

—Marilyn Ferguson,
The Aquarian Conspiracy:
Personal and Social Transformation
in the 1980s

Contents

Acknowledgments   xi
Preface   xiii

**PART ONE: The Dynamics
of Human Programming**

1: Your Destiny Is Self-Determined   3
2: Coming to Grips with the Inner Saboteur   16
3: Looking Back to See Ahead   35
4: How to Be a Potent Person   51
5: Positive Thinking Is Not Enough   64
6: Self-Motivation—the Pathway to New Decisions   79
7: Getting On with It   89
8: Transition   102

**PART TWO: Making Your
New Programming Work for You**

9: Your Words Can Make or Break You   117
10: Positive Listening   132
11: Managing Your Mind   151
12: Friendly and Unfriendly Stress   164
13: How to Be Up on a Down Day   178
14: Permission to Prosper   194
15: Being Your Own Boss   207
16: Growing Up as You Grow Older   222

17: Handy Hints for Positive Action   238
     Appendix: Which Way Next?   258
     Glossary   261
     Notes   263
     Bibliography   266
     Index   269

Acknowledgments

This book began when I was born to a spunky woman on January 15, 1916, in St. Francis Hospital in San Francisco, California. I call her spunky because she was a suffragette, a pioneer in the ranks of women who have fought so long for equal rights. I never really understood her until I understood myself, and it was too late then to thank her for her three great gifts to me. I hope she knows how much I appreciate being given curiosity, determination, and the willingness to challenge life.

The great appreciation of my life is for Rowena, who has been my partner and my support for so many, many years.

Thanks to the psychologist whose name I've forgotten. When I talked about going back to college to earn a master's I said, "But I'll be fifty-two when I finish." His reply was, "How old will you be if you don't go back to college?" That was the turning point for me.

Neither Gordon Haiberg nor Donald Duns believed the old saying about the impossibility of teaching old dogs new tricks. They started me on the path to a greater realization of my life potential.

A special thanks to Eric Berne, Fritz Perls, and Carl Rogers for looking at human behavior in new ways and to all of those whose thinking and writing expanded the fields of transactional analysis, Gestalt therapy, and client-centered therapy.

My appreciation of Mary and Bob Goulding can be better expressed with a hug than in words. With much caring and patience over a two-year period they taught me the process of redecision therapy. Out of that experience came the redecisions I needed to become successful in my own eyes—doing the work I love to do and living the life with Rowena in the beauty of Pleasant Valley.

Susan Bagby's belief in what I say here added to the quality of her editing, and I am thankful for her help. Craig Caughlan encouraged me to get started and urged me on. Thanks also to Andrea Stein for her help in putting the final polish on the manuscript.

Two people gave me special help in its creation. Thanks to Lee Dunn for her careful editing of the chapter on stress, and to Ed Frost, whose assistance over the last few years has led to a friendship very special to me. Dave Toshikian's support came in an unusual way and was the catalyst for writing this book: A workshop titled ''A Process for Positive Living'' for him and his associates made me realize I had a potential book that demanded writing. The spark for these ideas came from the monthly articles I had written for over a year and a half for *Positive Living* magazine, and I am glad the people there let me bring my ideas to light in my own way.

Some of my information was gleaned from seminars, workshops, conversations and personal correspondence. For this material a special thanks to Donald M. Dible, Mark Victor Hansen, Austin M. Elliot, Dottie Walters, Jerry Buchanan, Stanley J. Woollams, Jim Elliot, Jules Archer, Jay van Andel, Rich De Vos, and Lay Levinson.

Acknowledgment is also due to all my peers, clients, and participants who taught me so much about human behavior in workshop classes and in the intimacy of one-to-one counseling.

And my appreciation for Lynn, Whitney, and Mark is beyond expression for letting me become their friend instead of merely their father.

Preface

This book is about discovery: my discovery that I could become the person I wanted to be and live my life the way I choose to live, and that I could have fun and be paid for it. In order to do that, I first had to learn how to become self-directed rather than other-directed. Most of the time I live by my own standards, but I am a part of the human network, and now when I do follow the standards of others, I know I do it as a matter of choice. I am free from the resentment and rebellion I had for so many years when I did things because I felt I "ought to" or "had to."

A part of my discovery was the realization that I could choose my destiny if I was willing to take the positive action necessary to achieve it. So many times in my life I had set out with high hopes and wild abandon only to end up later in boredom and even despair. Four times I embarked on careers with such enthusiasm that I would wind up being "somebody" by others' standards, only to end up restless and move on like an ancient knight in search of the Holy Grail. I learned to acquire material things, but they did not bring me happiness. I found I could be president of "this" or lieutenant governor of "that" but felt I was only "getting by." I seemed to be caught in a cyclical trap and felt doomed to make the same mistake over and over again. I wanted more out of life, but I didn't know what my "more" was.

About age fifty I began wondering. What will my life be like five years, ten years, from now? Will I still be going along with our family motto, 'Life's a struggle'? Will I find my enjoyment in my Golden Years? Finally, with Rowena's encouragement, I stopped everything. For a year I wrote and thought and went to every conceivable kind of group on the human potential movement. For the first time in my life I trusted myself to go with the river instead of against it.

Somewhere along the way I read *Games People Play*, the best-seller by Eric Berne, and it made so much sense to me that I became a trainee at the Sacramento Institute for Transactional Analysis. TA, a system of human behavior and communication, was specific and rational (in my view), and I could validate theory by my experience and observation of others. Wanting to know more about human behavior, I enrolled at the University of the Pacific to earn a master's degree in interpersonal communications, and concurrently began two years of training at the Western Institute for Group and Family Therapy and interned as a counselor at a family service agency.

Slowly, what "more" was began to take shape in my mind. I rediscovered many things from my childhood that I had lost when I put aside my toys to become a "man." I had forgotten the thrill of being alone, reading a book, and dreaming childlike fantasies. I had forgotten that I liked the feeling of importance I had when I could show the other kids how to do something. I had forgotten the ecstatic thrill I'd had when my mother praised one of the short stories I wrote when I was ten. Out of those rediscoveries I came to understand what my "more" was: It was to have a purpose and meaning in my life by teaching others what I had learned, and what I had seen others learn.

I do that now as a free-lance writer and a free-lance teacher leading workshops on constructive change. I am no longer anxious about "what comes next," because that, give or take the relatively small effects of fate, is up to me. Now, at sixty-eight, I am in my Golden Years, and they are golden because I decided I would make them that way and accept responsibility for doing so.

I have the "more" I want out of life and hope that this book will help you define and achieve the "more" you want for yourself.

PART ONE

The Dynamics of Human Programming

Chapter 1

Your Destiny
is Self-Determined

*You are the manager of your life. You
decide whether or not your life will be
other-directed or self-directed.*

Destiny, in the minds of many people, is an outside force that
irrevocably controls the direction of their lives. They feel
they must accept whatever life has in store for them. They
believe the message in the axiom "As the twig is bent so
grows the tree" so strongly not even the thought of constructive change in their lives seems futile. They grow up believing that if they just do the right things, go to school, get a
job, get married, then somehow, someway, happiness will
come to them.

But unless some crisis clears their vision of reality and they
accept self-responsibility, these kinds of people unfortunately
go through life just getting by, mere survivors who miss out
on the real joys of successful living. Their life-style is one of
"groping and coping" rather than achieving the well-being
that comes from a comfortable balance of winning in all
departments of life: work, family, friendships, and health.

*The reality is that most of us can be in charge of our
destinies through a personal policy of self-determination.*

3

Self-determination isn't easy. It requires a great deal of personal thought and work, but the rewards are great. Still, we often wonder why people aren't naturally able to manage their destinies. Why do we have to work at it? After all, in childhood most of us are taught that if we just do what we're told to do, we'll all grow up and happiness will magically come our way. Why isn't that really the way things work?

The reality is that most of us grew up in family environments that were more negative than positive. Our childhood development was distorted by casual put-downs (or not so casual put-downs), sarcasm, ridicule passed off as teasing, and even, in some cases, cruel and unusual physical punishment. That's why the names and numbers of so many people-helpers are listed in the Yellow Pages. That's why a multitude of people flock to self-help groups. That's why so many of our educational institutions offer a host of personal development courses that might be labeled "Self-Management Training." That's why about one and a half billion dollars per year are spent on Valium in this country.[1] And, finally, that's why depression is so common. Psychiatrist David D. Burns, a specialist in mood therapy, says, "In fact, depression is so widespread, it is considered the common cold of psychiatric disturbances."[2]

When life doesn't magically work out the way we think it should, we reinforce our disappointment by playing blame games. We often blame others—or circumstances—for our unhappy condition. Rather than face responsibility for our condition, we look to a Great Rescuer—a guru, an evangelist, a Pied Piper politician—to lead us out of the swamps of mediocrity or failure and the morass of depression.

This amounts to a negative aspect of reality. But the positive aspect of reality is that people can change and they do change when they have the desire, the willingness, and the necessary information and techniques to do so. We can lead *ourselves* out the morass; we can unlearn the myths that crippled our childhood development; we can find our own paths to successful living.

We can reprogram ourselves to live the life we want.

Reprogramming the human mind is basically the same process as reprogramming a computer. When computer results are not satisfactory, a new program is used or changes are made in the existing computer program. Programs, or software, tell a computer what to do, when to do it, and the way to do it. Your human software does the same for you. Think of your mind as a kind of human computer.

When information is fed into a computer, it is translated into zeros and ones. These numbers are then stored in an internal memory system or on tapes or disks. When the results of a particular program are desired, it is fed back into the computer and the numbers are translated back into written information—as print on the video display screen, in the text of a book, on paychecks, as business correspondence, or as instructions to a robot welding machine. These are only a few examples of a computer at work. The point is, barring malfunction, they give what they get. If the results don't meet expectations the program can be changed or rewritten.

Now lets take a look at the human computer. If you are not getting out of life what you want, the fault probably does not lie in the actual human computer, it probably lies in its programming—your programming. (I have qualified the statement with "probably" because there are humans whose human computer effectiveness is diminished by irrevocable damage or disease).

The major difference between you and a computer is that *you write your own program.* You make the decisions about your programming. Throughout this book you will be reading much more about human programming, particularly in Chapter 5, but this short list of steps will introduce you to human programming.

1. *Stimulus:* The situation or person that triggers a positive or negative response.
2. *Interpretation:* What this information means to you and what kinds of feelings are generated.

3. *Decision:* What you will do about this situation or person.
4. *Storage:* The filing of the thoughts and feelings connected with the stimulating experience in the internal memory system. You might even think of each brain cell as being similar to a microchip that holds the data, thoughts and feelings, concerning the originating stimulus.
5. *Response:* The habitual reaction when the appropriate key is punched to recall the stored information.

The importance of this analogy between the computer and the human computer is that in both cases, once the information has been recorded and stored the response becomes automatic. Over the years, the actual steps in the human programming process are forgotten but an automatic response to some stimulus becomes a habit. We become the creatures of our stimulus response system.

Fortunately, when we find our standard responses are not contributory to our well-being we can *change* our programming and make new decisions; we can respond the way we *choose* to respond rather than in conformance with our old programming.

Let's use Alice as an example. As a child, a garden snake slithered across the lawn in front of Alice and her mother. Alice's mother screeched, "Snake! Snake!" Her screams frightened Alice as much as the snake. Alice developed a phobia about snakes that made it almost impossible for her to enjoy nature. She gave up Girl Scouts to avoid going to camp, because she didn't like being teased by other kids about her fear of snakes. In junior high school, a kindly natural sciences teacher taught Alice how to tell a harmless snake from a dangerous one. Over a period of time she gave up her phobia. She made a new decision about snakes: "I can tell which snakes to be careful of, so I don't have to be afraid of all snakes anymore."

Of course, she didn't realize she was reprogramming. For her it came as a part of growing up. Many of us do that unconsciously and change our programming in the process of maturing. But when that does not happen, our childhood programming is replayed over and over and we can cripple our potential for living a productive life.

If you want to make constructive changes in your life, there are two important points to keep in mind. The first is that it will take time and determination. The second is that you have the power to make new decisions and to carry them out. If you have any doubt about that, talk to someone who has quit smoking, overcome obesity, or given up dependency on alcohol or drugs.

Unlike a computer, you can decide not to follow the feeling, thinking, and acting habits of the past. You can develop new habits. When Alice went through her reprogramming process to overcome her unreasonable fear of snakes, there were still many times when she automatically felt her panic rise. Yet she exercised her will until she formed new habits that made her comfortable about her ability to take care of herself. Soon she became competent and confident about being able to take care of herself. Developing competence and confidence are the two greatest gifts, you can give yourself as you develop your new programming for successful living.

Remember when you thought life would just magically work out? Well, you can work some magic in your life by putting total faith in believing: "I am responsible." *That* is the magic formula. But until the belief in your own responsibility becomes a commitment, no source of help can become much more than a psychological Band-Aid. You can change, but only when you want to. Thomas A. Harris, M.D., author of *I'm OK—You're OK*, suggests that people want to change only when they become bored, are hurt, and/or find a method that others have used to bring about constructive change in their lives.[3] If you are reading this book, then chances are that you sense that in some way you are not getting the results you want from your human computer. Chances are you want to change your programming. I hope it can help you decide to make that change.

This is the way it went in my life: I didn't start a serious search for a better method of managing my life till the experience of fifty years had brought me to the point of hurt and boredom. Then, and not until then, did I accept my responsibility to me and make the decision that enabled me to embark on the grandest period of my life. And in the process of reprogramming myself I encountered many others who have been able to do the same thing. For those readers who doubt that we can be masters of our destiny; here are some facts that have changed the thinking of some of the greatest skeptics of them all, the medical profession.

- Some people are able to lower their blood pressure by meditation or self-hypnosis.
- There are cases in which paralysis can be overcome through biofeedback training.
- Visual imagery has aided in the remission of cancer.
- Norman Cousins, editor, author, and lecturer, has spoken so convincingly in favor of humor and medicine that he is an adjunct professor at the School of Medicine, University of California at Los Angeles.

These examples are a powerful demonstration that the management of our minds can beneficially affect our health. If a person can overcome cancer, certainly it is possible for him to manage the mind to enhance well-being. Statistics are hard to come by concerning those who have rescued themselves from failure, mediocrity, loneliness, or the many phobias that block people from achieving their full potential for successful living. Over the years, hundreds of people have passed through my own life who refused to let their lives be marred by the negativity of their childhood programming. The case histories cited in this book are only a handful of examples.

One saying that was repeated over and over to me as a child was: "What man has done, man can do." Feminism motivated my mother in many ways, and I'm sure that "man" to her meant "mankind." Nevertheless, I say it now in a different way, more in tune with our times: *What others have done, you can do*. But only when you have the desire, when you have the willingness, and when you are willing to be responsible for your future. And that is the Truth, a truth that you can find for yourself.

SELF-TRUTH

Many believe they have the truth. I had to determine my own truth to make my life right, and my truth came only when I began to "know myself." The longer my pursuit of self-understanding (and that pursuit will continue as long as I can read and breathe), the more powerful my truth will become for me.

Your truth is that you alone are the determiner of your truth. Living by the truth of others can only lead to disillusion and frustration unless you have thought about that truth and willingly adopted it into your belief system.

"To be or not to be" may have been an appropriate question for Hamlet. It is not appropriate for me. My questions are: How to be? How do I comfortably survive today, caught in the crush between negative assumptions of my belief system and the reality of the world and my pragmatic observation of the people in that world? How much longer do I go on distorting the truth of my experience by seeing the world through the eyes of those who taught me to see it their way? How do I make sense out of a world whose dichotomies and paradoxes frequently make no sense to me?

MODEL OF PERSONALITY

The following visual model of personality will be helpful to you in understanding your life. It is meant, in a very simple way, to demonstrate how belief systems develop in a person and the conflict that can be programmed into the self during the early developmental years.

I Am

This is what you were at birth, your integrated experience, and what you are today. Whether or not you came into this world influenced by genetics, by the stars, or by the numbers, you have since become what you are now, the sum total of everything that has gone before.

I Ought to Be

At birth you immediately became the target for other people's expectations. Parents or surrogate parents, siblings, teachers, ministers, and significant others began shaping you to meet standards and values of their world.

I Want to Be

This is a mixture of I Am and I Ought to Be. It can be reasonable, rebellious, or autonomous (autonomy meaning personal objectivity in self-awareness). Being who you want to be is a matter of choice. To go passively along with the standards and values of others is one thing. It is quite another thing to examine those standards and values and evaluate them. Choosing to accept them can lead to a comfortable accommodation of them. To reject them objectively in a dispassionate letting-go leads to freedom. To rebel against them may provide the energy for other directions, but not necessarily freedom, because rebelliousness stays linked to its source; hate is as binding as love.

With the exception of those people who seem to have a natural permission to find a comfortable way in life, being who we want to be is a lifelong struggle. This struggle is complicated by constant exposure to the changing world outside of us and the inexorable internal metamorphosis as we are confronted with the reality that the world is not what we were led to believe it would be. Only by facing the conflict between other-values, and self-values can we choose who we

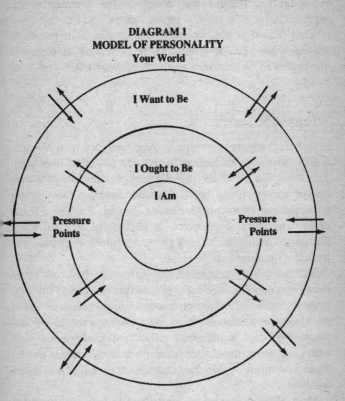

DIAGRAM 1
MODEL OF PERSONALITY
Your World

want to be and what we want to do, or, when the conflict is apparently inescapable, live graciously with it without negatively stressing our minds or bodies.

Your World

This is a personal rather than a global world. It includes the people and things visible in your environment. It also includes that unseen world of economics, politics, legislation, ethnicity, and religion that composes the commandments, representing a view of how people "ought" to be.

Your World is the totality of the system as it relates to the individual. The developmental tasks of adult development are generated by the interface between your I Am and Your World.

Pressure Points

Just as pressure develops a long time before a volcano erupts, so it is with humans. Crises do not erupt overnight. The straw that broke the camel's back was the last of a long line of straws. Being fired, divorced, having a heart attack are symptoms of long-neglected, or ignored, wants and needs of self or others. Fortunately, it is possible with sufficient self-understanding to identify or foresee pressure points, and to deal with those that do erupt.

This model of personality recognizes that for most of us there is an ongoing need for the resolution of internal conflict. Only a handful of people go through life continuously meeting the expectations of others with no apparent ill effects. Another handful is the small group, previously mentioned, who have that natural permission to enjoy themselves and be successful in life. When they do encounter conflict it is easily resolved.

Most of us, however, lie somewhere in between the group of survivors just getting by, and achievers who meet their own expectations but suffer dis-ease because they are not clear regarding their "wants" versus their "have tos." This group includes those who succeed by the norms of others, and those who meet the criteria of "normal mental health" but do not necessarily achieve the pleasure of positive living.

LIFE SCRIPTS

The roots of the turbulence encountered in establishing comfortable life directions lie in our childhood programming—a process involving the expectations projected on us and our decisions concerning those expectations. Combined, they constitute a life script, an unconscious plan that may positively or negatively affect the course of a life. It is similar to the script of a play and has elements of drama. On the stage and in life there are turning points that provide excitement and provoke emotions. Without such turning points a script soon plays to an empty house.

The key to deciphering a life script is the uncovering of early childhood decisions about survival. The only way infants and youngsters know how they are getting along is by the kind of attention they attract. They gradually learn which actions draw positive or negative reactions. If positive attention is not forthcoming, negative attention is invited. Hence the saying "Any strokes (attention) are better than no strokes." The deadliest environment of all for a child is one in which there is a poverty of attention. The subconscious question for the child is "How do I get my strokes around here?"

The answer to that question is one of the script decisions, made at a tender age, that influence the direction and quality of a life. Uncovering, examining, evaluating, and, when appropriate, changing those decisions is the key to unlocking a life script that might diminish the potential for self-determination.

CHILDHOOD PROGRAMMING

Turning points in adult growth arise when conflict develops between our illusions (based on childhood expectations and decisions) and the adult reality of our experience. When the "shoulds" and "oughts tos" in our belief systems disrupt the harmony of our lives, when our "wants" clash with the demands of our childhood programming, internal dissonance occurs. Unfortunately, when we are not aware of childhood programming, life scripts, or belief system, we fight desperately to regain our balance. We want to feel "good" and not feel "bad." We fall back on our childhood programming, believing that if we just do so and so we will be all right. We forget that most of our feelings (and you will be learning more about this later) are learned responses. When we dismiss these feelings as childish and resort to our supposed logic we may gain temporary respite, but this rarely results in beneficial change. We forget that feelings of guilt, irritation, anxiety, fear, self-pity, and the like have been repeated over and over since childhood and have become habits.

RECOGNIZING FEELING PATTERNS

Few of us have ever been told that we can change our feeling patterns and that unless negative feeling patterns are changed there is little likelihood that positive change will be made permanent.

Would you like an example? Maybe you are one of those who enjoys receiving a well-deserved compliment. At times you even extend yourself to earn recognition. Yet surely you've met people who brush away such compliments. Time after time in my management workshops I've heard people say, "I don't know what to do with this guy. He does a good job but when I compliment him he brushes it aside." People often do this because a compliment generates feelings of embarrassment or distrust and those are familiar feelings to them. In order to go on carrying out this familiar script, they turn aside any suggestion that they are capable or deserving. To accept a compliment comfortably they would have to change their feeling patterns and think of themselves as winners rather than losers, not as the victims they like to think they are. It is far easier to go on as before, carrying out the script of a victim.

Recognizing feeling patterns in yourself provides clues to the understanding of a script. The next step is to identify how such patterns develop in childhood so that you can independently determine whether or not a given current feeling is appropriate to the situation or merely a replay of an old tape.

One of the first steps in moving toward self-determination is to decide how you would rather feel in any given situation than the way you habitually feel when things don't go your way.

A great example today in America of a man who never let his feelings block his progress is Nido Qubein. He came here from the Middle East at age seventeen, with $50 in his pocket and could barely express himself in the English language. He knew what he wanted to do and set about doing it. In the next six years he put himself through junior college, college, and graduate school, where he earned an M.B.A.

As a new graduate in 1972, Nido went into the business of publishing books and producing cassettes on leadership. He now grosses about $1 million a year from sales and speaking and consulting fees. He is rated among the top three speakers in America, and among his clients are twenty international companies.

Nido says self-determination is both a choice and a personal responsibility. Successful living is available to all of those willing to ignore the bad feelings that can deter us when we listen to negative inner voices. The energy to reach our goals is generated through the self-confidence that comes from developing competence, learning from our mistakes and celebrating our victories. Successful living is not a born-again experience but something that arises from taking positive action, over and over again.

Chapter 2

Coming to Grips with the Inner Saboteur

The Inner Saboteur is the negative voice that urges us into self-defeating behavior. Listening to that voice often makes us our own worst enemy. Self-determination brings freedom from self-sabotage.

In my goals workshop, I show people how the Inner Saboteur works. When a participant says she or he has made a decision to change her or his life and to achieve certain goals, I ask: "This is what you want and you are willing to take the steps necessary to get what you want?"

The usual response: "Of course."

"Fine. Now, *according to your past performance*, how will you sabotage your future?"

Bingo. Up pops the devil, the Inner Saboteur. Some are so stunned they look at me blankly and say, "What do you mean?"

Most, though, say, "Wow. Is that the way it is?"

Yes. That is the way it is. It is not difficult to set sensible goals. Millions do it every New Year's Day. They just have never considered the darker side of their nature that harbors the Inner Saboteur.

Think of the Inner Saboteur as a sly character skulking around in the shadows of the mind, a forgotten voice that reflects long-forgotten childhood programming. Tracking down the messages behind that voice provides the information needed to counteract its negative influence, to prepare new programs for the human computer.

Unmasking the Inner Saboteur gives you the chance to challenge your opponent. It is the difference between shadow-boxing and climbing into the ring with another boxer. It is the difference between generality and specificity.

Jack would say to his wife, "I wish we didn't quarrel so when we go out to dinner."

On the defensive she'd say, "Well, quit complaining about the high cost of everything."

After a particularly bad evening she said, "That's it. I'm not eating out with you anymore."

Jack didn't want that. He earned good money and thought his wife deserved a break from cooking. They tried going out a few times after he promised not to say anything about the prices. That helped a little, but choking back his irritation resulted in an upset stomach.

One day she asked, "Do you act like this when you're out with a client?"

He didn't. He thought a lot about that and finally realized it was the situation, not the prices, that upset him. He could remember having the same feelings when he and his brother went to a restaurant with his parents. He wondered if it just had become a habit of getting irritated when eating out with his wife.

On a vacation visit to his parents he told them about the problem. His dad laughed. "I know how you got that habit. Mom used to say you kids needed to eat out once in a while, good for your manners. Times were tough. I'd tell her we could teach you manners at home. Then we would get to fussing at each other."

His mother said, "Business got better. You boys grew up.

Moved away. We eat out all the time now and Dad never gets upset.''

With that information Jack realized he had been reliving his childhood programming about eating out when he went to dinner with his wife. He changed his programming so that his Inner Saboteur could no longer spoil his fun. He set up a generous budget for dining out. Knowing his wife was not extravagant he trusted her to do the ordering and didn't look at the menu. He broke the habit of being irritated when he quit automatically reacting to feelings acquired in childhood.

Too simple? Who knows? Check yourself out. What is something you enjoy doing but often find ends in bad feelings? Ask yourself, ''According to my past performance, how will I sabotage myself from achieving my goals?'' Ask yourself this about any problem in your life that consistently reappears. A sure sign of the Inner Saboteur at work is behavior that results in bad feelings.

Once you have brought your Inner Saboteur into the open, you can consider plans and methods to acquire the competencies necessary to attain your goals. Think right now of one of your goals and ask yourself, ''According to my past performance, how will I sabotage myself?''

Another way to track down the messages from your Inner Saboteur is to imagine it is seated in a chair opposite you. Ask it questions like this:

- How did you creep into my life?
- If you have your way, how will my life go from now on?
- What decision on my part will help the most to overcome you?

You might want to change chairs and play the role of the Inner Saboteur. Think a bit and give voice to the negative messages you have in your belief system. Give the Inner Saboteur a voice and be aware of what is said.

The Inner Saboteur provokes the internal, and eternal, civil war between ''shoulds'' and ''should nots,'' between ''have

tos'' and ''choose tos,'' between ''I will'' and ''I won't.''
The Inner Saboteur controls a memory bank filled with negativity about self, situations, and others. It reflects childhood decisions to go along with negative expectations until they become a reality. When a bright little kid is called ''stupid'' enough times, he or she may decide the big people are right and go along with everyone by acting stupid and incorporating stupidity in his or her life script. All of this programming is then available for instant replay later in life whenever a situation arises that invites the Inner Saboteur to whisper, ''You can't do it, kid. You're not smart enough.''

CHILDHOOD PROGRAMMING

The integration of negativity into the self is the consequence of a childhood decision that is often a distortion of reality, but it seems realistic to the child. Once a young child decides on his or her self-image, the child develops thinking, acting, and feeling habits consistent with the decision. The negativity is incorporated in the belief system and reinforced by behavior and emotions that may not be logical in an adult frame of reference, but that ''make sense'' to a little kid needing attention and a feeling of approval that comes with living up to family expectations. In later life what made sense as a youngster clashes with the reality of life, but the Inner Saboteur inhibits the potential for constructive change.

DEFENSIVENESS AND PROJECTION

Defensiveness and projection are two of the most powerful tools the Inner Saboteur musters up in the effort to sabotage your best intentions. Defensiveness and projection are in your belief system because you used them as protective devices as a child. They protected you against the pain of criticism, the fear of rejection or abandonment, the shame of feeling inadequate. Maybe you remember saying things like "Brother did it" or "The teacher isn't any good." Children often feel that if they can assign blame to others or to circumstances, they won't be held responsible or won't lose any of their parents' love.

As they grow older, some realize through experience that making a mistake doesn't threaten the bond between them and their parents or other people who are important to them. In adulthood they are able to handle problems without denying responsibility for them. Those who do not learn this continue to defend themselves by posing as blameless or by projecting the blame on others or the world. *To ignore tendencies toward defensiveness and projection is an open invitation to your Inner Saboteur to work against your best self-interest.*

Defensiveness is not easily self-measured, but if you become upset or irritated frequently or easily let yourself feel hurt, you are probably reacting to some person out of your past rather than the person you are dealing with in the present. When you get those feelings in response to criticism, first check yourself out. What are the messages you have in your belief system about criticism? How did you react as a child when criticized? With that in mind, check the validity of the criticism. Is it valid or invalid? What are you willing to do about it, either way?

Whatever you do, don't brush it away. The unwillingness to hear and process criticism destroys marriages, wrecks careers, and alienates friends. Such unwillingness arises when parents demonstrate a lack of sensitivity to a child's feelings and a child's desire to please parents. When children perceive themselves as failing or when criticism and/or punishment are harsh, they become defensive. This trait is then carried forward into adult life. Few people are taught in school how to overcome their defensiveness; most never come to examine it until some severe problem has arisen in their lives. Understanding the childhood programming that triggers defensiveness is one of the most positive steps you can take in moving toward your goals.

Projection is an extreme form of defensiveness. Some children find criticism so painful to deal with that they refuse to accept their faults and instead project them on others, thereby transferring what they perceive as blame to others. "Mr. Perfect" is that way because he simply does not "own" his faults. Headline examples are the stories often seen in the newspapers about a self-righteous reformer who has been revealed as a practitioner of the vice he or she so strongly attacks.

Extreme defensiveness and projection are not easy to recognize in ourselves. The people in Alcoholics Anonymous have a saying that stimulates self-examination: "If you hear anything here that makes you mad, go home and look in the mirror." Think about it. You might open up the way to some of the most positive steps you could possibly take to getting more out of life. And while you're doing that, take it easy. Don't push yourself with the process of self-understanding. Intellectual awareness of defensiveness and projection is one thing, and understanding it on a personal level is another, but simply knowing about such psychological concepts may alert you as you move through your transition and provide you with a constructive learning opportunity.

Arnold

Arnold's family programmed him to believe he couldn't figure anything out for himself. When he did try to figure something out and made a mistake they said, "There you go again. Here. I'll have to do it for you." Arnold's decision whenever he tried something and didn't initially succeed was: "I'm stupid. I need help." Once the decision has been made he quit *really* trying and was willing for others to help him with everything. In time he became very clever at manipulating others but felt bad inside about himself; he felt he was being "dumb."

In his career, Arnold did well as an assistant manager, but

despite the fact that he did a good job of problem-solving when the boss was on vacation, Arnold avoided opportunities for promotion. Over the years this negative thinking about himself became quite distressful, but whenever he felt he wanted to change, the voice of his Inner Saboteur echoed in his mind—"You'll never make it." That negative thought was in conflict with the reality that Arnold had solved many business problems in the past by taking positive action.

Bored with his job, Arnold enrolled in some evening community college classes, and in a psychology class he took an intelligence test. He scored on the borderline of genius. It was a shattering experience for Arnold. He thought of all the opportunities he'd passed up in his career because of his negative belief system about himself. Feeling he had to know more about his potential as a manager, he went to an executive search service. The service felt he was eminently employable in a manager's position. Arnold's new decision was to recognize his competence and move to another firm.

His positive actions with the new firm have made him a successful manager. From time to time Arnold has the old feelings of low self-esteem but recognizes them as feelings not based on reality and soon gets over them. One of his positive actions was to find a reliable mentor and, when appropriate, bring in a professional helper, a management consultant, to help with some complex problems.

Of course, Arnold didn't do this overnight, but he persistently built a better image of himself each time he handled a problem of the kind he'd once avoided in the past. Had he known about the Inner Saboteur and how childhood programming can affect adult behavior, he might have accomplished his positive change earlier in life. Regardless, Arnold resolved what might have become an extremely intense pressure point.

Before

I Am: I am only good enough to be an assistant manager.

I Ought to Be: Topflight, even if I usually need someone to help me.

I Want to Be: Competent, respected, promoted.
The World: I've been in this company so long they see me
  only as an assistant manager.

After

I Am: I am intelligent and can solve problems.
I Ought to Be: No longer relevant.
I Want to Be: I will be a competent manager.
The World: My new employers respect my ability.

Keep in mind that this appears deceptively simple and logical in print. It is more difficult to describe the gradual change in Arnold's feeling patterns. For years he'd accepted mild feelings of depression about not being able to move up the corporate ladder. His luncheon buddies laughed when he complained and called him Old Dependable. His wife gave him sympathy and reminded him of the job security he had and the pension waiting at the end of the rainbow. When he changed to the new employers his friends were startled and his wife fearful. But Arnold knew what he was doing and went on despite their fears.

To use transactional-analysis terms, Arnold changed his "stroking pattern." He exchanged the sympathy he received for praise, and in the beginning that was uncomfortable for him. However, as he examined his past and accepted the many times he had demonstrated competence, he gradually let go of his negative thinking and filled that mental void with positive thinking until he became a full-fledged positive thinking/positive action person. Arnold had learned how to manage his feelings by himself and not be trapped by his Inner Saboteur.

GARBAGE IN—GARBAGE OUT

"Garbage in, garbage out" is a chiché in the electronic data processing business. It means that when a human makes an error in computer programming and the error is fed into the computer, the results will be erroneous. The same is true of the human computer. When it is fed inappropriate information the result is inappropriate action and/or inappropriate feelings. The potential of the human computer for making decisions and solving problems is diminished when it is fed garbage. And the negative information from the Inner Saboteur is garbage.

Symptoms of garbage are negative attitudes, actions, and feelings. Once the garbage has been "locked into" the childhood programming the child/youth/adult will continue to be the victim of the Inner Saboteur until, or unless, new decisions are made to free him or her from it.

John and Jim

Here's an example of two brothers whose choices in life directions were seriously affected by the garbage of their early programming. They grew up in a family where sarcasm was considered humor. They were constantly put down and discounted by their stepfather. Both developed deep feelings of inadequacy, but each made a different decision based on the principle of fight or flight. John, the older of the two, chose to fight back, talk back, be bold and aggressive, thereby cloaking his feelings of inadequacy. Jim, the younger, chose the route of flight, becoming very quiet and walking away from any unpleasant situation. Both passed up many chances for improvement because of the feelings of inadequacy they had come to accept as reality.

Ironically, that sense of inadequacy was the rankest form of garbage. In fact, both of them had ample intelligence to become whatever they chose to be. But their Inner Saboteurs, each in its own ways whether it was "fight" or "flight," did their dirty work. Jim used his inclination to fight to make a stand against the world. He had a successful career in law enforcement and in sales and is now a teacher. Jonn went along with the messages of inadequacy from his Inner Saboteur in the beginning years of his job. At that time he didn't see himself as having a career. Gradually as he went along doing the requirements of his work he recognized his creative ability and his competence in translating his thoughts into the design and development of new tools for experimental work. Now his company sees him as a well-respected technical expert and pays him far more than he had ever dreamed of earning.

Experience taught each of them reality: They were intelligent and could master new challenges. They recognized that the messages from their Inner Saboteurs were not consistent with their abilities. They both changed their childhood programming. Jim's changes were harshly made. When he realized his potential was greater than any job, he'd quit and then go through a tough struggle reestablishing himself in a new field. John quietly grew in his chosen field and moved up one step at a time.

Each made his life changes in his own way. This is important to everyone who wants to make constructive change in his or her life. There is no *one* way. There are many ways to overcome the influences of the Inner Saboteur. It is up to each person to chart their own path.

SELF-DETERMINATION

Self-determination is the capacity to make autonomous choices and exercise options appropriate to our lives as we want to live them. It means making choices free from the influence of the Inner Saboteur and untainted by garbage. It means living in accordance with our conscious choices of the present rather than reacting to the programming of the past. It means the clarification of values: the rejection, modification, and selection of those values we feel will be most fitting as we seek to live a satisfactory life. It means to be "inner-directed" rather than "other-directed," even though at times we may choose to go along with the values of others.

Few people will challenge the reality that they can change their behavior, their thinking, or their physical bodies. Millions go to work every day to engage in a form of behavior that might not be of first preference. Millions go to school every day and change their thinking in response to the belief that education will enhance their potential for earning money. Thousands more are voluntarily changing their bodies daily as they jog by roadsides or through the parks. All have made a choice and exercised an option in favor of change. All of this makes sense in their belief systems.

Unfortunately, their belief systems do not include recognition of the possibility that feelings and emotions too can be changed. They do not see feelings and emotions as learned habits that can be unlearned. But if you have any doubt about your ability to change your feelings, think of any time when you were angry at someone and the phone rang. You probably answered in a courteous manner, immediately setting aside your anger until the phone conversation ended. In other words, you decided that for one reason or another you would not direct your anger at a party not involved in the angry situation.

NATURAL RESPONSES

Fortunately the stress of constantly making choices is greatly eased by many responses that seem natural to us. Two types of natural responses are the way in which we automatically react to regain our balance when our physical equilibrium is disturbed, and the way in which we blink our eye when an insect flies too close. These are instinctive, natural responses that work automatically without the need for conscious data processing or decision making.

However, there are times when the natural response may not be favorable for us. An innocent bystander involved in a burst of gunfire between police and robbers could endanger his life when abruptly thrust out of the line of fire if he followed his natural inclination to maintain his balance and remain standing. The natural response of blinking an eye might be unfavorable while undergoing an eye examination.

CONDITIONED RESPONSES

Another set of responses is learned and is called the conditioned reflex. We smell a pie baking in the oven and our mouths water because as children we learned that an apple pie tastes sweet. We associate the delicious smell of the baking pie with satisfying an appetite for it, and therefore we salivate. A person raised in the country without apples or sweets would not make the same association and would not salivate. There are places in the world where the smell of a baking apple pie would not turn a single head.

PROGRAMMED RESPONSES

This reaction pattern is more complex. When Jon was very small his mother baked many apple pies and at first always gave him a small piece. Then she began to use a piece of pie as a reward or a punishment. She would say, "If you're a good boy today you get a piece of pie after dinner," or "You were a bad boy today so you don't get any pie tonight." She never announced her verdict until dinner had been eaten and it was time to cut the pie. Sometimes he would smell the pie all afternoon as its odor drifted through the house, but then felt anxious all through dinner wondering whether he'd be punished or rewarded.

Jon didn't understand what "good" and "bad" meant, and there were no clearly defined rules of conduct around the house. He had to guess whether or not he was pleasing his mother. In time he began to feel apprehensive whenever she began rummaging around the kitchen for the ingredients of a pie. It was painful to be continually wondering if he was "good" or "bad." In order to make sense out of his confusion, Jon decided his mother loved him on some days and gave him a piece of pie. On the days she didn't give him pie and said he was "bad" he felt she didn't love him. To him issues of conditional and/or unconditional love centered on dessert.

As a grown man Jon is decidedly overweight. He always has dessert with lunch and dinner. If his wife doesn't give him dessert he pouts. When he makes halfhearted efforts to diet he jokes, saying things like, "Gee, if you really loved me you'd give me just a little piece of pie."

The dynamics of his situation are these: His conditioned response to the smell of a baking pie is a watering mouth and hunger, a physical reflex. His programmed response concerns thoughts of being loved or unloved, a mental reaction. As an adult he has long since forgotten his decision about this situation and confuses his habitual anxiety reaction with something natural. He does not know he was responsible for the original decision and that by stuffing himself with sweets he avoids the feelings of anxiety and the thoughts of guilt. He has lost his power of autonomy in this situation and surrendered to his programmed reactions.

Stimulus: Dessert.

Interpretation: Dessert is a symbol of self-worth and love.

Decision: Eat dessert and feel worthwhile and loved while avoiding feelings of anxiety, guilt, and rejection.

Positive thinking: I work hard to earn my just reward.

Negative action: I refuse to lose weight despite a physician's warning that I should reduce and slow down.

Jon continued to let his emotions and feelings control his life, unaware that he was a victim of his thought process and that he could change that process. It never occurred to him that his childhood decision could be redecided. He never realized that his misinformation and inappropriate decision was the garbage in his programming, and like "garbage in, garbage out," his computer turned out results that were self-damaging. He'd never learned that with his mind he could reprogram his mental and physical responses in favor of his self-interest.

For Jon to make constructive change would require the use of his selectivity powers—his ability to make choices and exercise options, to make new decisions and take positive action to achieve the goal of improving his health and living longer.

His options are therefore continuing to eat excessive amounts of sweets, disregarding the doctor's warning, and having a heart attack; or changing his thinking/feeling habits regarding overeating.

Jon's efforts to diet always failed because he addressed the wrong problem. His Inner Saboteur led him to focus on symptoms (obesity) rather than causes (childhood programming and his belief system). His problem is not eating in itself, but how eating figured in his relationship with his mother and how it does the same with his wife. His "crooked" thinking precludes the possibility of the straight thinking and straight talking required for evaluating his self-esteem and communicating with his wife.

WHAT'S THE QUESTION?

Jon's problem is not uncommon. In an address to the Central States Speech Association in 1941, Dr. Coyne Campbell said that his patients showed one chief symptom: *They were unable to tell him clearly what was the matter.*[1] Gertrude Stein put it more simply. On her deathbed when asked, "What's the answer?" her response was, "What's the question?"

Either/Or

The reason the right questions don't get asked is that Inner Saboteur keeps us trapped in the "either/or" syndrome: We are either right or we are wrong. We are either a success or a failure. We are either good or bad. We are either happy or sad. We do not like the uncertainty of middle ground. As children we were not able to discriminate ourselves from the assumptions we made about ourselves. When Momma said, "You are bad," we assumed that we were bad, bad, bad—all the way through. That carried with it an implied threat of lost love or abandonment. So when we were good we tried to be very, very good, and overlook the point that on a scale of 1 (bad) to 10 (good) we might have only been a 7. How did that childhood poem go?

There was a little girl
Who had a little curl
Right in the middle of her forehead.
And when she was good
She was very, very good
But when she was bad, she was horrid.

As if

The "either/or" syndrome is an assumption treated "as if" it were an absolute. In our speech and thoughts we use words as the means of creating or reinforcing our illusions and assumptions about self. Because words are what we define them to be, they are imprecise in meaning, bending to the intent of the speaker or thinker. When Jon thinks of himself he pictures himself "as if" he were only a little chubby. His doctor pictures him as obese.

The principle of "as-ifness" is not new. Aristotle wrote about it. However, the principle of self-examination to expose "as-ifness" brings with it the obligation of self-responsibility, and that has never been a popular principle. The best tool chest the Inner Saboteur has ever been given is the set of labels coined by psychologists in their efforts to create a scientific language of human behavior. Terms like "neurotic," "inferiority complex," and "maladjusted" are handy in professional language, but they are very disturbing for anyone who is, or suspects he or she is, the target of them. They are "bad" words.

It is too bad we can't deal with psychologists and behavioral scientists as we do with automobile mechanics. There is no difficulty in saying, "I think the carburetor is a little out of whack. Maybe I need a tuneup?" How many of those who counsel others have ever had someone come in and say, "I think my mind is a little out of whack. Maybe I need a tuneup?" Only a few of the so-called "crazy" might say something like that, but even they are more likely to assign responsibility to an external force:

- My wife said to come in and see you.
- The judge said I'd better see a psychiatrist.
- My boss said I'd better do something.

A young woman who was doing a beautiful job of "messing up her life," by her definition, once said to me, "I think I've got the picture. I'm doing it to myself and I'm ready to change. But first, tell me, why did Christianity screw me over like it did?" When I said, "What do you think about that?" she stalked out and never came back. I'll never know what her Inner Saboteur said to her, but it was clear she was locked into a compulsive blame game and not yet ready for self-responsibility. The strong message from her Inner Saboteur was: "If it weren't for Christianity your life would be OK." Acting "as if" that were a valid message helped her avoid the pain of becoming a self-directed person.

SEMANTIC CONFUSION

Semantic confusion is a ripe field of garbage for the Inner Saboteur and derails many from getting on the track of positive action, leaving them faced with the many quandaries of life management. In *People in Quandaries*, Wendell Johnson wrote, "Quandaries, then, are rather like verbal cocoons in which individuals elaborately encase themselves, and from which, under circumstances common in our time, they do not tend to hatch."[2] Seeking to clarify the confusion of words, Johnson established three laws arising from his understanding of Aristotle's views:

1. The Laws of Identity: We talk and act *as if* things are what we say they are.
2. The Law of the Excluded Middle: Everything either is or it is not.
3. The Law of Noncontradiction: It is taken for granted that if something is one thing it cannot be another.[3]

For some this represents a form of logic that makes sense—that makes it possible to live by an imaginative self-concept that precludes evidence of reality. They say:

An inferiority complex is bad.
I am not bad.
Ergo, I do not have an inferiority complex.

For others, such simplistic thinking does not make sense. They ask questions, of themselves, and others, like "If I don't have an inferiority complex, how come I can't talk in front of a group?"

The first step in unraveling the latter kind of verbal cocoon is to rephrase the question according to unlogic: "How come I *won't* talk in front of a group?"

This kind of question brings a person face to face with his

or her Inner Saboteur, which insists on the use of non-responsible sabotage language: "I can" or "I can't" implies that some external force precludes the possibility of the desired action.

TWO BASIC WORDS OF SELF-RESPONSIBILITY

"I will" and "I won't" are the two basic statements of self-responsibility. Here's an example: a paraplegic says, "I can't exercise" and withers in a wheelchair, another says, "I will exercise and plays wheelchair basketball.

Switching to "I will" or "I won't" instead of "I can" or "I can't" opens up the door to the acquisition of the competencies needed to get all the things you want in life—when you are *willing* to get on with doing so, when you accept the reality of the negative influence your Inner Saboteur may be exercising on your life.

Here are three simple steps to take as you begin to dispel your Inner Saboteur's tool of "as-ifness" in your life:

1. Be aware of negative thoughts or bad feelings that are consistently connected with similar situations. In other words, what goes on over and over?
2. Think back about the times in your life this has happened before. If possible, connect these thoughts and feelings with appropriate childhood incidents.
3. Then ask yourself, "How do I want to think and/or feel in this situation now?"

Don't muck up this simple process with the garbage of precise analysis or what you've always considered "logical thinking." Don't rush it. With persistence the questions will come to mind automatically, so you needn't consciously force the process. Go about your business as usual and let your thoughts flow as they will. Trust the part of you that yearns for balance in your life to bring the answers you need. And when it seems appropriate, act on those things that make sense to you. Don't be afraid to take a few thoughtful risks as you do so. There is no such thing as mistake-free learning, but you can minimize the hazards by acting independently of your Inner Saboteur.

Bear in mind that one of the deadliest traps you face in your effort to make change is to succumb to the part of your belief system that says nothing less than perfection is acceptable. Love yourself for your courage and willingness to seek the rewards of becoming a self-directed person.

Chapter 3

Looking Back to
See Ahead

> *Knowing how we got where we are
> today can be the key to knowing where
> we will be tomorrow.*

Maybe the reason people respond unfavorably to clichés is
that they so often speak the truth.

- History repeats itself.
- Some people never learn from their mistakes.
- As the twig is bent, so grows the tree.

These are powerful statements because they arise from
people's experience in observing one another. Folk sayings
do not attempt to prove a theory; they simply report the facts
as people see them. They come from the wisdom of experience rather than from book learning.

What you can discover about your childhood programming
by looking back can help you greatly in your efforts to see
ahead. Eric Berne said, "Self-analysis is like giving oneself a
haircut; with sufficient practice it can be done."[1] Looking
back does not suggest the undertaking of a deep-seated attempt at psychoanalysis or a total preoccupation with one's

inner being. Nor is it wise to get lost in a "Why, why, why" trip.

The question is not why but how. How did I learn this so it is now a part of my belief system? How come I get irritated every time dinner is a little late? The why of that situation is meaningless. The how may be because your daddy did exactly that over and over again for all the years you lived under his roof and you've adopted it as standard operating procedure. That is a sample of a common situation/feeling pattern that a child may imitate and, in time, forget where or how it was learned. Once a child decides to follow a pattern, that pattern is applied to other similar situations, triggering irritation automatically whenever frustration is faced. The frustration/irritation pattern becomes a persistent part of the personality. The corresponding life-script theme might become "Why does this always happen to me?" and the major role played is that of martyr or victim.

My convictions about life scripts and childhood programming arise out of my own experience. At the age of 50, I looked back to discover the reasons behind having embarked on four challenging and interesting careers and, each time I reached the point of getting along fine, having quit. I always found some reason that I was in the wrong business and charged off into another, sure that I was on the right track. Finally tired of that, I stopped everything and gave myself a year to write, think, and explore the fields of the human potential movement. My only goal was to find out what my goals were, to find a way that work could be play if I could do what I *wanted* to do instead of what I felt I *had* to do.

During that first year of searching, my tutor was Dr. Gordon Haiberg, who, with W.R. Sefness and Eric Berne of *Games People Play* fame, had written an article titled "Destiny and Script Choices." The first time I heard him talk about it I was ecstatic. I had it. I knew it. Somehow just the thought of destiny's being self-determined made sense to me. It was also a little sickening to think that Mother had been so right when she'd said, "Sometimes you are your own worst enemy"—a pattern I had followed for half a century.

Haiberg made me want to know more. At that time, life-script theory had been more conjecture than theory. It was talked about at transactional analysis groups and journal pieces had been published, but no books on it had been published. I began my own research. My subject was me. As I studied my lifescript I began to see the way to my future life was as a student and teacher of human behavior. In the ensuing eleven years I've seen at least a hundred therapists work out their life scripts, I've helped probably three hundred students and clients work through theirs, and I've listened to at least a thousand or more people talk about scripts in workshops and classes.

Over and over again I've seen the startled look, the almost disbelief, when someone connects his or her grown-up feelings and actions with a long-forgotten childhood experience. Many of them have said, "I don't have to do that anymore." That is right. No one is condemned to hang on to a self-defeating life pattern arising from childhood decisions once he or she understands childhood programming and is willing to make new decisions and be responsible for his or her destiny.

THE LIFE SCRIPT QUESTIONNAIRE

The life script questionnaire is used by behavioral-change therapists to help people uncover their feeling patterns, along with the actions and attitudes accompanying those patterns. The purpose is to link old feelings and behaviors to current feelings and behaviors that will facilitate making new decisions and constructive change in the life plan. Because work is such an integral part of personality identity and life satisfaction, these questions are taken from a Career Script Check. The purpose of these questions is to open the doors of the unconscious mind and bring the hidden messages there into the light of your conscious mind. With this information, the next time you have a bad feeling and realize that it is the same feeling you had during a similar childhood situation, you can do something about it. You can decide to take action appropriate to the current situation. Analysis and insight alone rarely produce change. But if you add action, faith, and determination, the combination is unbeatable.

If you find you have difficulty remembering back beyond a certain age, do not be concerned. With some people the cellar doors of the mind are stuck more tightly than with others. Time and awareness will open them when you are willing to change. In twelve years of conducting workshops and counseling I've never encountered a person who might be considered "normal" who could not eventually recapture many childhood memories—once she or he was *willing* to do so. Just reading these questions, and thinking about them, can produce a great deal of useful information. There are many safe techniques for exploring the mind. Some of them will be described in detail later in the book.

The following questions will help you examine your own career and life script. You might want to have writing material handy so you can jot down any thoughts that come to mind that might be helpful in the future as you get on with getting more out of life.

1. How do you feel about your job or your career?

If you have anything less than good feelings, identify them. Are they boredom, futility, hopelessness, despair, panic, lack of confidence, anger, or some other? How long have you had these feelings? Have you ever had them before with other jobs? Did you have any of these same feelings while getting through school? Did you ever have these feelings as a child when assigned chores and tasks by parents, older siblings, teachers, or others?

Do any of these reactions and feelings describe the way
~ings were with you as a child?

- I can't do anything right around here. [Futility, hopelessness, despair, lack of confidence.]
- I don't want to be given away just because I can't make
  my bed right. [Panic, fear of abandonment, vulnerability
  to people in power.]
- You can make me do it but you can't tell me when.
  [Rebellion, anger.]
- Nobody appreciates me around here so I might as well
  run away. [Restlessness, fear of failure.]

Some, or all, of these feelings can bring people to react
~npulsively, taking actions not in their own best interest
~ithout realizing that they are surrendering control of their
~fe to archaic feelings. Others are so afraid of their feelings
~at they become desperate workaholics, believing if they just
~ork hard enough and please enough people they will be safe
~om abandonment (unemployment) or will look good by
~ving up to the expectations of others, even when it may be
~amaging to health, relationships, or family.

. Did your parents reflect pleasure in their working roles?
~hat kind of models were they?

One fellow who had changed jobs five times in fourteen
~ears reported, "I can still hear my dad saying it again: 'I
~ld them where to head in today'." Many women have a gap
~n their belief system here because they didn't have a working
~nother, and the only message they got was that a woman's
~lace is in the home.

~. What kind of feelings do you get when you have scored a
~uccess in your work?

The natural tendency is to say, "Great." If that is valid fo you, fine. Some people express other feelings. You may hav heard them:

"If it wasn't for the others I wouldn't have made it." Thi can be a straight message where cooperation was called for but it can also be a crooked message that says, "I fee uncomfortable when I get praise." Were you ever told as child, "Don't get a big head just because you did it right fo once," or "Don't toot your own horn?"

"I was lucky." Some people have great difficulty accept ing their competence and will insist that only luck brough them through. It is a disclaimer carried forward from child hood when parents and peers may have implied incompetenc by saying, "Here, let me do it." When the child doe anything right they call him or her "lucky."

"It really wasn't anything." This may offend the perso offering praise, thereby cutting off friendship and intimacy Many men report feeling embarrassed when their mother hugged or kissed them for doing a good job and struggling t get free. They suffer the same embarrassment when they ar praised as grown-ups.

5. What was the response around your family when you di a good job?

Did you get sincere praise? How did you feel then? Was i disregarded or did it go unnoticed? What did you think abou that?

6. What kind of feelings did you get the last time you were criticized at work?

Frequently the feelings about criticism are the ones mos easily identified with childhood. Defensiveness, humiliation worthlessness, hopelessness, rebellion, and self-deprecation are some feelings reported. A young bank executive said "Wow. It's just like I am seven years old again and my dad on my case." However, some people recall that their childhood errors were dealt with compassionately and they do not suffer much when criticized at work. Others were criticized so much they reached a point of turning off when they were being told what was wrong. A young lady lost a highly coveted job because she refused to pay attention when her supervisor tried to teach here the new skills required. When she was let go she was very upset and disturbed. Her Inner Saboteur had whispered, "They're wrong. You're right." All she could say was, "I just don't see it."

How were you dealt with as a child when you made mistakes?

What kind of feelings did you have? What did you say to the grown-ups? How did you act? What did you say to yourself? What did you want to say and do that you didn't say or do? Sometimes people have so deeply buried the things they want to say and do they simply freeze and walk away from any hint of criticism.

How do you feel when asked to express yourself verbally in a group or to superiors?

Psychologists consistently report that the fear of speaking in public rates number one in the minds of those responding to questionnaires. The feeling of fear and/or inadequacy is another feeling that is easily connected with childhood. "Silence is golden" and "Children should be seen and not heard" are two messages that continue to be passed along from generation to generation despite many changes in parenting in recent generations. The fear of speaking up is then reinforced in school when volunteers are labeled "teacher's pet."

What did your parents say to you when you tried to express yourself?

Were they patient or impatient? Were you encouraged t
state your views? A successful salesman said, "I was told
was wrong by my father so often I finally decided it wasn
any use to talk to grown-ups." Fortunately his mothe
encouraged—even pushed—him to take public speaking in hig
school and college. At the time he entered sales he got col
knots in his stomach when he called on strangers. Those ba
feelings finally disappeared with time, experience, and success

10. What are your feelings when you're faced with a diffi cult problem at work?

One person says, "Hot dog. Here's another chance t
prove myself," exhilarated with the challenge. Another per
son says, "Holy cow, what do I do now?" and is panic
stricken. Between those extremes, is an entire range of thought
and feelings. What are they for you?

11. How did your folks handle it when you were given new task as a child?

Were you encouraged or put down? When you faltered i
your performance, how did they react? How did you respon
to their reaction? How similar are the feelings you have now
when faced with the uncertainties of a new assignment or
new job? Or maybe of that long-held dream of getting int
business for yourself?

12. Are any bad feelings you have in a new situation consistent with the reality of your competence and experience?

If you have handled challenges in the past there is no
reason to allow old feeling habits to hamper your current
performance.

13. How did your parents handle their problems?

Parents are models, and children tend to adopt the opera
tional style of their parents, or others in authority. Children

rarely know all the facts behind a parent's behavior. They just see what the parents do and follow suit, believing it is the way to solve their problems. In a family where the parents react to problems with anger, children will learn the same habit, with the exception of those who are fearful of speaking out or showing their feelings.

Two children of the same parents may come to different conclusions about behavioral patterns even though they live with the same models. My brother and I demonstrate the difference in handling life problems that can exist between two boys raised in the same family. Our stepfather handled his career problems by quitting and looked for a better job. Mother's watchword was "Charge!" When things or people got in her way she pushed, hauled, or shoved till she got her way. Though I'm not a job-jumper, by the age of fifty I'd had four careers. My watchword was not exactly "Charge," but it was "Do something."

My brother is the opposite. He is a quiet man and has worked for the same company for more than thirty years. I followed the model of my parents. He turned against it.

As you consider the way your family handled its problems and whether or not that is your style, be aware that if you operate in the opposite manner it may be rebellion rather than true freedom. Becoming aware of your style in dealing with life problems is best arrived at by examining habitual responses. If you have handled problems the same way over the years and that has not worked well for you, it may be time to give up repeating yourself—to give up following childhood programming. You are free to operate in the style best suited for you once the Inner Saboteur has been exposed and new decisions have been made.

14. What did your mother and father say about work?

In this country, with its Puritan work ethic, comparatively few people realize that work can be fun. They grew up in households where the sayings about work were:

You have to work.

Life's a struggle.

Keep your nose to the grindstone.

Work first, play later.

A man makes a living.

A woman keeps a good house.

Learn a trade.

Get an education so you won't have to work the way I do.

Some women have been repeatedly told by their mothers, "You'd better learn to do something. You can't rely on a man to take care of you." This programming can influence the kind of career a woman will choose as well as her relationships with men or her spouse.

Then there's another set of messages that have the implication that if they are followed everything will be all right in life:

Be a doctor.

Be a banker.

Be a dentist.

Be a fireman.

Be a lawyer.

Sometimes these messages reflect a parent's envy and frustration with his or her disappointing career. Sometimes, coming from a mother, there is a roundabout slap at the father. "Be a professional" may have the implicit meaning "Don't be a failure like your father." Such messages also may have a heavy "Make me proud" message cloaked in them, so strong that young people are pushed through college to get a degree only to find later in life that they don't like their professions. Any resort or vacation area in the country has a sprinkling of people with doctoral or master's degrees working as bartenders or waiters while they search for what they really want to do. They got tired of making others proud.

One of the most baffling messages parents give is "You can be anything you want to be." The implication is that their child is especially talented or brilliant and that life's choices will be simple for them. People who have absorbed this message frequently find themselves frustrated because they haven't found the right career and feel it's their own fault they haven't.

Even more confusion may result if the message goes like this: "You can be anything you want to be. I don't care, as long as you are happy." One person with this programming said, "It's bad enough not to know what I want to do at age 37. It's worse to feel guilty because I can't tell Mother I'm happy. Around my house it was a sin to express unhappiness. I had to act as if I was happy even when I was miserable. Mom always told me everything would be all right, just wait till tomorrow. I guess I'm still waiting for tomorrow."

15. What were the predictions for you in your grown-up life?

Parents say many things to their children that forecast their future. These forecasts can be either gloomy or joyous. The parent who says "Life's a struggle" and demonstrates it to a child is reflecting his or her lot in life and how he or she feels about it. Unless something fortuitous happens, that doleful outlook on life is imprinted in the child's belief systems. The parent who says "You can, within reason, be anything you want to be" and encourages a child to test his or her capabilities, to make mistakes without feeling discounted as a person and to see what the child is good at and enjoys doing, is literally giving a child permission to seek a successful career of his or her choice.

Here are some predictions reported by people in classes, workshops, or counseling sessions:

- You ain't never goin' to amount to nuthin! [From a highly talented and intelligent man who messed up and moved on every time he began to be successful in his work.]

- You better learn something because you'll never keep a man the way you keep house. [From a woman who'd been divorced three times but was competent in her work.]
- Security is the most important thing in life. [From a government worker who hated his job.]
- You don't have to live like us if you go to college. [From an unemployed man with a Ph.D. in English literature.]

Once children have accepted their parents as the source of all truth, they tend to slant all outside information in a way that conforms with their emerging belief system. Therefore, the child who believes his parents when they tell him "You never do anything right" might say "I just lucked out" when told he's done something good in school.

Another influence on childhood programming is the manner in which a child is taught to obey the rules. In my own experience, my mother and grandmother were both powerful women who taught elocution. They did readings on crude wooden stages erected inside circuslike tents. I remember rooms lighted only by the dancing flames that reminded me of witches' dens. With the facial gestures of a powerful dramatic actress, Mother recited the poems of James Whitcomb Riley. When she thundered, "And the goblins'l getcha, if you don't watch out," I expected scary little demons to come charging out of the chimney. When she wanted to keep me in line all she had to do was scowl, shake her finger at me, and say, "Watch out for the goblins." I grew up dreaming about goblins and emerged with a fear of rule and law. I was 37 before I got my first ticket for a meter violation.

16. What predictions did you make yourself when you were little?

In thinking about the influence that affected your decisions and predictions about your future, think of your childhood heroes and heroines. Who did you think was living a good life and didn't have to follow all the rules imposed on children? Remember the kinds of feelings that led you into dreams of living like So-and-so someday. You might want to take a pad and complete this sentence: "Someday I'll grow up and then I'll live like . . ." This person could be a favorite storybook character, a folk hero, a movie star, a political figure, the protagonist of a novel or play. You might also consider what TV shows pictured the life you wanted to live someday.

As you consider this, think of familiar situations that arise in your life over and over again and that either follow the pattern of your model or trigger thoughts similar to those you had in your childhood. One man in his fifties who described his life as rather dull said, "I grew up in the West. Some of my family came out in covered wagons. One of them was in the Gold Rush. I seem to just go along, figuring someday I'll strike it rich." A woman reported, "I'm always into lost causes. My heroine was Joan of Arc. I guess I like to be a martyr."

Think of some of the people you've known or encountered in your life that could be simply described as:

Cinderella	Goldilocks	All-American Girl
Sir Galahad	Gary Cooper	Superman
Elmer Gantry	Hercules	Superwoman
Babbitt	Abraham Lincoln	John Wayne
Errol Flynn	Hamlet	Florence Nightingale

These people may be following typecasting from their childhood heroes and heroines. Shakespeare said: "All the world's a stage, and all the men and women merely players," but remember that life is different from the theater. None of us auditioned to fill our roles. Our character directions were set in childhood, and before puberty passed we settled into our roles and began living them out. Yet we live without the benefit of a playwright or director to guide us or perhaps to suggest we play a different role. Examination of the consistency with which you play your roles—worker, parent, lover, loafer, friend, or fighter—will give you clues to the plot and directions your life has taken.

17. If you sat down today to write a play, a song, or a novel, what would the title be?

This exercise will assist in summing up the theme of your life in either your career or your total life plan. Before doing this, think about the kind of books, plays, and songs that you have always enjoyed most and the feelings connected with them. Early in the exploration of my life script I encountered a strange contrast: I had good feelings when I listened to sad songs; I luxuriated in misery. I also loved to read about active heroes who did things and came out winners. I guess my title then might have been "A Sad Man in Second Place." Now it is "The Happy Comeback Kid."

Play around with this exercise. Don't force it. Don't ask anyone to help you. Let your thoughts come and go until something that seems right for you emerges. Whatever that title is, accept it as real for you at the moment, regardless of the feelings connected with it. When you have identified the theme of that title you can begin thinking about what you'd like that title to be five or ten years from now.

18. In your relationships with others, do you mostly tend to be Persecutor, Rescuer, or Victim?

These are general descriptions, but people very definitely tilt toward one out of the three. Remember, it is consistency and intensity that mark *the degree* of the inclination. These descriptions also define the different ways in which people act their roles in life. For example, a Persecutor boss would be domineering, authoritarian, critical, and punitive, pounding the table to get his message across. A Rescuer boss would be overly helpful, offer unsolicited advice, and feel hurt when his or her suggestions were rejected. A Victim boss would avoid responsibility by blaming upper management for any unpleasant task he or she had to handle.

To the extent that you can operate free and clear of these characteristics, you can be objective. You may choose to adopt one of these roles for a specific situation, but in doing so will be acting rather than reacting. You will be autonomous. You will be in charge of yourself and your relationships. You will be laying the foundation for a new direction and a new life drama.

All of these questions are linked to your childhood programming and your decisions concerning yourself and your relationship to your childhood world. The amount of negativity in your belief system and the strength of your Inner Saboteur are also reflections of your life script. Some of the questions may not apply to you but may suggest other questions as you give consideration to the childhood conditioning that was the foundation for your current position in life.

The process of self-discovery is not an overnight exercise. It would be nice to make a Great Discovery that would miraculously change your life, but it is not likely that this will occur. You are far more likely to be picking up clues all along to help you understand how you got to be the way you are and to help open up the way toward positive action. Each experience that leads to negative thoughts or feelings provides you with an opportunity to say to yourself, ''I don't like what is going on with me and I'm not going to go on like this just because this is the way it has been in the past. From now on when this happens I will . . .'' Finish the sentence by saying what you will do differently in the future. Doing this will link your discoveries with new decisions and help you forge a new chain of experiences for the life ahead.

Be careful of getting bogged down in self-analysis for its own sake. You are simply looking for discoveries as you go about experiencing life. When you discover you are reacting in nonfunctional ways, you can consider the sort of change you want to make and get on with taking positive action. To make discoveries and not to do something about them is a form of avoidance that keeps you floundering in the trap of your old ways. The process of self-discovery is most rewarding when engaged in for a purpose, not as a diversion or something to talk about at cocktail parties. Some people get so mired in self-analysis that they never get around to getting on with the consideration of new directions. Wayne is one of them. He's been groping along now for about ten years. He knows his script backward and forward. He says he knows what he wants out of life "if" he could just find the right way. Seeking the right way has taken him through some extensive territory in the human potential movement. He's done Esalen and est, sensual massage and Silva Mind Control, transactional analysis and transcendental meditation, the Tarot and the *I Ching*, and a few less identifiable philosophies and practices connected with even less identifiable gurus.

Last time I saw him he was still selling used cars—and hating it. He just hadn't gotten around to establishing a new career, because "After all, I might not like that, either." Wayne's inability to make decisions blocks him from taking any positive action to move him forward.

Here's another suggestion. It's probably best to keep your search to yourself. To go around talking about your new life can be distracting to others, even perhaps damage your image in their eyes, or it can be just plain boring. If you have a trusted friend or mate to talk to—preferably one involved in the same process—they may be supportive listeners. Support is helpful. But if you need more than that, find an appropriate professional to talk to.

Chapter 4

How to Be a Potent Person

> *Potency is the sum total of your life competency. It is a measurement of your personal power and how you use that power to get what you want out of life.*

Potent people know who they are, what they want out of life, and how to go about getting it. A few seem to have come by it naturally, their childhood programs containing a minimal amount of the negative garbage that fosters the Inner Saboteur and prevents complete potency. These people reflect a quiet confidence in their ability to meet their goals in life and enjoy themselves. They are not confined to the ranks of the rich and powerful. Their potency may or may not be measured in terms of material gain. Whatever their station in life, it is based upon personal choice and not something that fate has thrust upon them. Because they feel in control of their lives they have no occasion to play Blame Games, or thrust aside personal responsibility in other ways.

Most people, however, who become more potent in the management of their lives have had to struggle to make improvements in their attitudes and performance. They have demonstrated flexibility when things did not go right in their world and have undertaken the task of *making* things go right For any of a thousand reasons their world told them some thing was not quite right—a business failure, a job loss, a strained relationship, discomfort with their role in life, a poor job performance appraisal—some turning point separated the high road from the low road. They chose to take the high road of personal growth and positive change. They accepted responsibility for themselves, did what they needed to do, and found appropriate means to improve themselves in whatever way necessary.

One mistake potent people don't make is to consider working hard the only secret to success. They are observant enough to know they are surrounded by workaholics who live a dreary, joyless life confusing effort with effectiveness. This observation is reinforced by the work of Charles Garfield in his research concerning optimal human performance. He found that optimal performers tend to take more vacations than workaholics, regularly play tennis, jog, or engage in some exhilarating exercise, and always make time for family and friends.

This is important in considering positive change. Making it a grim program, ignoring the child within, is a high price to pay for enhancing potency. After you've examined those areas in which you wish to make some improvement, accept it as a challenge and enjoy your improved personal competence as you go along.

The purpose of this self-examination is to provide information for your mind. The mind can bring about personal miracles, even to the extent of reversing terminal illness, when it is given appropriate verbal and/or non-verbal information. Verbal information is expressed or recorded by the conscious mind as words, phrases, and sentences. Nonverbal information is expressed or recorded by sensing, feeling, or emotional experience. When information from the unconscious mind is translated into thoughts in the conscious mind, it is then available for the problem solving and decision making necessary for positive action.

Potent people have a special presence, an awareness of themselves as productive people who know how to get the job done whatever the task. They are good listeners who reason rather than argue and get results from their communications. They are upbeat and optimistic, projecting a great deal of vitality. They radiate a sense of personal power but use that power in a way that is never damaging to themselves or to others. Potent people are comfortable people to work with or for.

SELF-AWARENESS

Think of yourself as you really are rather than whoever you think you should be. Your parents used many labels in many ways as you developed your self-concept. Some of those attributes may be realistic today and some may not be. Without getting into analytic nit-picking, begin to think of yourself as others see you. Do it objectively and remember *you* are in charge of your feelings. You don't have to feel bad because you honestly face the fact that your clothes are a size or two larger than the size you wore in high school, or that sometimes you are unduly biased in your viewpoints. Yes, those are wrinkles you see in the mirror, or maybe a receding hairline. Yes, you did get irritated with your bridge partner last Thursday night when it wasn't called for. Yes, you were late coming in on Monday and it wasn't the fault of the freeway traffic.

As you go along, become more aware of the picture you have of yourself in your mind. There will be differences between that picture and the reality of your presence in the world. You may not like some of those differences, but to avoid acknowledging them is to create disharmony within, as well as externally with the people in your life. No need to punish yourself with what you're not.

Again, no nit-picking or self-punishment. Rather, go gently, but persistently, as you acquire an awareness of yourself as you really are, rather than as you were programmed to be. *This is the foundation for one day becoming the person you want to be, the one you choose to be.*

OPEN-MINDEDNESS

Learn how to receive information or criticism from your boss, a client, an employee, a friend, or a family member without becoming defensive or angry. The Inner Saboteur does not want to hear information inconsistent with your self-concept, because he must protect you against change. Don't buy it.

Often people will resist new information or feedback. They will focus on the faults of others and thereby feel no need to examine their own attitudes or behaviors. They protect themselves from blame or guilt by finding fault with others. Resistance can range from mild defensiveness to the total denial of reality.

There are two ways to check yourself out on the extent of your own open mindedness. The first is simply to be aware of your thought process when you are confronted with new information. Are you immediately open to it, or do you resist? Is the resistance legitimate, in favor of rational problem solving? Is there a fear of risk? How frequently do you feel you are right and others are wrong? Is that a familiar thought to you? Is it a thought you had a lot as a child? Does your belief system permit tolerance for feedback from others even though it may be critical?

The other way to check yourself out is through your feeling system. What others say and do may be a reflection of your own personal style. When we are reminded of things we do not like in ourselves, our protection may be the bad feelings of anger, irritation, or indignation. As self-awareness increases you may recognize some sayings and actions of others that trigger bad feelings. Check yourself out on the possibility that you may be agitated by a reminder of your own behavior.

Evaluating your degree of open-mindedness is a tricky business. Being open-minded is such a highly valued characteristic that most of us would like to think of ourselves as possessing it to a high degree. However, to be aware of the extent to which we are not open-minded can be a milestone in the march toward personal growth.

SELF-DIRECTION

Being self-directed means operating free and clear of garbage in the mind and the influences of the Inner Saboteur. It means freedom from childhood programming and permission to see the world as it really is, rather than the way you were taught it was supposed to be.

Being self-directed does not mean rejecting all the standards and values learned in childhood. It is a consequence of a values clarification process in which you choose to have those attitudes, actions, and feelings that you decide are appropriate to you in the present. It is achieved by giving up old habits and acquiring new ones. It calls for taking responsibility for choice and even keeping old habits because you feel they are appropriate, rather than letting yourself be manipulated by your Inner Saboteur. It is to find a comfortable balance between what you are, what you want to be, what you feel you should be, and the "have tos" of your world.

Here are some thoughts that come out of negative programming and reflect the influence of the Inner Saboteur. They are all other-directed and, if strictly adhered to, can sabotage the potential for being comfortable with one's self. Some may apply to you:

- I tend to go along with others' views even if I don't agree.

- I often feel embarrassed even though I've done nothing wrong.
- It is more important to make a living than to find work I enjoy.
- It seems as if I'm always explaining myself to others.
- I don't think very many people like me.
- I'm always trying to help someone even when it's not convenient.
- I worry about what people will think about my house if they drop in.
- I am almost obsessed with punctuality.
- It bothers me terribly to ask where the bathroom is.
- I can't ever get anyone to do anything right.

These are examples of the kind of thinking that psychologists link with an inferiority complex. You can change this kind of thinking. Recognize such thoughts as the voice of your Inner Saboteur and realize they weren't built into you at birth. They are a part of your childhood programming and are learned in the experience of survival as a child. They are rarely appropriate to the life of an adult. There are many ways to change negative thinking discussed throughout this book, but right now, today, you can begin to make constructive changes in your life. Start thinking of yourself as being a potent person, and begin planning to take the necessary steps to achieve your goals.

POSITIVE SELF-IMAGERY

It is important to have a positive mental image of yourself that is based on reality and not on illusion. In other words, when it comes to a positive self-image, don't kid yourself. If you are a functioning person and getting by, then you are capable of being honest with yourself. You know what you can do based on your experience. What you don't know is that most likely there are many things you can do you have never tried because of some negativity in your self-image.

You have learned many new things in life, either through education or training or through the experience of trial and error. You have a demonstrated capacity to learn and translate that learning into positive action. Where you are in life now is a result of having taken many positive steps in the past. What you did yesterday you can do tomorrow. People faced with change often forget how many times they have successfully solved problems in the past and surrender to the influence of negative thinking.

If you graduated from high school, you made that happen. If you graduated from college, you made that happen. If you got a job, began a career, began a business, you made that happen.

Whatever you want to make happen in the future, you can make happen and facilitate that positively by keeping a positive self-image in mind. One way to do that is to write out a list of your positive accomplishments in the past. Write down all the positive characteristics in your personality. Stick it up on a bulletin board or on a door—someplace you will see it and read it every day. Whenever anything negative creeps into your mind, think of the positive deeds of the past and the positive aspects of yourself. In time the positive imagery will become a habit.

Regardless of your goal, remember that if it is realistic, someone else has probably attained it before and there's no reason you can't do the same. Be careful how you apply terms of reality to yourself. Negative messages coming from your Inner Saboteur may lead you toward self-imposed limitations, and that is not reality. Though a mentally retarded youth may compete in the Special Olympics it would not be realistic to aspire to the Olympic games. The chances that a tone-deaf person can become an opera star are probably nil.

See yourself in your mind positively doing what you want to do and you can accomplish your goals.

POSITIVE THINKING

Accept responsibility for your thinking process, keep all channels tuned to positive thoughts, and be aware of the negative thoughts that cross your mind. Positive action is precluded if you surrender to the negative thoughts you have about yourself. Potent people recognize negative thinking as part of their childhood programming and just let it go by when it comes up. They don't dwell on negativity and they stay away from people who do. They know what they want and they get on with the positive action needed.

RESOURCEFULNESS

To be resourceful means capitalizing on the situation at hand, dealing positively with strange situations, or creating opportunities not apparent to others. The phrase "street smarts" is used by some people to mean a kind of resourcefulness. They are talking about the informal education that comes from experience, which when coupled with the ability to "figure things out" allows a person to employ new or different procedures to solve problems instead of running away from them.

Resourceful people recognize desirable opportunities or discoveries when they run across them, and often create desirable opportunities or discoveries on their own. They are not afraid to take risks, or to capitalize when these opportunities arise, whether they're self-created or not.

You can increase your resourcefulness. The first step is to make every reasonable effort to solve problems on your own before seeking help from others. Have other people faced this problem? Maybe they've written books about it. Gather information. Think of several solutions. Stimulate your creativity by thinking of "crazy" ways to solve the problem. Be a devil's advocate and argue the opposite side. Ask advice from peers—advice, not help. When possible, take a risk and try some experimental solutions. But avoid at all costs the pretense of helplessness in order to get things done.

When asking for extensive help is appropriate, look at it as a learning opportunity that can be utilized the next time you're faced with a challenge.

PERSISTENCE

Be determined enough to achieve appropriate goals, yet be flexible enough to change directions when called for. The U.S. automobile industry is an example of inappropriate persistence: Manufacturers doggedly clung to the belief that big cars would come back and lost billions of dollars because they were too inflexible to change to the production of small cars.

Appropriateness and flexibility are very important as you consider the use of that energy known as persistence. You undoubtedly have seen people who stubbornly cling to habits, actions, or beliefs that have obviously been damaging to their careers or personal lives. However, once you have decided on a goal, be persistent. When you encounter setbacks, check yourself on the messages that come to mind, the things your parents said about making mistakes and the feelings you had. You don't have to feel crushed or rejected now just because that was the way you felt as a kid. Get your positive thinking in gear and persist in the pursuit of your goal.

ATTENTION

This is the capacity to be sensitive to what is going on at all times and to keep track of little things. On a long drive, have you ever suddenly realized you'd driven ten or twelve miles, maybe even through a small town, and not seen anything but the road ahead? You'd been paying attention to the big thing—driving the car—and missing a lot of little things.

Many people go through life this way, at work, at home, and in their relationships. They miss out on their environmental feedback. This can be deadly when that feedback indicates a tough road ahead. Many a middle manager or executive has found himself or herself on the outside after years of inattention to the management environment. Over and over again marital counselors have heard it said, "But I never knew. I didn't realize he (or she) felt that way."

Of course, it may be difficult to pay attention to everything going on around us. Not to do so may lead to more difficulty. Increased attention can be taught and learned and is basic to many kinds of individual and group therapy.

Here are some questions to check your attentiveness:

- Do you listen for the message in vocal tones?
- Do you evaluate the messages delivered by facial expressions?
- Have you learned what the body language of your associates means?
- Do you hear the message when you are being criticized by people who hide their critique behind a smile?

Insensitivity to others works in the best interest of self-sabotage, reinforcing attitudes and assumptions in your belief system that interfere with relationships and career progress. Not giving sufficient attention to others is a way of avoiding hearing things we would rather not hear. This may preserve the psychological status quo, but can be deadly when the boss is telling us to shape up, or when spouses, children, and friends need attention.

Giving up defensiveness opens up the mind, clearing the channels for new information. For the moment, just be aware of your tendency to think what you are going to say next instead of hearing what is being said to you. You know how your ears seem to plug when you make changes in altitude in a plane, or driving in the hills? Do you remember how your ears "pop" and suddenly clear at times and you hear everything with clarity? The next time you are listening to someone, pretend that has just happened and let the words come through, just as though you were a radio receiving unfiltered communications.

POSITIVE COMMUNICATIONS

Being assertive rather than aggressive in the expression of wants and needs does not arouse anger or resistance in another reasonable person. Assertive and potent people express themselves in a calm and rational manner that creates trust and confidence in others. Aggressive people express themselves in a demanding, sometimes arrogant way that triggers defensiveness in others. There is a fine line between being assertive or aggressive, and circumstances may dictate the difference. An aggressive style might be suitable for a successful salesman but fail him miserably when he becomes a sales manager.

Aggressiveness frequently is evidence of the Inner Saboteur on active duty. Some people are consistently aggressive, even when the situation calls for a milder approach. There are people who report that when they face resistance, angry aggressiveness is the only operational style they know. Aggressiveness inhibits the potential for positive action, but you would be an unusual person if you had never acted aggressively and later regretted it. In any situation when that happens, check yourself out on righteous indignation. There are certain basic standards of justice and ethics that apply to all of us. When those standards are violated there may be justification for anger or aggressiveness, but assertiveness will more appropriately resolve your problem. Again, the surest indicator that your Inner Saboteur is at work is a pattern of past performance. Do you habitually overreact in certain situations? Do you regularly react with anger toward people in authority? Do you regularly react with irritation when faced with views contrary to your own?

If you answer yes to these questions, think back a bit about your childhood. Is this the behavior your parents demonstrated? If so, you are reacting in conformance with your childhood programming rather than acting autonomously. A positive change in your programming will permit you to be assertive rather than aggressive and open up the way to more pleasant and effective relationships with others.

VITALITY

Having abundant resources of physical and mental energy is evidence of enthusiastic acceptance of the challenge of living and growing. Vitality is the power to live and grow. Living requires physical health, and growing requires mental vigor. Mental vigor is the more important of the two. Many a physically healthy person stays stuck in a rut for a lifetime because he or she lacks mental vigor. History is replete with examples of people in poor health who achieved their highest goals by virtue of mental vigor. Franklin D. Roosevelt didn't let polio keep him out of the White House.

Why some people have more mental vigor than others cannot be answered with certainty. It's possible it is connected with childhood programming and it has been shown that mental vigor can be improved by almost anyone. Enthusiasm, the quality of being "turned on," is a dynamo that produces mental vigor in quantities that are restricted only by individual limitations. Boredom is the blanket that stifles mental vigor.

Vital people have faith and they have hope. They feel they can manage their destiny and go about it enthusiastically. When stuck in a dull job they find ways to make the work interesting, they find off-hours activities that generate excitement enough to carry them forward into their work, or they find work that is enjoyable. They exercise their minds as well as their bodies.

These qualities—I have discussed ten of them in this chapter—show that potent people have a sense of moving ahead based on a belief that what they are doing is meaningful and important. When anxiety creeps in, it is short-lived. What is meaningful and important is a personal decision and a sign of inner direction. Whether by instinct or deliberate design, potent people choose their life directions and get on with the process of enthusiastic living. They have succeeded in facing down their Inner Saboteurs, purging themselves of the negatives in their belief systems.

You can do that too by becoming a more potent person through the process of positive change.

Chapter 5

Positive Thinking is Not Enough

The next step after positive thinking is to "do it." Positive thinking not followed by positive action is little more than wishing. Inaction is the handiwork of the Inner Saboteur and diminishes personal potency.

Positive living is not attained until positive thinking has been translated into positive action. Positive thinking is a process that may stimulate growth, but nothing concrete happens until someone does something constructive. The strength of a positive persuasion cannot be tested until some behavior results from it. Insight without action is simply a pastime. Uri Geller's claim to be able to bend metal with his mind would remain a theoretical concept if he had not risked public action. It is his performance, not his thinking, that has made him famous. Even the famous thinkers of all time might have died anonymously if they had not sought the public eye— spoken out, or written down their thoughts.

Positive action is emphasized in this book because various forms of positive thinking have been around for quite a while, yet the percentage of unhappy and frustrated people appears to remain constant. Emile Coué, a French pharmacist and psychotherapist, taught people autosuggestion in his clinic at Nancy beginning in 1910. His position was that we are what we think we are; by imagining ourselves well we can become well. Although he used some hypnosis in his work with patients, he gave them responsibility for imagining themselves well by persistently repeating the positive affirmation, "Every day in every way, I'm getting better and better."

When word of his work spread to the United States in the 1920s, Couéism swept the country. People went around murmuring to themselves over and over, "Every day in every way, I'm getting better and better." My mother was one of them. As well as practicing the incantation, she had it written out on little cards pasted about the house as constant reminders. Only in recent years have I realized that Mom and my stepfather put their hearts into positive thinking but steadfastly sabotaged their potency by negative actions.

In 1952 the first edition of Norman Vincent Peale's *The Power of Positive Thinking* was published. By now almost eight million copies have been sold. Many people have undoubtedly gained greatly from the book, but a question remains: If positive thinking, by and of itself, could easily be translated into joy and contentment, why hasn't the world's quota of misery been lowered to reasonable standards? The same could be said about the abundance of motivational books in the fields of business and sales, and the do-it-yourself school of psychology that some professionals discount by calling it "pop psychology."

THE POWER OF POSITIVE ACTION

What do the people who make positive thinking work for them do that the hangers-on and losers fail to do? *They take positive action.* Sounds simple, doesn't it? It isn't. Perhaps one of the most difficult phenomena to explain to people is what psychologists call "fear of success." Because of traditional belief systems and programming for "success," it is hard for many people to believe that they can be their own worst enemy. It is so much easier to blame others or circumstances than it is to recognize the Inner Saboteur that drives us to act or think in ways inconsistent with our perceived goals. When we say, as an afterthought, "Now, why did I do that?" or "Why did I say that?" we are recognizing our Inner Saboteur at work. The Diagram 2 will help you to recognize your Inner Saboteur.

Positive Thinking/Positive Action

This is the *only* response that is free and clear of the influence of the Inner Saboteur. Only a few fortunate people are raised in a sufficiently nurturing environment to evolve into adulthood with positive-thinking/positive-action characteristics. Most people in this category learned it by trial and error or reeducation. Some, with a stubborn Inner Saboteur, have only reached that stage with the assistance of psychotherapy. Regardless of the manner in which people have reached this state, they are highly effective in managing their careers, their relationships and their interactions with their world. They are peak performers.

Negative Thinking/Positive Action

These people have various feelings of inadequacy but through schooling and experience have learned to take positive action. Regardless of any negative feelings about self, they do the things necessary to achieve their stated goals. When their positive action proves rewarding, the power of the Inner Saboteur may be diminished or eventually extinguished. If the negative power does not weaken, or if it intensifies, a pressure point develops that can invite negative action. The classic example is the successful person

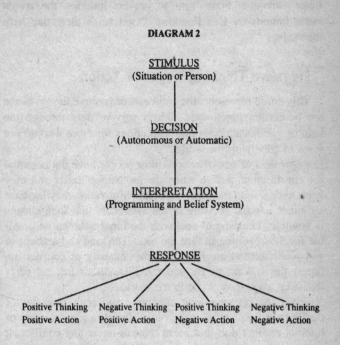

DIAGRAM 2

STIMULUS
(Situation or Person)

DECISION
(Autonomous or Automatic)

INTERPRETATION
(Programming and Belief System)

RESPONSE

| Positive Thinking | Negative Thinking | Positive Thinking | Negative Thinking |
| Positive Action | Positive Action | Negative Action | Negative Action |

who destroys his or her own career by certain types of negative behavior—excessive smoking or drinking, reckless driving or flying.

Positive Thinking/Negative Action

These people are blind to the reality of their actions and how those actions keep them from achieving stated goals. Brushing aside feedback from their environment, they project self-confidence and say, "Someday my ship will come in." Unwilling to take responsibility for the condition of their lives, they smile brightly and send out good thoughts while ignoring the influences of the

Inner Saboteur. Some turn to prayer, ignoring the words made famous by Ben Franklin: "God helps them that help themselves."

Negative Thinking/Negative Action

This group represents the antithesis of positive living. Some are borderline functionals. Others survive only through the help of various agencies and institutions for those who do not learn to cope with the world.

Regardless of classification, most people have the potential for constructive change when the motivation exists and they learn to deal with the Inner Saboteur. Motivation may increase by either internal pressure or the awareness that such change is possible. Learning to deal with the Inner Saboteur is possible for those willing to face the task. The kind and amount of assistance needed are related to the intensity of conflict between the I Want to Be and the I Ought to Be and early decisions about how to be in the world.

The lines between low, medium, and high intensity of conflict are frequently overlapping. Having a low intensity of internal conflict does not mean there is never any conflict. It means that such a person effectively deals with such conflict and is a positive-thinking/positive-action person *most* of the time. Remember that all of us have a little craziness in us sometimes. It is also very possible to be a positive-thinking/positive-action person in business and be something less in other aspects of living.

Here are some case histories that demonstrate the three different levels of intensity of conflict:

LOW INTENSITY

Consider Bill. "I loved my work when I came here: creative research and development. Then, when my boss left, they made me lab manager. I hated it. I knew all about things and nothing about people. I had made it all the way through a Ph.D., but I have never taken a course in why people act the way they do. I'd have quit, but, you know, starting over at 40 didn't seem such a good idea.

"I had a couple of warning signs that the stress was getting to me—palpitations. So I had to do something about gaining more confidence as a manager. I figured if I'm smart enough to design a new computer I'm smart enough to learn more about people. Even about myself. Two years ago I started reading, going to workshops and seminars with titles like 'Organizational Effectiveness.' I took a class on 'Transactional Analysis in Supervision and Management.' I learned a lot of my trouble with people was in being too authoritarian. When I began to practice active listening, really listening, then hiring, firing, and doing employee appraisals became almost fun, challenging.

"I feel great now. No more palpitations. I look forward to going to work. And another thing: that communications and human behavior stuff works at home. It really produced new vibes around the house."

Bill's conflict was between a want (to be a loner) and his should (to get ahead). For years his father had said to him, "Did you get a promotion yet?" Once Bill understood his belief system and acquired some new communications skills he was startled to realize that he did want to get ahead for himself, not just to satisfy his father's expectations. With that awareness and persistent application of his new knowledge, he linked positive thinking with positive action and he began a new style of positive living. Now he says, "I just didn't realize how I'd blocked out my ambitions because of my fear of dealing with people."

MEDIUM INTENSITY

People in this group have the desire to improve their lives but are not self-starters. Usually it takes some kind of prodding from others to get them going on ways to change, and frequently they need the assistance of a mentor, a friendly manager, a counselor, or in some cases, a supportive spouse.

Take Helen's case. "I knew what my pressure point was. I had had a lot of messages in my programming about 'being somebody.' That meant work. But my husband used to say, 'A woman's place is in the home,' until he realized the stress I was suffering. I didn't know what I wanted to do, be a mother or try to make a career for myself. I went to a feminist counselor for awhile. She helped me understand my conflict. I almost went back to secretarial work but realized that it wasn't for me for the rest of my life. I took a test that showed me that my interests were in being creative and getting things accomplished.

"Now I'm going to the community college during hours when my children are in school. I'm taking advertising and commercial photography this semester. Jack minds the children one night a week while I'm at my support group. I'm busy, but I love it. I feel I have some control over my life. I get along better with the kids, and Jack and I are more like partners. I don't feel so one-down anymore. In about a year I'll be ready for part-time work, and when the girls are in high school it'll be full steam ahead on my new career."

In resolving the conflict between her "ought tos" and "want tos" Helen got herself out of one of the worst psychological traps that exists: the either/or trap. She discovered she had options and the power to make choices. She didn't have to be either a housewife or a business person, she could do both. She also discovered that some of her assumptions about her husband were wrong, and that discovery greatly enhanced their relationship. In the course of this change process, Helen cleaned a lot of garbage out of her old programming that opened up the way to positive living for her. She says now, "I'm glad I had the spunk to get myself going. I used to read a lot of psychology books, but they just kept me messed up until I decided to do something about my life."

HIGH INTENSITY

People included in this group are those whose lives are marked with crisis, for themselves and/or others. Their self-image is not consistent with the reality of their world. They act "as if" their belief systems are law and they are compelled to follow the law. The concept of self-determination is foreign to them and frequently difficult to understand when they have been exposed to it. They have a variety of mental devices they use to avoid self-responsibility. Some just barely get by, hanging on the edge of functionality. Some have periods of crisis. Some live in constant crisis. Some bury their conflict under a blanket of tranquilizers or alcohol or drugs until the blankets themselves create a crisis.

Whatever the causes for their self-defeating programming, thousands of people in this category do make constructive change. It may take a little bit longer and maybe a little more work is involved, but once a new decision is made, including the willingness to carry out the decision, miraculous change can occur. Whatever the reason, there comes a time of readiness when the desire and the determination to make change are activated. One way or the other, people just get sick and tired of the conflict in their life and start looking for ways to resolve it. Looking through his case file one day a parole officer realized he hadn't seen Jerry, a regular repeater, for ten years. Curious, he stopped by to see Jerry one evening and asked what had happened. Jerry said, "Hell, I just got tired of going to jail so I got a job."

Few high-intensity people find a solution as simple as Jerry's. Usually they need the help of others. Alex is testimony to that. His childhood had been one of deprivation, and he often dreamed that his father, an erratic provider, brought him all the things a normal boy desires. At times the dreams seemed so real Alex actually believed his father did bring him the things that the other kids had in school. One of his childhood decisions was that he would always work hard so that if he had children he could give them what they wanted.

After high school Alex worked hard, so hard that by age twenty-three he decided to live by his wits rather than his brawn. He went into sales and did very well. By age thirty he was earning more than he'd dreamed of as a child. He was married and had two adorable children. He also had a wallet full of credit cards and was on the verge of bankruptcy. Every time Alex saw anything he wanted for his family or himself, his Inner Saboteur urged him, "Go ahead. You can afford it. You deserve it after all you did without when you were a kid."

One day his wife said, "That's all—I've had it. I'm tired of getting calls from bill collectors when you're not here. This place is filled with things we don't need. I didn't need that new car you bought me for Christmas. I need some peace of mind, some stability. I'm frightened. I still love you, but I can't live like this."

They talked almost all night. Alex was shocked. He hadn't realized he was acting out a fantasy of what a father "should be" or how unrealistic his spending had become. Reluctantly he agreed to see a psychologist, and his first visit was another shock. When asked to forecast his future if he didn't change his spending habits, Alex had no reply. His "wants" were so mixed up with his "shoulds" he had no rational answers. The first rational step he took was to see a financial counselor at the local credit bureau and work out a plan to repay his debts.

It took time, hard work, and sacrifice, but Alex regained his balance and saved himself from the horror that a bankruptcy or a divorce would have meant to him. With the help of the psychologist he gradually made his own decisions and became the master of the Inner Saboteur.

Speaking of that experience now, Alex says, "It was as if I were blind." And he was psychologically blind—a common problem with people suffering a high intensity of internal conflict.

A change in the level of intensity may be gradual, building

slowly with awareness that an individual's life experience is not providing the pleasure of living desired. Change can also be precipitate: loss of a job, a divorce, the loss of a loved one, an accident, or any of those things called destiny or fate. Few of us are given a ticket to a smooth trip through life. What we are slowly learning is that there are foreseeable trouble spots in life's passage, and through awareness and self-understanding we can enhance our potential for a pleasant journey.

Hal

Now you have some ideas about what positive living *isn't*. Let's get on with what it *is*. Here's a case history demonstrating how one man resolved a crisis in his life and is approaching the point where he can totally live the way he wants to rather than the way he's supposed to.

Hal's dad had been a construction worker. The family followed his wandering path and the economic roller coaster that goes with the construction life: feast or famine. His mother was a quiet woman who simply went along. As a kid, Hal had no religious or intellectual guidance to give him any sense of self. He was of average intelligence; school was a chore to him, and he didn't do very well as a student. He never had any encouragement about his future work or career.

The messages from his father were:

- A man makes a living. A man supports his family.
- Be independent. Don't work for somebody else if you can help it. Stand on your own feet.
- Be a man. Don't let anybody walk over you.

The messages from his mother were:

- Get an education.
- Settle down and stay in one place.
- Don't fight the world. It doesn't do any good.
- A woman's place is in the home.

Hal's dad was a model of machismo. He worked hard, fought hard, and drank hard. Many Sunday mornings he wore the battle scars of Saturday night at a working stiffs' beer joint. Hal's mother was a model of passivity. She never complained. Keeping house and raising children were all she knew.

After high school, Hal joined the army, hoping to learn a trade, but spent most of his time shuffling papers in an office because he had learned to type in school. He didn't mind the army life but left it after his first hitch, responding to his programming about being independent. His last army station was a medium-sized California town. Hal liked it there and decided to stay.

At age 22 his belief system was:

I Am: Vague, nothing certain.
I Want to Be: Independent but with no ideas on how to do that.
I Ought to Be: A college graduate. Independent. A family man.

At this time of his life, Hal had no internal conflicts. Getting a job, any job, was paramount, and he took advantage of his army clerical work by going to work at a branch of a major bank. Two years later he resigned and joined a local savings and loan firm, feeling somehow that a smaller organization moved him a little closer to being independent.

The next twenty years slipped by smoothly. Two sons grew up; one landed an athletic scholarship at a college, and the other went in the air force to learn computer programming. Despite Hal's feelings that a woman's place was in the home, Marian, his wife, faced the empty-nest syndrome by going to a community college to get a certificate in business administration.

At 44, Hal was settled in as assistant manager at the savings and loan. He knew everyone in town, had been president of the Lions Club, and played golf Wednesday and

Saturday. Once in a while he felt he really should be in his own business, and Marian's talk about her school stirred some thoughts about getting a degree, yet there was never enough pressure inside him to generate the energy needed to get him started. He'd long since forgotten that he'd given up going to college because he didn't feel he had the intelligence for it. Buried under his positive action, the negative feelings he had about himself rarely came to the surface.

Fate disturbed his equilibrium. With no warning, his company merged with one of the savings and loan giants in California. Hal's manager retired, and the post Hal had dreamed of attaining was open less than twenty-four hours. The shock of being passed over for promotion was compounded when the new manager arrived: a woman with a master's degree in business administration.

Hal wanted to quit and wondered if maybe the new outfit wanted him to quit. He remembered how his dad had told him to be independent, how his mom had always preached, "Go to college." Further, he now felt embarrassed around his friends. For a month he didn't go near the golf course and skipped the meetings he'd once enjoyed at the Lions Club. In the evenings he stayed glued to the tube with a highball glass in his hand. Alcohol sedated the inner voices that scolded him for having failed to put more effort into his career.

One night his wife said, "You know, I'm worried about you. This just isn't like you to sit here staring at the TV and drinking night after night. You can't go on like this."

That was reality, and Hal admitted it. With some encouragement he said, "Maybe there's still time to get on my own."

Hal got started. Slowly he began to face the reality of his position and what he wanted to do about it. He'd often chattered about the real estate business over the years, envious of the independence of the real estate people he met in his work. He admitted to himself that he'd blocked his drive to get more education with his negative feelings about his ability to learn. He also realized how terribly difficult it was for him to talk to anyone about his feelings.

His first positive step was to take a night-school course in business psychology at the community college. While learning a little about himself he was able to camouflage his intent to his macho friends under the guise of studying management. The next step was a course in career development, ostensibly to help his employees in their career directions. His wife got him to take a course in transactional analysis that she had taken. For the first time in years they had a common interest and topic of conversation. While all this was going on, Hal was learning something about himself and his belief systems and saw how he had been keeping himself from doing what he wanted to do most: be indepenent and enjoy life with Marian. At the same time he was exposing some of his internal mythology to the light of reality. He was as capable of learning as the other adults in his classes.

Ultimately he decided it was time to get on with doing what he needed to do to satisfy his urge to become independent and resolve the internal pressure point that might otherwise have totally disrupted his life. He began taking courses in real estate that would eventually lead to getting his sales license. Once he was doing something to answer his inner voice, his negative thinking began to fade away. Positive thinking coupled with positive action helped him feel better about himself, enhanced his supervisory capabilities, and enriched his life with Marian. That's what positive living is.

Let's look at the five phases that Hal underwent as he made his way toward increased positive living. Note that none of them were sudden "aha" experiences; there were no overnight bursts of enlightenment. There was no talk of "personal growth" or "maximizing human potential" or "midlife crisis." To Hal the steps he took were all rational moves to improve his career. But the personal development, his increasing personal potency, and the revitalization of his marriage were benefits that came with Hal's decision to take positive action. The five phases are:

1. Motivation

A career crisis made Hal realize that motivation comes from within. It was up to him to become his own rescuer. Although he received very welcome support from Marian if he vacillated, whenever he seemed to push her to give him the answers she'd say, "It's your life, Hal."

2. Decisions

The complexity of Hal's life problem did not lend itself to clear-cut decisions. His decisions evolved more than they were produced. He began thinking positively about himself and his future without having made a conscious decision to be a positive thinker. When he earned an A in his business psychology course he decided he was smart enough to take more classes and he ignored the old messages in his belief system that had condemned him to mediocrity. As his confidence increased he made major decisions more easily as well as the secondary decisions needed to carry out his desire to become independent in the real estate business.

3. Organization

Hal's planning had no formal organization for the first two years of his new way of living. Flashes of the old low self-esteem made it difficult to state his goals specifically for fear he would not achieve them. Then he came home from a night class at the junior college one evening and said, "I enrolled in the real estate course tonight." That committed him to a course of action. In effect, he had made a new decision to fulfill his wants in life and ignore the negative programming of his Inner Saboteur. At that point his plan for fulfillment became organized and he knew exactly which steps he would be taking to achieve his goal.

4. Action

Once Hal felt he had to "do something," his life became a series of positive actions: going to night school, improving his job performance, establishing new communications with his employees, even with his new boss. There were many risks—some real, some imaginary. He made mistakes and learned from them. He persisted, feeling good about himself, because almost every day he was taking a positive step forward. He made a giant stride forward when he quit the country club in order to begin selling real estate on weekends. That was a tough move for him to make, because belonging to the country club had been a big part of his identity, a wall between him and his Inner Saboteur and all the messages of insecurity and inadequacy.

5. Transition

Hal's transition was eased by the support of his wife and an older friend in real estate who became his mentor. His greatest enemies were the friends who said, "What in the world are you doing this for? Your kids are raised. You love golf. Your wife's working again and you make a good living." Wisely, Hal soon gave up trying to explain his actions. He didn't waste his energy inappropriately. But the wisest move of all was Hal's decision to continue working on salary after he received his real estate license and began to sell properties on the weekends. He didn't quit his savings and loan job until he'd saved enough commission money for six months' living expenses. He'd known others who had sabotaged their new careers by striking out on their own without enough financial reserves to pay the bills when sales were slow. Hal will continue to develop as long as he faces the challenge of overcoming his Inner Saboteur.

Chapter 6

Self-Motivation—the Pathway to New Decisions

Motivation comes from within, not without. Others may inspire you, influence you, or even command you, but your motivation is self-determined. Self-motivation generates the energy and willingness available to make and carry out new decisions about your life.

Making New Year's resolutions is one of our great popular pastimes. Each year we want to throw out self-defeating habits as we toss away a faded Christmas tree and begin again with the bright hope that "this year things will be different." Unfortunately, most of these resolutions are made without resolve and don't last much longer than the children's Christmas toys. Resolutions, made with the best of intentions and reinforced by positive thinking alone, soon begin to crack and crumble as they are assailed by the insidious force of the Inner Saboteur.

THE SEMANTICS OF PERSONAL CHANGE

What goes wrong when all the logic in the world does not provide enough energy to push us forward in our own self-interest? For centuries this question was brushed away by people who said, "You can't change human nature." One obstacle to change is the problem of semantics: We think we know what we mean by the use of certain words, but those words frequently do not fit with actions, attitudes, and behaviors. When a person says, "I changed my mind," it doesn't mean the *mind* was changed. It usually means that a planned action was changed. To change the mind is to change the self, or the programming that rules the life of an individual. In order to change the *mind* there must be:

- The means to change
- The motivation to change
- The will to change

Willingness opens the door for motivation. It is the difference between wishing and wanting, between dreaming and acting.

WISHING, WANTING, WILLINGNESS

Failure to separate wishing, wanting, and willingness in the mind is another obstacle to change. Wishing means dreaming about taking action. Wanting means making a decision and taking action. Willingness means giving yourself permission to achieve your goals.

This kind of willingness may be difficult to understand when considered only from the viewpoint of logic: "Who doesn't want to be a winner?" seems a logical question. The reality is that for many people their Inner Saboteur has condemned them to a lifetime of being happy only when they are sad. They get their feelings out of being martyrs and victims. They put a lot of energy into fishing for strokes by engaging in Games of Ain't it Awful, Poor Little Me, and If It Weren't For Them.[1] Next time you run into a Constant Complainer, notice how much animation and vitality he or she puts into the items from his or her gripe of the day. Pay attention to the fact that the Constant Complainers tend to "flock together." Give one a compliment and notice how it is quickly brushed aside, sometimes earning a negative reaction. Some may have the willingness to get ahead but not the willingness to enjoy either their working life or their retirement. Others never get started on their way because they are not sufficiently motivated to accept total responsibility for their destiny. They never reach the point of testing their willpower, instead, giving up, blaming others, or discounting their potential for potency is standard procedure for them.

Consider the difference in these statements:

- I wish my life were better.
- I want my life to be better.
- I am willing to make my life better.

The differences in these statements may seem subtle, but consider the power and meaning of the last statement. It is the only one of the three that leads to new decisions and the appropriate exercise of the will. The most powerful of all statements is: "I am willing to make my life better and I will make that happen by my willingness to . . ."

Finish the sentence for yourself. Be as specific as you can possibly be at this time.

EXERCISING YOUR WILL

That last statement is a declaration of an individual's responsibility for his or her destiny, and it's the first step toward exercising willpower in the management of a positive living program. In *The Act of Will*, Robert Assagioli wrote, "The function of the will is similar to that performed by the helmsman of a ship."[2] Just like a helmsman, you too can chart a course for your life's direction, using the knowledge and experience of those who have gone before you as well as the reality of your own experience. Psychological navigation is available to those who have the willingness to exercise their will and reinforce it with will*power*.

CHOOSING YOUR DESTINY

Once you establish your willingness to move in new directions, the next step is to have a sense of purpose and destination based on your motivation and your new decisions. Even an addict who says something like "I don't care where I'm at, man, as long as it isn't here" knows he is "getting away from" rather than "getting on with" the struggle of his life.[3] His drifting reflects a decision not to make decisions about his life. Cursed with deep feelings of inadequacy, his only goals are relief from the daily desperation of coping. His motivation may be functional in his present circumstances, but without further decision making, progress toward a more positive life will not occur.

His is a despairing example, but only different by degree from the life situations of millions of people struggling through life who lack the willingness to "get on with" positive living because they don't know how to go about it. Despair is the possession of an individual by her or his Inner Saboteur. And it can be exorcised by those who are willing to do so.

ESTABLISHING A FUNCTIONAL BELIEF SYSTEM

The matter of being functional or nonfunctional is a personal one. It is also a product of our belief systems and in many cases defies logic. A person who looks for positive payoffs finds it difficult to believe that some people are driven to seek negative payoffs. There are a great many people who seek put-downs, failures, and disappointments in life. Their belief system commits them to a low level of personal esteem and a poor self-image; from them, a negative thought or action is functional. For them to believe something good about themselves is nonfunctional: It disturbs the balance of their belief systems and results in mental stress. Saying or doing something positive confronts some people with a sense of personal responsibility so strong that they will never put forth the effort to make constructive change.

EXAMINING YOUR PAYOFFS

It is imperative to examine your payoffs in relation to your belief system if you want to make a permanent change. *Negative thinking is no more than a habit acquired in childhood and is not based on reality.* In adult life it is an unconscious reliving of childhood experiences which may have been functional at that time but are not connected with reality in the present.

Leslie

Leslie grew up in a family that made fun of him and repeatedly called him "stupid." But his IQ showed that he was of better than average intelligence. His parents discounted the evidence, and he continued to avoid belief in his ability to learn. In military service he was forced to learn new knowledge and skills. Eventually he could no longer challenge the reality of his experience and gradually gave up the negative parts of his belief system.

"Goofing up" had been his way of conforming to his poor self-image and getting laughter and sympathy from his buddies. The "goofing" had been functional for his old belief system, but as he gradually became aware of his potential he began the process of positive living. When his military service was over he took advantage of his veteran's benefits and went to college to become a teacher—a childhood dream he'd never mentioned since the time his father told him he wasn't smart enough to be one.

Once Leslie realized his wish could become a reality, his motivation changed. He gave up his old negative thinking/ negative acting pattern that had got him a lot of attention from people who either laughed at his antics or sympathized when he was in misery. As he changed to a positive-thinking/positive-action pattern, Leslie's willpower was tested, because he discovered that people who are getting along don't draw the same amount of attention as those who are messing up their lives. Negative thinking and negative acting were habits that once had held some reward for Leslie. When Leslie goofed up as a kid his family and friends paid attention to him, and therefore his behavior was functional. When he did it in the army the same behavior was not functional, because of the negative reaction from his sergeant. Paying attention to his actions, Leslie gradually gave up the impul-sive behavior his Inner Saboteur suggested. His motivation changed as he learned to enjoy promotions and increased pay instead of sympathy or laughter.

WHY DO YOU WANT TO CHANGE?

Understanding your motivation for change is the key to making positive thinking work for you. It makes the differ-ence between hopefulness and willingness. Simply to hope you will get what you want out of life is not much more than wishing. The willingness to get what you want out of life calls for answering hard questions about your desired goal:

- Am I doing this because I feel I ought to, or have to, or really want to?
- Will this new goal satisfy me or simply move me to go on satisfying others?
- If this new goal will satisfy me as well as others, can I do it without feeling rebellious?
- What are the positive payoffs for moving in this new direction?
- What interests and values will be satisfied by such change?
- Will this process of change create new pressure points between I Am, I Ought to Be, I Want to Be, and My World?

Seem complicated? Well, it is. But so is anything worthwhile. Except for a fortunate few who have a natural facility for making appropriate adjustment to the problems in life, most of us fail to get what we want because we've been trained to believe we only need to set a goal and drive toward it with true grit for success. The reality is that successful living requires a complicated system of thought that is just beginning to be universally understood. A part of that system is recognition that people *can* make new decisions and *can* make positive changes in their lives when they are *willing* to.

DECISION MAKING

Life is a daily round of decisions. The flow of decisions goes on from getting up to going to bed, and for some who have learned to utilize their dreams, the decision making goes on in the course of sleep. Fortunately much of this decision making is habitual, an instant response to childhood programming, so that action does not require conscious forethought. If this were not so, we would be exhausted and overwhelmed by the psychic energy loss of directing our muscular responses to conform to the reasoning of our minds.

Once a person has been motivated to choose a new course of action, to change a habit, or to rearrange a belief system, he or she is suddenly faced with the static energy of the status quo. It's like drifting downriver in a canoe and turning to head back upstream only to find that despite furious paddling it is only possible to hold one's place against the inexorable force of the river. Only the truly motivated, the ones who understand what the positive payoff is for the attainment of the goal, will manage to paddle upstream.

The success of that upstream journey depends on the power of the will and the seriousness of the decision to explore new options in life, to live positively, and to maximize the link between positive thinking and positive action. Adults forget that when they were children, each new school year required strenuous change and mental growth as they moved up a grade at a time. Growth shouldn't stop because we are no longer in school.

One reason that growth stops for many is the myth that to express or pay attention to emotions is childish. Not knowing how to be in charge of their emotions, people bury them or avoid them, creating a major obstacle to giving up negative thinking.

Feelings and emotions do not recognize childhood or adulthood. They are what they are, whether expressed or repressed. They are habits. The child who learned to feel bad when he or she broke the family rule. "Children should be seen and not heard" can be the adult who suffers bad feelings anytime he or she is asked to make an oral report at a staff meeting. The feeling is genuine, *but it is only a habit* and is not relevant to the adult situation. In fact, it is not even appropriate at the staff meeting, where everyone is encouraged to speak up.

YOU CAN CHOOSE TO CHANGE YOUR FEELINGS

It is only recently that psychologists, psychiatrists, and behavioral scientists have taught that an individual can learn to change her or his feeling responses. After one workshop a professor said, "I've been in this behavior business twenty years and you are the first person who ever suggested I could change my feelings."

Mary and Bob Goulding are directors of the Western Institute for Group and Family Therapy, where hundreds of therapists from all over the world have come to learn redecision therapy. The basis for their teaching is that we are responsible for our feelings; that we have the choice of being angry or calm, sad or happy, anxious or tranquil. In their book *Changing Lives Through Redecision Therapy*, they say of the choice to be angry, "This is one of the most significant statements in this book. The notion that we are in charge of our own feelings is counter to literature, our songs, and our upbringing."[4]

People say, "It made me mad," or "They made me mad." They suffer from the delusion that some outside power generated their anger, when in reality they are reacting to a situation in the same way they did as children. They avoid responsibility for their feelings and blame anger, guilt, depression, or even happiness on an outer situation.

This can be easily checked out by reading a newspaper or watching the TV news programs. When people are triggered by their pet peeve they say things like "Those politicians really burn me up." They may talk about it the rest of the evening, feel the anger in their bodies; or perhaps end up in a fight with their mates, and all because of something happening a thousand, two thousand miles away. Yet the body stress is genuine; it can be felt. But it is an absolute indication that the Inner Saboteur is at work.

Understanding that we give ourselves our bad feelings is essential to positive living. When we understand our responsi-

bility for our feelings and recognize the stimulus that gener-
ates them we can begin learning to act in a positive rather
than a negative way.

Each time one has been motivated to a new decision about
a way of being or acting in the world it is always imperative
to recognize the signs of the Inner Saboteur at work and the
feelings connected with that decision.

But once we are motivated to think about new life decisions,
we must be aware of how getting on with the change includes
taking a risk and facing our shortcomings, admitting responsibility for them, and doing something constructive about them.
I'll discuss getting on with it in the next chapter.

Chapter 7

Getting On with It

After organization comes action. Until something happens, nothing can be measured. Motivation, decision, and organization are a waste of time unless followed by positive action.

Once motivation has led to a new decision about positive living, the next step is the organization of a plan or blueprint for achieving your desired goals. Organization is the dividing line between wishing and wanting, the difference between dreaming and acting. It is a time of surrendering impulsiveness in favor of total responsibility for your future. It is the point of no return beyond which life will never be quite the same. To go uphill is to embark on an exhilarating journey. Not to change after having once honestly admitted the desire to do so leads only to the accumulation of more psychic garbage.

PERSONAL CONTRACT FOR CHANGE

The process of writing an organized plan for life managment is the devil's playground for the Inner Saboteur. It is a time when procrastination is most powerful; when the mind searches for all the negative reasons for not going forward. It is a time for messages like:

- Oh well, I' not doing too badly after all.
- What can you expect without a master's degree?
- I'd like to do it, but . . .

Or for wishy-washy statements like:

- I think I might be able to if . . .
- I'll see what I can do about it tomorrow.
- If only I . . .
- When the kids are raised I can . . .
- I don't know what this will do to my family.
- People will think I'm nutty to . . .

Except in rare cases the mind will not accept constructive change easily. To overcome inertia disturbs the mind's balance and the strong desire to cling to the comfort of the status quo. Even when life is miserable there is a sense of security in dealing with the known, and great insecurity when venturing into the unknown. There is a great temptation to keep on being stuck in a rut until a crisis demands change.

Organization offers us the opportunity to look ahead and forestall crisis, to alleviate pressure points before they become volcanic eruptions. Having a plan offers security, especially if it is a plan that others have used to get what they want out of life. There are very few experiences in life so unusual that they have never been explored by another human being. There is solace in the saying "What man has done, man can do."

VISUALIZING YOUR FUTURE

An entertaining way of breaking through the barrier between decision and organization is to make a futures collage. Out of some old magazines, cut five or six pictures of people doing the things that represent a positive and good life. Paste them on a large piece of poster board and mount it where it will be seen regularly. Do not use more than six or at the most seven pictures. To use more invites confusion. Many people never reach their goals because of the tendency to give up after they bite off more than they can chew. A collage serves several purposes.

It will help bring to the surface subconscious desires that have been buried under a negative belief system. By treating your desires as make-believe, barriers such as "I don't deserve it," "I'm not smart enough," or "I never really wanted it anyway" can be bypassed. A game of "What If" will help fantasize a picture of a good life. "What if I *do* deserve it?" "What if I *am* smart enough?" "What if I do want it and I am tired of kidding myself?"

The collage will focus on the reality that other people are doing the things you dream of. People do drive nice cars. People do own nice homes. People are successful. People do have good family relationships. You can see images of people doing all these things in advertisements and recognize that you too are a "people" and can have and do the same things.

It will help sort out and set goals. Look at your collage daily for a couple of weeks before tackling your written organizational plan. Think of the prices to be paid to achieve your goals. One man who felt he "should" be at the top realized he'd have to give up his small-town life and move to the big city to become president of his company. He took that picture off his collage and replaced it with a photo of a successful real estate broker. He's living now in the same small town, enjoying the life a small town offers while earning as much as he would have as the president of a small company. By picturing the life he wanted he brought his dream to the surface and accomplished the things he needed to do to make it happen. He made a plan and followed it.

Some people want "real-life people" rather than models in their collages, so they clip out newspaper pictures of real people. Whichever method you use, you will be creating a positive picture of yourself. It will help in the development of a new self-image reinforcing the awareness that other people, ordinary as you and I, have made their dreams come true.

Another worthwhile prelude to writing your self-management plan is to look at the lives of people who can be a model for you, just as athletes study their heroes and heroines. Read autobiographies and success stories. Gather as much positive information about people as you can. Constantly be aware that somewhere there is someone who has made the kind of change you want to make. Your Inner Saboteur may be saying, "Oh, that's OK for them but I couldn't do that." Not so. You *can* do it. There are too many others living life on their own terms to deny this.

Having a written plan, a personal contract for change, will help you clarify goals, identify needed steps in your plan for change, and check your progress. It will establish a date to begin and a date by which your goal will have been achieved. Be sure to identify positive payoffs you expect to gain for making change as well as the ways in which your Inner Saboteur may sabotage your efforts.

STATING PROBLEMS CLEARLY

Changing your belief system about your capabilities and competence is an important part of your new programming process. The written word also tends to be more specific than the spoken word. In *People in Quandries*, Wendell Johnson's viewpoint was that troubled people fail in the solution of life problems because they are not able to state their problems in specific terms. Without specifically stating the problem, a contract for performance is impossible, whether it be with yourself or with significant other people in your life: mate, children, friends, counselors, or employers.

I WILL AND I WON'T

To say either "I will" or "I won't" is the shortest, and most specific, way of saying "I have made a commitment." It means you have examined the consequences of your decision and you are willing to accept responsibility either for your commitment or for your decision not to make a commitment. This is quite different from the ordinary usage of the words "can" and "can't," which usually discount an individual's personal power by implying that some external force either permits or prevents the possibility of commitment.

Take smoking as an example:

- I can quit smoking any time I want to. [Of course, thousands do it every day, but this statement does not resolve the question. "Will you, or won't you, quit smoking?"]
- I will quit smoking. [This is a decision and a commitment to a future course of action as well as an acceptance of responsibility.]
- I can't quit smoking. [Ridiculous. This does not jibe with the reality that thousands of people have quit smoking. It implies, "It is outside of my power to quit smoking." It really means, "I am not willing to quit smoking."]
- I won't quit smoking. [This is an honest statement that in effect says, "I understand the consequences of my decision and I accept responsibility for that."]

Be aware that as you use these words in making personal decisions they may send your Inner Saboteur into action. To say "I will" may provoke doubt, anxiety, procrastination, or other negative feelings or actions. To say "I won't" can provoke guilt, depression, fear, or other feelings that originated in childhood. It would be a rare person who as a child was able to say "I won't do that" to his or her parents, without suffering negative consequences. To say "I won't" will bring to the surface the difference between being "other-directed" and "inner-directed." It may spark rebellious thoughts about not doing what others want of you. "I won't" is a reflection of your ability to make choices and be responsible for those choices. It confronts any tendency to play Blame Games in the form of "If it weren't for . . ."

TAKING RESPONSIBILITY AND GETTING STARTED

Once you've decided "I will," you begin shaping your personal contract for change. This is the point at which you accept responsibility for your life. Remind yourself that there is probably at least one person in the world, maybe in your town, who has accomplished what you want to. This is the time to give up dreaming, wishing, and fantasizing. It is the time of decision.

Hazel

Here's the story of a woman who had for years vaguely expressed the desire to go back to work when the kids grew up. With the children in high school she realized she was near a dividing line in her life. She had four options:

1. She could go on talking about her wish and feel bad because she wasn't doing anything.
2. She could go on talking about her wish and quit feeling bad about not getting on with her dream.

3. She could make a decision to go to work and feel bad for not being a "better wife."
4. She could go back to work and feel good about herself, knowing that she had enjoyed working earlier in her life.

She was motivated in several ways:

- Working outside of the home would give her a better self-image than keeping house.
- She wanted money of her own to spend that did not pass through the family budget.
- She wanted to set up an investment plan for travel after retirement (she doubted her husband's pension plan was keeping up with inflation).
- She wanted to build her Social Security account so that she would have retirement funds of her own.
- In her previous work as a legal secretary she had felt great compassion for people in trouble and wanted to help them.

Her decision, or primary objective, was: "I will be a paralegal professional with a certificate in Legal Assistantship from the state university extension division."

Her secondary objectives were:

- To make time for attending school. She did this by giving up bridge, and bowling and by asking her husband to cook dinner the two nights a week of classes.
- To take the step necessary for enrollment at the university committing herself to beginning her program with the scheduling of the first available class. It was a two-year program, but not wanting to risk failure by overloading herself she set a three-year period for obtaining her certificate.
- To earn money to pay the extra school expense. Hazel decided to do some part-time legal typing at home. In

order to do that she signed up for a brush-up typing course at the local junior college.

- To plan specifically for "together time" with the children and her husband.

In order to establish guidelines for progress, she worked out a schedule with a career counselor at the university and agreed to come in once every ninety days to be sure she stuck to her program.

The last paragraph in Hazel's personal contract read: "According to my past performance the ways I can sabotage myself are:

1. Trying to do too much too fast, to bite off more than I can chew, as my dad used to say to me.
2. When the pressure gets tough I have a tendency to give up and say, 'Oh, well, it was a good idea while it lasted.' Then I lose respect for myself and feel unhappy.
3. I can be a martyr and say, 'I really shouldn't take this time away from my family.'
4. Sometimes in the past I've felt I wasn't really smart enough for law. But I accept the reality that in the past I had been given great responsibility as a legal secretary because of my comprehension of the law."

By writing out these sabotage techniques Hazel faced those areas in which she was "her own worst enemy" and identified them as potential pressure points that could hamper or negate her efforts.

Once Hazel had signed and dated her contract she was ready to move on and take action.

HOW WILL I SABOTAGE MYSELF?

Like Hazel, although you may have a very clear picture of your future, keep in mind the messages the Inner Saboteur whispers to woo you from your goal—messages like:

- You silly kid. You're daydreaming again.
- Who do you think you are?
- Don't make waves.
- Look at us—we got by OK.
- You're pretty uppity, trying to be better than Mom and Dad.

If you are not in touch with your internal dialogue, pay attention to your feelings. If feelings of guilt, anxiety, depression, or hopelessness come over you, think back to the times when you had these same feelings as a child. A good way to make contact with this old programming is simply to sit and let your thoughts come through your head freely. Don't get into an internal argument or ask yourself "Why?" Just let the thoughts come in. Let the memories flow and be aware of what is coming on the TV screen of your mind. Try not to make judgments. You are simply working at identifying those situations in your childhood that provoked feelings similar to those connected with the current situation in your life.

Harriet

Harriet can tell you what she told her women's support group while training for a job after seventeen years of homemaking:

"I'm doing well. I catch on quick and my instructor says I'll never have a problem getting the job I want. Trouble is, every time he tells me that I wake up the next day and want to give up. It doesn't make sense but I just want to quit."

When Harriet began to track down this feeling of hopelessness she remembered things her dad had said to her when she bragged about her progress at school. She remembered the feelings that she had then and realized what was going on within her now.

When she came home with five A's and a B on her report card, her father used to say, "Why didn't you get all A's?"

When she told him about winning the spelling bee, he used to say, "Women are only good at details."

When she won an award in her science class, he said "Science won't do you any good. That's a man's job. A woman's place is in the home."

Harriet realized that even though her instructor praised her just as her teachers had, she later felt the hopelessness she had felt as a child. She was still hearing her father's voice and reacting to it without processing the reality of her current situation. With that realization and with practice and determination, Harriet made it through her training and is now happily employed as an engineer in a computer manufacturing firm. Once she had identified the origin of her negative thinking she replaced it with positive thinking, and positive action followed.

ACTION AND DOUBT

But taking action presents risks and doubts. The mind searches out old memories, and subsequent thoughts provoke the bad feelings that go with taking a risk when the belief system is disturbed.

Action is the common denominator of everyone who achieves his or her goals. Nonaction is the common denominator of all the losers and hangers-on in life. You've met them. They sit around in bars and tell you of all their grand schemes. At parties they bore you with tales of the book they could write, the action they plan on taking "someday." They are the ones who are seduced by their Inner Saboteurs; they are like those companions of Odysseus who turned to swine on drinking a magic potion offered by the enchantress Circe. Nonaction is the course of mediocrity, unhappiness, and boredom.

Motivation, decision, and organization mean nothing when they lead to a dead-end street. Only action can take you on the journey toward the life you aspire to. Do something appropriate and constructive, and do it every day. Take some action that will move you forward. Action is the test of determination that goes beyond willingness. Like motivation, action generates more energy and enthusiasm to sustain you in the early stages of your transition.

> *Anxiety:* I wonder if I'll really be able to make it.
> *Fear of failure:* Everybody will laugh at me if I don't make it.
> *Fear of success:* I'll lose all my friends if I get the promotion.

This style of negative thinking frequently relates to the basic message "What will people think?" It is a message that suggests your wants and needs are secondary to those of others. The end result is a feeling of guilt or anxiety over having failed to meet the expectations of others. Feelings of inadequacy are heavily reinforced when Mother says, "You make *me* feel ashamed every time *you* go out in public."

TAKING THE FIRST STEP

Once you've written out your plan for accomplishment and put down your primary and secondary goals, take the first step in the appropriate direction. Keep it up. Again, do at least one thing every day that will move you in the direction of your new goal. Accept the fact that you're not perfect, that there will be missteps along the way, and that you'll probably not give up all of your bad feelings overnight. It took years to develop and integrate your negative thinking habits, but as you recognize that they were acquired in childhood and are not related to the reality of your current world, you will use less time and expend less energy feeling bad. When something goes wrong, figure it out objectively and go on with your action plan.

KEEP ON KEEPING ON

While you are taking constructive steps you are also strengthening your will. Every time you act in favor of your plan you increase your potential for successfully exercising your will in the future. You are developing your will just as you would develop your body. It gets easier as you go along. Every time you resist the invitation of the Inner Saboteur to give up, procrastinate; avoid responsibility, or rebel, you increase your skills in self-management.

In the execution of your action plan you are developing increased potency and the ability to appropriately exercise your power to be in charge of your life. There will be stress. Some of your pressure points may intensify when the Inner Saboteur is uncomfortable with the new You. Your world may resist you, dumping "shoulds" and "ought tos" on you as you change the I Am and make yourself the person you want to be, living your life on your terms.

When internal friction occurs, go back over your plan. Remind yourself of your decision. Think of your expected payoffs and how you will enjoy them. Then keep on keeping on, bearing in mind that what you do must be appropriate to the situation—and that sometimes doing nothing is appropriate. Pushing the world too hard can be self-sabotage if misdirected and becomes a negative force blocking progress. People often bite off more than they can chew, say yes to every request, frantically carry the weight of the world on their shoulders, and then collapse. The ultimate triumph of the Inner Saboteur is the obituary notice announcing death due to heart attack of a high achiever in his or her thirties, forties, or fifties.

MAKING TIME FOR FUN

If you did not schedule time for fun or relaxation in your action plan, give that a thought. Most of us have a child within that needs care and nurturing, and even the "very serious types" can find a hobby or pastime providing some enjoyment or amusement—something that provides for a change of pace. Mental activity can be compared to a muscle expanding and contracting; alternating between concentration and relaxation is important to building up strength and endurance while reducing the possibility of burnout.

Motivation, decision, and organization are all a part of your positive-thinking process but will only add to life's discomfort until appropriately linked with positive action. William Thackeray put it this way: "Let the man who has to make his fortune in life remember this maxim: *Attacking* is the only secret. Dare, and the world always yields; or if it beats you sometimes, dare it again and it will succumb." Persistence is the key to the joy and satisfaction of those who win out over the Inner Saboteur.

Chapter 8

Transition

The only thing we can count on in life is change.

Transition is the process of getting from here to there, and it includes departure, arrival, and the necessary travel between the two. Departure means goodbyes, arrivals mean hellos, and human transition can be a period of grieving for the past as well as anticipation of the future. It can be a time of torment or a time of excitement. For many it is a time when encouragement is needed and determination is tested.

FINDING MODELS FOR CHANGE

A great source of encouragement is the experience of others who have made a desired transition, whether it be as mundane as making more money or as traumatic as divorce. There may be difficulty in finding a model whose transition seems as ordinary or as commonplace as we feel ours to be. Reading about the rich, the powerful, and the famous can be inspiring for some and create feelings of hopelessness for others. Glowing "how-to" books on becoming an instant millionaire or overnight success raise many doubts that are easily seized on by the Inner Saboteur and work to your disadvantage.

I would like to mention here a few people who are ordinary in the sense of being just like anyone on the block, but who are extraordinary in the sense of having arrived at the point of being totally in charge of their lives and happy with their situation. In the last twenty years I have been greatly involved with people making changes in their careers and lifestyles. For example:

- Alcoholics and drug addicts who've regained their ability to live a normal life.
- An almost illiterate man who is now successful in business.
- Failures who just had enough of failing.
- Women programmed to be satellites of men but who now have claimed their own power and potency.
- A teacher who turned his back on teaching and became a mechanic so that he could also live a life of creativity in art.
- Burnouts and dropouts in business and sales who had reached a point of no return and needed to "do their own thing."
- Priests who have left the church to become psychologists.
- Ministers who have left their ministries to go into business.
- Therapists, who I once naively thought had an automatic claim on happiness by virtue of their education, who now have found the way to enjoy life.

All these people had one thing in common: consciously or unconsciously they learned that the secret to positive living is only a secret because it is deeply locked inside each one of us.

Roughly, these people fall into four categories:

1. The Only-Road-Is-Up Types

These are people who just get fed up with their status quo. They may be at the bottom of the barrel, in the middle, or at the top as far as success and economic comfort, but for reasons usually outside their awareness they are driven to make changes in their lives. It's either go up or go down—and they are not willing to go down any lower.

2. The Frying-Pan Types

These are the ones who jump out of the frying pan into the fire. In some cases they are thrown out of their pleasant niche in life by unemployment, divorce, technological change, and such vagaries as Proposition 13 in California, which has abruptly terminated the illusion of security so frequently held by public employees. Whether voluntary or not, all bridges have burned behind the frying-pan types.

3. The Wanderers

By and large these people are fairly comfortable with their lives and ease into the transition mode only after encountering something in their lives that suggests a different life-style or career. Do not confuse them with drifters. The wanderers have a purpose and goal, but it takes them time to find that out, to discover that they have wants and needs different from those imprinted in their belief systems. Their internal stirrings may come about through a book, a political event, a lecture, or such dramatic occurrences as the Vietnam War or Three Mile Island. Whatever the stimulus, they develop that "divine restlessness" that energizes change.

4. The Adaptors

Adaptors are pragmatic realists who sense where they want to go in life and create or follow opportunities that will take them there. They operate from an "I want to—I need to" position rather than from "I ought to—I have to." Adaptors don't expect the world to be perfect, and they are willing to make compromises while they figure out a way to make their own life better when conditions are appropriate. They understand their priorities in life and recognize the prices that must be paid to attain them. For example, an adaptor might want a better marriage, but would keep the peace until the children were raised and gone. An adaptor might dream of independence and security, but hold on to current income until the time was right. An adaptor might go to night school, take a correspondence course, or develop a hobby or craft leading to career extension after retirement. A prime example is a New York policeman who underwent nursing training while still on the force and simply moved from one job to another the day after retirement. Adaptors tend to think ahead, plan their progress, and negotiate with life as they move toward their desired goals. They do this with comfort, a balance different from the manipulators who wrangle their way through life or risk their health and relationships as workaholics do.

Change is accepted as a constant in the dynamics of life by the adaptors. They either foresee change and take appropriate steps to deal with it, or handle change rationally if fate thrusts it on them. In the midst of the Depression a Los Angeles man made a fortune putting hot-dog pushcart vendors on the streets. He was an adaptor. A young San Francisco executive was abruptly ordered to a position in the Chicago office of his company. He and his family didn't want to go, so he resigned and became a successful investment account executive. He was an adaptor. Neither wasted time on resentment or feeling sorry for himself. They simply let go, an important early step in successful transition.

Gayle

Gayle is an only-road-is-up type. In her twentieth year her Inner Saboteur led her into a total rebellion against the standards and values she felt her parents represented. The family connection broke down completely. Gayle embarked on an adventure of wild excitement that took her along the edge of the drug scene. She was swept along by the crowd, her bold front covering her insecurity and inability to be decisive about anything. From time to time her "old man" got steady work in a lumber operation, construction, or a mine, and she'd find herself dreaming of life as a housewife and of having some security.

In her late twenties she began to tire of the excitement, of the constant hustle to provide bed and board and seeing every dollar go for another party. The arrival of a baby boy tempered Gayle's rebellion, stirring dreams of a different existence if her man would settle down. Living in the void of illusion, she functioned almost automatically, doing what she needed to do to keep the little boy fed, even when it meant getting a meal at a mission or clothes from a church. She learned to become a survivor, to hang on without dropping completely out of life.

Then, in her own words, "Everything came down at once." She called her folks, not knowing they had undergone their own transitional struggles escaping midlife crisis, and in that passage had vowed that the door would always be open to Gayle if she ever needed sanctuary. Gayle come home. She walked off the airplane completely whipped, with everything she owned in the world: a four-year-old boy in her arms, a suitcase, and a bag of clothes tied together with an old rope.

Slowly coming out of shock, she began to work out the standards and values she wanted for her life, so that they were not the "shoulds" or "oughts" with which she'd been programmed, and against which she had rebelled. She learned that anger and rebellion were the energy produced by her Inner Saboteur. She also learned a great deal about her programming through long talks with her mother and sister, and realized how two kids in the same family can see the world in different ways and make very different decisions about it. She found a female counselor who helped her make sense out of her new discoveries.

There were times when she felt bad about drawing welfare

assistance, and times when she felt inadequate because her parents helped her with housing and transportation. Then an employee-development counselor told her, "It's like insurance. You're getting training now, and once we get you a job you'll pay taxes a long time." She's paying taxes now. After having undergone career counseling and testing to uncover her skills and abilities, Gayle trained for hospital work at the local community college. She's working in a hospital now, living life her own way and enjoying being a mother. When her Inner Saboteur makes a pass at her, she has supportive people around to listen while she works things out.

This is how Gayle's plan might appear:

1. *Motivation:* To achieve a feeling of security based on her ability to earn her own way without relying on others.
2. *Decision:* To develop an independent life-style based on her needs and wants rather than meeting the expectations of her world.
3. *Organization:* Gayle went to the community college career counseling center, an employee development counselor, and a nonprofit community agency to get assistance in working out her plans for the future. Based on the information she gathered, she set her primary objective as employment in the health services field. Her secondary objectives were to enroll in training courses, to give up television time for study time, to rearrange her budget to pay for the gasoline needed to get her to school and her son to preschool, and to lose some surplus weight that was siphoning off her physical energy.
4. *Action:* She enrolled in medical-terminology and typing classes at the community college and began a work-study training program in procedure at the county and began a work-study training program in procedure at the county hospital. She also took a course in assertiveness training so that she could handle personal interactions and not be triggered by the anger with which her Inner

Saboteur had often undermined her efforts to state her needs. A turning point came when she told her father, "I won't get angry at you anymore, because when I do I give up my power."

5. *Transition:* The immediate transition was completed when Gayle started work at the hospital. She now realizes she is in a new transitional phase: working, nurturing a boy in grade school, and making friends in her community. Gayle will be in transition for many years as she moves through the developmental tasks of life. But she looks forward to them with anticipation and excitement. For her, the only way is up.

Larry

Larry is one of the frying-pan types. He's only 35 but on his fourth "career." Larry never has jobs, he always has careers, and each time he starts a new one he works on it like a professional. He studies hard, listens, and goes through all the right motions. He is bright, personable, and clever in his relations with others. Then, after about two years, he discovers:

- He is smarter than his boss (he thinks).
- His work does not sufficiently challenge his creativity.
- He is bored.

He suffers his boredom because his Inner Saboteur traps him in an "either/or" syndrome: either he must go crazy from boredom or quit and get another job. He is not able to energize his objectivity and think out clear solutions to his problems. He tends to be more other-directed than inner-directed and asks friends what they think he should do. His wife said little when he made his job changes, because Larry earned a decent enough income, but on the third one she expressed some worry. "You just get going, I begin to feel some security, and then it's time to jump again."

This worried Larry and kept him on the third job five years, but eventually his Inner Saboteur got to him and he impulsively quit the best job he'd ever had. His wife suggested he see a psychologist, but Larry didn't believe in "that Freudian crap." It didn't make sense to him that his grownup life might be influenced by his childhood programming. He simply would not have believed in a phenomenon known as "fear of success" or understood that as a boy it would have been unthinkable for him to surpass his father at anything and that could now influence his career.

Larry would start each career with his renewed efforts to conquer the world as a positive thinker taking positive action. Then, just as he unconsciously sensed he'd be asked to take on more responsibility, his mind searched out the negative points in his belief system, and he used "dumb bosses" and "boring jobs" as excuses to avoid his potential for successful living.

Fortunately, everyone's entitled to a little luck in life. Larry had a bachelor uncle who had always favored him as a boy, who took a great interest in Larry's family, and who had attempted to serve as a mentor from time to time. Distressed by his wife's reaction to his last job departure and worried about his future, Larry went to see Uncle John, the successful owner of a printing business.

Larry asked, "How do you do it? How do you stay in one thing so long?"

"I like it."

The simple response was overwhelming for Larry. It had just never occurred to him that there were people who enjoyed the privilege of doing work they liked. Larry once had dreamed of being a writer, but put that aside as not being practical. He took work he could get, not work he wanted. Without making a decision about goal setting, he drifted into what was really a career-counseling process with Uncle John, who knew about Larry's interest in writing. The two of them brainstormed the options open to creative writers other than starving in a garret while writing the Great American Novel.

Uncle John said, "I've seen your writing. You're clever.

You express yourself well and you dress decently. How about the advertising business?''

Larry wasn't sure. He'd have to think about it. His Inner Saboteur raised some immediate objections:

- That's selling, isn't it?
- You can't afford to work on commission.
- How do you know you'll like it?

However, he talked more with his uncle about it. He talked with his wife about it. Most important, he talked with himself about it. For the first time he felt some power over his career directions as he realized he would like to use his writing talents and enjoy the personal responsibility he would have for managing his work. In an informal way he was taking the steps necessary to intelligent career planning. Finally he said to his uncle, "I'm interested. How do I do it? How do I support Bobby and the kids while I get started?''

"That's what I've been waiting to hear," Uncle John laughed. "Sounds like you've made a decision.''

Larry had doubts, but when he learned many people in the advertising business are paid salaries and bonuses, he made a decision—not just a decision to try, but a decision to succeed. Uncle John had him get a book on copywriting and then write several sample advertisements. With those in hand, he went to several ad agencies with permission to use his uncle as a referral. He's been an account executive for three years now and loves it. For once, he's jumped out of the frying pan without landing in the fire.

Larry's transition was fairly rapid and was positively influenced by an element of fortune, his uncle. At the same time he was able to seize an opportunity that was right for him. He is now able to identify the signs of the Inner Saboteur at work when he feels a fear of tackling a new project or account, or procrastinates in servicing an account. Sometimes his wife recognizes the old signals of his Inner Saboteur and alerts him. He listens now and has even read a few "pop psychology" books that have given him new ways to keep on his chosen path. And when someone questions why he is in the advertising business, he says, "I like it."

Wayne

Wayne is a wanderer. He goes with the flow, enjoying life without feeling the need to strive for a particular goal. He grew up in a mountain town and figured someday he'd work for the U.S. Forest Service, because it was outdoor work and because it offered a career compatible with the environment and it had the security of civil service.

He is an uncomplicated man, and it came naturally to him to be a positive thinker who took positive action. He studied, through special courses offered by the Forest Service and took the promotional exams he felt were appropriate to his ambitions and the needs he had for increased income as his family grew in size. In his thirties he became a district ranger, managing a small district in a remote mountain town. The work was challenging, especially during fire season. Slowly, though, Wayne became increasingly aware that he was managing people rather than things and situations.

After a week-long group training session in organizational development, a humanistic management technique, he came away with a new vision of himself and his relationship to his workers and his family. He read all the books he could find on the human potential movement. He wandered through the field of human behavior, taking every course the Forest Service offered having to do with human relationships. He involved himself with the county mental health association. When courses were offered in transactional analysis, he attended every one he could, and for a while his friends called him a TA freak.

Wayne was a wonderful example of the hierarchy of human needs proposed by Abraham Maslow.[1] Wayne had met his basic needs for food, shelter, sleep, sex, safety, security, love, belongingness, self-esteem, and esteem by others. Now, in order to grow, to become self-actualized, he had a growth need: the need for meaningfulness. For years his line and staff duties provided the needed meaning in his life. Then, with the change in his duties, he was challenged by the responsibility to know more about the interaction of management with people and human behavior, on and off the job. Meaningfulness came when, instead of shirking his duties, Wayne faced the challenge they presented.

He was also an excellent example of one who takes responsibility for growth. He continued his studies of human nature without really knowing where it would take him, but trusted his instinct. When a position opened in the regional office of human resources management he applied, fearful he might be denied for lack of formal training. It was ruled that his personal learning program was the equivalent to college courses, and he received the coveted appointment. Wayne's primary objective was to learn more about himself and others. His secondary objective was to take the training and get the needed education. Now he is the man he wants to be, doing the work he wants to do and enjoying it immensely. And by staying with his own organization, he accomplished all this without cutting off his options or sabotaging himself.

Jacob

Jacob is a descendant of a long line of Middle European merchants. All of his relatives were thrilled when he decided to go to college and get a degree in business. He was the first of the family to get a degree and was a great source of pride to all of them. He landed a good entry-level management position with a national firm, married, and had three children.

All of this kept him happily busy until his late thirties. Then, nearing middle age, some new thinking crept into his consciousness. Over a period of time he became uneasy with his vulnerability to the power of the corporation. They could transfer him. They could merge with another corporation and eliminate his job. Approaching forty, he also thought of the difficulties faced by the plus-forties in the management world. He remembered when he was a boy all the praise lavished on is relatives for being independent merchants and began to feel the answer to his situation was to get into business for himself.

Analyzing his dilemma it appeared like this:

- He had a good job with good pay.
- He had a wife and three kids to support.
- He did not have much capital to risk.
- He had a good pension plan if he stayed until eligible for early retirement.

Being realistic, he began to explore businesses that could be developed and run part-time. He subscribed to a newsletter specializing in reports of such businesses. From his bank he obtained a portfolio of small ventures. He got appropriate information from the Small Business Administration. He looked up some people who had successfully set themselves up with their own organizations while retaining their current jobs.

His decision was to team up with a national advertised company specializing in direct sales of home goods to consumers. Working with, and for, people had always given him satisfaction. He liked the idea that he could help himself by helping others earn extra money or build their own distributorship. Jacob now has an average of thirty people working with him and earns almost as much in his side venture as he does in salary. He had these three options for the future:

1. To leave his job and become a full-time entrepreneur.
2. To work until early retirement and claim his pension.
3. If asked to transfer, to step out on his own and stay in the community he loves.

Of course, he paid some prices that people who are just getting by don't want to pay. He doesn't bowl or play golf— most of his spare time goes to his private venture. But he is not a workaholic. He takes time to enjoy his family. He enjoys going to conferences, and his wife takes an active part in their venture. They have the kind of mutuality many of his relatives had in their mom-and-pop stores.

As an adaptor, Jacob examined the payoffs he wanted from his life, made decisions, organized a plan for his future, took action, and successfully made his transition from employee to employer. He is winning in life. Of course, he has problems. He doesn't live in paradise any more than you or I do. But when problems arise he knows the "how-to" of keeping himself on the track of getting more out of life.

PART TWO

Making Your New Programming Work for You

Chapter 9

Your Words Can Make or Break You

> *Your words are your image—in your own mind as well as in the minds of others. You can make positive changes in that image by the selective use of words.*

There are two things about you that cry out your message to the world: your appearance and your speech. Your body image (and the clothes you use to cloak it) and the way you use words are two ways by which people judge you. And, rightly or wrongly, you are judged by the assumptions locked in the belief systems of others. The color of your skin, your sex, your bearing, and your apparent age all send signals that are interpreted by others to fit you into their belief systems.

You may share many of the assumptions that are prevalent among others of your world. A suntan is the look of health. Clothes make the person. Thin people are more vigorous. Tall people make better executives. You can't teach an old dog new tricks. You can trust anyone who wears a clerical collar. Beards and longish hair are the brand of a liberal. A Cadillac is the mark of a successful person.

MENTAL SELF-IMAGE

These assumptions are all superficial and often mistaken, but there is enough reality in them to support a sizeable industry offering you assistance with your appearance. High-quality clothing stores suggest that if they dress you, you will project confidence and success. Cosmetics, for both men and women, are promoted by Madison Avenue advertising agencies. Diet pills, vitamins, and health supplements are hawked on television. You can hire a consultant to train you and turn you out in the style deemed appropriate for your career. You can go to a health spa to develop the body image of an energetic striver. There is a plethora of sources that will help to enhance your image, style, or pizzazz.

There is also an equally large network of assistance available for people who realize that getting more out of life is dependent upon the ability to communicate.

Harrison

When Harrison pulls his Mercedes Benz away from his handsome two-story home on his way to work, his suit, shoes, shirt, tie, and haircut represent about a $450 investment. He looks like a $50,000-a-year man on his way up. Yet he has never considered taking a course to improve his communication skill. He's done all right so far, but his Inner Saboteur is moving him into a trap. Harrison's progress has been based on his technical brilliance in electronics. If he moves up he will need to change from a "thing" person to a "people" person. He will not make it to the Executive Suite if he does not change his authoritarian manner of speech and give up his sarcasm with subordinates and glee on winning arguments in staff meetings. Harrison needs to know more about his choice of words, the way to use them, and the manner in which his speech affects his belief system and reinforces some negative aspects of that system.

"Poppycock" would be Harrison's response if told that his communication style was abrasive—that instead of a willingness to cooperate, it generates resentment and distrust in others—or that his management wonders if he could be a "good team player." He doesn't realize that *looking* like the well-dressed executive does not alleviate the distress of others when he says, "You have to" (banging his fist on the table), or "Everyone knows that" (with a slight sneer that implies stupidity in others), or "You'd better get it right" (scowling).

These were the phrases he heard most from his father, a naval officer. Because his father's word was law, Harrison adopted the same style and is unaware of how others feel about his dictatorial attitude. Nor is he aware that his speech is also a reinforcement of his self-image as a "man who stands on his own feet and makes decisions." Often what he says serves more to reinforce that image rather than to communicate with his audience. And every time Harrison reinforces his image he becomes slightly more callous to the possibility of constructive change.

LISTENING TO YOURSELF SPEAK

Few people realize that their words reinforce their self-image, whatever it may be. You probably know someone who consistently presents the picture of a loser. Next time your are around the person listen for phrases like:

- Why does this always happen to me?
- I made *another* mistake.
- That's me, stupid Harry.
- If it weren't for [you, him, her, they, whatever] . . .

It might surprise you to find how many negative feelings about themselves people reveal in their daily conversation.

The most negative one I ever heard came from a fellow who felt he was born to lose. As a teenager he'd gone on a joy ride with friends. There was a robbery and a murder, and even though he did not participate he spent twenty-one years in prison. When things weren't right with him he said, "Man, I'm born dead."

Frequently such statements are accompanied by a grin or laughter even though the situation is not funny. They seem to be saying, "I'm a victim of my fate, so I might as well have a sense of humor." They do not understand that they could take a major step forward in improving their self-esteem by giving up the words with which they discount themselves. By hearing themselves speak in positive terms people can project a more confident picture of themselves, and they can also begin to make changes in their belief systems. Eventually, the negative messages of the Inner Saboteur could be ignored or, in some cases, given up entirely.

LISTENING TO YOUR THOUGHTS

By paying attention to the way you use words, you can also improve your self-understanding and increase your personal potency. Thinking is mainly talking to yourself, holding an internal conversation, and the selection of the words you use in your mind is just as important to your growth as the ones you use out loud. As you think of the words and the way you use them, be aware that some words are positive and some are negative. Listen to radio and TV commercials if you want examples of pleasant words. Ads don't say, "Hey, you turkey. Buy Super Soap and knock 'em dead." They say, "Fellow, the masculine scent of Super Soap will turn girls' heads—toward you."

Here are some words communications researchers say people like and dislike:

Like:

you	dependable	useful	enthusiastic
yours	efficient	responsible	reliable
benefit	justice	fair	genuine
easy	prestige	honesty	cheerful
healthy	success	desirable	admire
courageous	free	valuable	practical
service	wholesome	trustworthy	cooperative
conscientious	smiling	honorable	integrity
satisfying	popular	energetic	generous
capable	effective	appreciate	kind

Dislike

blame	hardship	allege	crisis
smelly	impossible	fraud	fear
extravagant	sloppy	hypocrite	failure
hopeless	prejudiced	obey	apologize
cheap	unfair	squander	beware
imitation	tardy	exaggerate	should
alibi	discredit	superficial	dispute
opinionated	flattery	decline	critical
rude	unsuccessful	negligent	censure
wrong	unlucky	idiotic	waste

In looking at this list, simply be aware of the feelings you have when these words are applied to you. The chances are that the words giving you good feelings or bad feelings do the same for others. Using pleasant words rather than unpleasant ones will raise your stature with others. It will also improve your own self-image when you clean the loser words out of your mind.

LISTENING TO SPEECH—YOUR OWN AND OTHERS'

Now examine how you communicate with others. How you use words makes the difference between talking to people and communicating with them. Conversation isn't always communication. How many times in your life have you had a conversation with someone believing you were in agreement, only to find out later there had been no meeting of minds? You and your respondent had certain assumptions about semantics (meanings of words) and syntax (the way words are put together). Frequently such assumptions are incorrect. I remember an unpleasant squabble one day in a post office because I asked for a roll of one hundred stamps. I was brusquely told there was no such thing; the stamps came only in rolls of five hundred. Having bought what I considered a roll of one hundred on several occasions, I insisted on it. It took the intervention of another worker to straighten out the situation. He said, "I think he means a strip," calmly stripping one hundred stamps off a five-hundred-stamp roll. He then rolled the strip into a small roll and put a paperclip on it so that when he handed it over to me it looked like a roll. How many times have you lost time and energy because of a misunderstanding of a word?

THERE'S MORE TO COMMUNICATION THAN WORDS

Most literate people tend to overemphasize the significance of words in getting their meaning across to the person you're talking to. It is a holdover from elementary school, when spelling and grammar were stressed by teachers. The reality is that words may be the least meaningful component of a successful verbal communication. In his research of verbal communications, Albert Mehrabian found that the words contributed only 7 percent of the total impact of a message. The balance of meaning was conveyed by tone of voice (38 percent) and facial expression (55 percent).[1] In other words, *how* you use your words affects a message far more than the actual words contained in the message.

Here's a way to test for yourself. Stand in front of your mirror and gently say, "Please." Hear the sound of your voice as you do so and look at your facial expression.

Now give yourself what might be called a huffy expression and sarcastically snap out, "Please."

Next, assume a scowl or angry look, double your first, and punch the air in front of you as you shout, "Please."

Get the idea? All three transactions are based on the same word, but three different responses are generated in the listener. You can check this further by asking your children, your mate, or friends how they respond to differences in your vocal tone and facial expressions.

Think a moment about the many times in your life people have talked to you in a way that left you with bad feelings. Your Inner Saboteur had been activated and the result was confusion. Old thought and feeling patterns momentarily blocked your capacity for objectivity along with your ability to accurately process the message sent to you.

Maybe you've had the experience of being around a person who is partially deaf and consequently talks in a very loud tone. Even though you know the person is deaf and doesn't hear the loud tones, it is easy to become cross or irritable; the loud voice may trigger your memory bank and activate old rebellious messages and feelings. Sometimes it takes a special effort to ignore these feelings and remain objective.

THE MODEL OF SPOKEN COMMUNICATION

For those of us wanting more from life, examining our communications process is imperative. To improve that process we need to know how we are affected by other people's communication. To walk a mile in our brother's or sister's shoes is to enhance our empathy, trust, and confidence in self and others. Once you firmly have in mind the ways you don't like to be communicated with, you can make a decision not to communicate with others in this manner. This does not mean you have to sacrifice your needs to express them. You can be assertive without being aggressive. You can learn that much of your body language, vocal tones, and appearance may contradict your intended message, thereby sabotaging your intended results. The goal is to make all aspects of your communication—your words, vocal tones, body language, and specificity (more on what I mean by "specificity" below) —blend harmoniously and reinforce one another.

Here's the model of spoken communication:

Verbal: Word selection.
Vocal: Tone of voice.
Body Language: Dress, facial expressions, body movements.
Specificity: The syntax of responsibility.

Verbal

Earlier in this chapter you read a list of words that people like and dislike. Make a list of words that *you* dislike when people are talking to you. You can be sure that if you don't like them used toward you, others feel the same way. Discard those words. Avoid them. Let them go. This won't happen overnight, but as you become aware of them you will gradually lose them.

How do I know? Because I grew up in a family where

sarcasm was mistaken for humor. I was very sarcastic until at age 37 a turn of fate left sales as the only career door open to me. I didn't need a communications specialist to tell me that a sarcastic salesperson has little chance of success. I knew nothing about the Inner Saboteur. But I do know that as I worked to clean sarcasm out of my speech for profit, the fringe benefit was an increased comfort in my family life.

Unless you are a bullfighter you probably wouldn't go into a bullring waving a red flag at a bull. There are words that are like red flags to many people. Giving those words up in the service of better communication is a worthy effort.

Vocal

Think about the vocal tones people use when talking to you. What tones do you dislike? What ones upset you? What ones result in confusion so that you do not get the message, or feel so rebellious you reject the message? For anyone to use those same tones to others is evident of the Inner Saboteur at work.

Vocal tones can easily distort the meaning of a message if they trigger automatic reactions in others. Pete supervised thirty-five women in a bank and worked hard at being a model manager. He took, and even taught, all the management classes he could in night school. But he was a big, burly man with a macho background and a voice that could make the walls tremble.

In a workshop he said, "Man, what's with these women? Every time I try to tell one about an error she bursts into tears."

The workshop leader said, "You know, with that tone of voice sometimes I feel like busting out crying too."

That made Pete think, especially when the women in the workshop said the same thing about his voice. He said, "Funny. My wife's been telling me that a long time but I thought it was just her."

It had never occurred to Pete that despite his desires to be a good manager the way he used his voice sabotaged his efforts. As he became aware of the internal stress arising within his employees at times of criticism, he worked hard at modulating his vocal tone. With his new sensitivity to the feelings of others, he overcame the Inner Saboteur's advice: "Just be yourself. If they don't like it that's their problem."

By paying attention to those vocal tones that trigger negative reactions in you, you can become more aware of your vocal tones that may be sabotaging your communications.

Body Language

Dress and appearance are tremendously important in human communications. Take the young college student, barefoot and clad in jeans and a tank top who went to a Rotary Club meeting in a small college town to talk sincerely about school-community relations. He clambered onto a table, sat on a table in yoga fashion exposing his dirty soles to his audience, and earnestly said, "What can I tell you?"

The unspoken answer was, "Nothing." The ones who didn't leave immediately were turned off and became lost in thoughts of what was becoming of the younger generation.

Appearance and body language trigger immediate reactions in your audience because they have so many assumptions about appearance based in their childhood programming. To illustrate this, a very successful management consultant who does two-day communication workshops always wears a $500 suit the first day with a group of executives. The next day he comes in wearing blue denims and jogging shoes. This always generates a heated discussion about the appropriateness of his dress. After listening, he says, "Listen. I'm the same fellow who was here yesterday. And I'm just as smart as I was yesterday." Then he talks about assumptions and how they can either benefit or disrupt communication, problem solving, and decision making.

It is up to you to determine the image you wish to project

and then do it in a way consistent with your intent and desired results. There'll be comments on ways to do that at the end of this chapter.

Specificity

This might also be called "semantic responsibility" and has to do with the fact that a great proportion of our conversation is a process of avoidance. Hidden behind the torrent of talk is the fear of exposing ourselves to others, fear of responsibility, fear of consequences, fear of getting what is wanted, or fear of not getting it. Paradoxical perhaps, but true. Few people's belief systems permit them to be honest and/or intimate with others.

Check it out during Happy Hour in any bar or gathering place. You'll hear things like:

"How are things going since the merger?"

"Oh, great, great. Say, the Dodgers really have a streak going." (Meaning: "I'm too scared to talk about it.")

Or: "How are you getting along since the divorce?"

"Oh, great, great. You ought to meet the fantastic woman I just found at a singles club." (Meaning: "I'm still hurt, angry, and lonely, and I don't trust you enough to talk about my feelings. Besides, I might cry.")

Or: "How do you like red?" (Meaning: "Do you like this new dress?")

"Oh, great, great. It's kind of in this year, isn't it?" (Meaning: "On that body it looks like a knockout but I'm afraid to tell you, you'll think I'm on the make and I'll be rejected again.")

Conversation is like a merry-go-round. Everyone goes around and around and up and down and the only one who knows what he's doing is the fellow who collects the tickets. That is what specificity is all about: knowing what you're doing, knowing what you want to have happen, and doing what is necessary to get your expected results. It is being self-directed. It requires the risk of saying what you want and just how you expect another to help you in fulfilling that want.

GETTING YOUR MESSAGES STRAIGHT

Every step you can take toward becoming more congruous in the transmission of your messages is a step toward meaningful and results-oriented communication. Dissonance or incongruousness occurs when your signals, including your words, your vocal tones, your body language, and your specificity, do not "fit" in a way that makes sense to your listener. How many times have you walked away from a conversation guessing, "I wonder what he or she really wanted to say to me?" You may not have doubted the sincerity or intent of the message sender but somehow the message didn't get through. The words said one thing and all the other signals said something else. It's like having your hostess, who served you chili beans not knowing you have an ulcer, ask, "How did you like dinner?" With a painful smile you reply, "Oh, fine. It was good." Later she worries, "He doesn't like my cooking."

Incongruousness in communications is not an accident, despite our good intentions. Paradoxically, our childhood programming recorded many counter productive perceptions in our belief systems.

"Don't be selfish" may translate into "Don't ask for what you want."

"Don't be rude" may translate into "Let other people have their way."

"Don't cry," "Don't be angry," or "Don't show your feelings" may translate into "I'm not important," or "What's the use of telling them?"

These are perceptions recorded early in life and replayed many times over later in life by the Inner Saboteur. It is these messages and perceptions that create perplexing problems in human relations. Sizable numbers of behavioral scientists, therapists, lawyers, and politicians would be out of work tomorrow if the world population awakened with a new skill of talking straight to one another instead of using crooked language.

Why can't we talk straight to one another? Fear. Plainly and simply, fear.

Fear of rejection
Fear of scorn
Fear of ridicule
Fear of criticism
Fear of being ignored
Fear of being put down

Most of these fears are leftovers from childhood. Certainly there are times when a fear is justified by experience, but that is a rational and valid fear. An employee working for a volatile and intemperate boss knows from experience that negative results are a constant threat. That threat is real and objective. Fears triggered by the Inner Saboteur, however, are not connected with current experience and reality.

Here's a personal research task. Think about some of the situations that provoke distress for multitudes of people. How do you feel when:

- You ask for a raise.
- You are asked to give a talk.
- You are interviewed for a job.
- Your supervisor does a performance appraisal with you.
- You ask an acquaintance for a date.
- You feel sexy and want to ask your mate to turn off the TV and come to bed.

If you are an ordinary sort of person there are probably dozens of times you've wanted things from others and beat around the bush, afraid to come right out and say what you want. The questions now for you are these: are these feelings appropriate to the current situation? Are they the same kinds of feelings you had under stress as a child? What terrible thing do you fear will happen if you talk straight and ask for results?

The reason for this self-questioning is simple. Once you recognize that most fear in grown-up communications is simply a feeling habit, your potential for taking positive action to improve your communications process is greatly expanded. As you read the following suggestions for self-analysis and self-correction, be aware of your *immediate* reaction. If you get any negative thoughts, it is your Inner Saboteur saying, "Uh-oh. This is scary. You're being asked to be responsible for yourself."

SEEING YOURSELF AS OTHERS SEE YOU

The single most important and powerful measure you can take to examine your communications habits is to see and hear yourself on videotape. Listen to your diction, reflect on your choice of words, hear your vocal tones, see your body image and watch your body language. One adult student in a communications class said, "Boy, I learned more in five minutes of watching myself in action that I've ever known before about how I come off with others."

Videotape training has been used to help salespeople improve their performance, managers and executives improve their communications, and individuals improve their human connections. Such training is offered in many community colleges, college extension courses, and a variety of private organizations listed in the Yellow Pages ranging from modeling schools to self-enhancement programs.

If video facilities are not available in your community or are too expensive, or if you just don't feel ready at this time for such an experience, you can very simply record your voice with a tape recorder. This is best done in groups but can easily be done while talking with your mate or a friend.

Find a subject in which you both have interest and talk spontaneously with each other. In short order you will soon forget the machine and the conversation will become relaxed and natural. Set the tape aside when you are through and wait a few days before you listen to it. Along with noticing your words, your sentence structure, and your vocal tones, listen carefully to the way you ask questions and why you ask them. Many people shield themselves from risk by asking questions. Try turning some of your questions into statements and notice how this makes you feel. If you will do this several times both you and your communications partner will learn a great deal about your speech habits and will find places for easy improvement. Two other resources available almost universally are public-speaking courses and Toastmasters International. Both are low in cost and offer high rewards that can be measured in terms of increased self-confidence and self-esteem—important contributions to your potency.

The stress on communications here is based on my own personal experience of getting more out of life through improved speaking ability. At age sixteen I was so shy I crossed the street to keep from meeting people. My mother said, "Take public speaking." She said it many times. So I took it in high school, thinking I'd faint before I got a word out. And I took it in college and acted as if I felt confident even though I was so afraid my stomach hurt. But I was a negative thinker who covered his trepidation by positive action. I kept at it until my capacity for verbal expression was my principal tool for earning a living in management and sales. Along the way I spent a couple of years in Toastmasters International and involved myself in community activities that had me speaking before at least one group a week for two years. You can do the same by giving more thoughts to the words you use, how you use them, and with whom you use them.

Chapter 10

Positive Listening

> *Really listening to what is said involves the mind and the heart. Not really listening is avoiding responsibility for results.*

How many times as a child were you told, "Keep quiet and listen"? And you couldn't listen. Your mind was a morass of confusion, filled with fright or anger. Maybe your body trembled or stomach tightened when someone said, "Children should be seen and not heard." And if you are like so many others, you couldn't hear what was really being said. Your thoughts were full of all the things you wanted to say:

- I'm a person too. Why doesn't anyone listen to me?
- I didn't really do it. It was Bobby's fault.
- I'm too scared to understand you.

Or when admonitions turned into a lecture or a diatribe, you turned it off by thinking about the kids playing outside. Then, in frustration, the older person would say, "Look at me when I talk to you." So you looked into that angry older person's face and tried to shield yourself from the glaring eyes. The greatest terror of all was when they said, "Look me in the eye."

The dilemma of the inquisitorial process that so frequently passes for "communications" between parent and child is that the child learns how to not-listen. Evasive action is learned; some children hang their heads and look at the ground, others learn to look into the parent's eyes without seeing the face, and the rebellious ones stick their chins out and glare back at their tormentor. With all the dynamics of the situation in full play there is little hearing going on. The listening habits and the body language of the future are gradually developed out of the one-up/one-down relationship between parent and child.

The process is later reinforced in the schoolroom in the teacher-student connection. But then a new confusing element enters. The child hears, "Speak up," or "Don't mumble," or "Enunciate clearly," or "The class can't hear you."

From having originally been told to listen, the emphasis becomes talk-talk-talk. First come the spelling bees and poetry recitals. Later came classes in English and grammar. Many are urged to take debate, and in some schools it is almost as prestigious to be a witty orator as to be a quarterback or a pitcher. Parliamentary procedure and rhetoric are often pushed. All of this generates the idea that good conversation is a form of combat, and that words are the weapons of winners.

Unfortunately, few are taught to listen, or taught the importance of listening. Listening is a behavior habit that can be as cleanly defined as talking but is nevertheless overlooked as part of the human communication. Until about 1970, listening as a communications skill had been taught only to psychotherapists and counselors. Then, suddenly, it was an idea whose time had come and books for the lay person dealing with the art of listening began to appear on the market. They dealt with kinesics, body language, coding and decoding, giving feedback, and transactions.

I began to find answers to my question "Is anybody listening, and if not, why not?" A dozen years of supervision and management in government and international business left me with the conclusion that what passed for management was a process of talking "to" or "at" people rather than "with" people. I found little done to measure the effectiveness of that process. It seemed as though everybody was always talking and few listeners were getting the message. The unilateral imposition of orders and instructions leaves the one-up person with the assumption that the one-down person will automatically comply. It doesn't work. Ask anyone who has been in the military.

EFFECTIVE COMMUNICATION

During my sales career I learned a little about talking "with" people. I also learned that the salesperson has an immediate criterion for the effectiveness of communications. Either a sale is made or it is not made. Period. No ands, buts, or maybes. An idea is transmitted from the mind of the salesperson to that of the prospect. The result is either negative action or positive action. Positive action results in a sale or a contract for a sale at some specified future date. Salespeople who survive learn two fundamental skills in communications: specificity (they ask for the order) and listening (they listen to a prospect's needs and fulfill them). In other words, they get a contract for results.

CONTRACTING FOR RESULTS

Getting a contract for results is the difference between conversation and communication. Good communicators, when not engaged in the pastime of conversation, ask for and expect results. They create a contract requiring performance and establish criteria for the measurement of performance. They take responsibility for getting their message across.

With all of the emphasis on talking, too many people *assume* that they have transmitted their message and fail to check it out with their listener. They do not get a contract. For example:

Boss: "Do you think you might be able to get this report out for me by four o'clock on Friday?"

Administrative assistant: "Oh, I think I might be able to do that."

No contract. No specificity. No listening. When the boss comes in on Friday to get the report he is furious to discover the report is not ready.

Administrative assistant: "You didn't say to do it. You just asked me if I might be able to and I told you I might be able to. It turned out I wasn't able to."

No contract. The boss is Mr. Nice Guy; he'd rather be liked than be a boss. He shies away from giving orders. Yet, at home he says things like "I sure wish I could find more competent people." His real problem is that he plays guessing games with his subordinates. He doesn't get contracts, or agreements, for performance.

This is a way he might have handled the report request:

Boss: "I need this report by four o'clock Friday afternoon. Will you have it ready then?"

Administrative assistant: "Well, I'm not sure. You know, yesterday you asked for the Xilcon report by Friday. Which has the highest priority?"

Boss: "I guess I forgot. The Xilcon thing comes first. When can you have the other done?"

Administrative assistant: "By noon Wednesday."

Boss (thinking): "Well, OK. I'll have to change my schedule a little bit, but upstairs they're hot about the Xilcon situation."

That's a contract, an agreement. You'll learn more about positive listening later in this chapter, but for the moment note that the administrative assistant took some responsibility for competent communications by asking, "Which has the highest priority?"

ELEMENTS OF POSITIVE LISTENING

These are the elements of positive listening that will help you become more effective in your communications at work, at home, and with your friends:

1. Clarification
2. Separating facts from feelings
3. The sending and receiving process
4. Positive listening
5. Communications contracts
6. Straight and crooked messages

1. Clarification

This step calls for thought and decision. You need to be clear about what you want out of your conversation or communications. There are appropriate times for "shooting the breeze," gossip, social chitchat, or bar talk. To attempt to analyze and use your communication skills in every human involvement might both leave you exhausted and give you a reputation as an amateur "shrink" or a bore. The question is: What do you want out of this contact at this time?

If you want something to get done or if you want to know what is really going on with your contact, clarification will help you do that.

2. Separating Facts from Feelings

Objective facts come in the form of words. Feelings are demonstrated by vocal tones and body language. Feelings are also demonstrated frequently by the lack of specificity—i.e., by avoidance or indirection.

Mother: "You do know why I'm sending you to bed early tonight, don't you?"

Child (looking down at the floor so Mom can't see his anger): "Oh, sure. Yeah, I know."

Mother (not hearing the angry tone in his voice or not being willing to recognize it): "Good. I'm glad you understand."

Intellectually, feelings are intangible. Realistically, feelings are a fact. It's a fact that when a person is angry there will be little communication. It's a fact that shouting and table-thumping are vocal and visible evidence of feelings that preclude clear understanding of the message. Another fact is that too often people attempt to deal with feelings by being logical. They fail to recognize that when nonrational feelings are uppermost, the logical capacity of the persons involved is diminished.

3. The Sending and Receiving Process

Differences in belief systems can present a major barrier to the clear transmission of messages. The word "bureau" may mean a chest of drawers to one person and the FBI to another. A vocal tone acceptable to one person may drive another up the wall. A slack-looking person may look depressed to one observer and relaxed to another.

Before I spoke to a group of business people in Brazil my interpreter took me aside. She said, "In Brazil you don't do this." She held her hand up with the thumb and finger closed in a circle, the typical American sign for OK. She closed her fist with the thumb extending at the top. "You do this. It means OK." When used in Brazil, the American gesture for OK is a very vulgar insult.

Words, vocal tones, and gestures can also have many regional variations in meaning. This also applies to differences in social classes. In one bar, "turkey" may be a humorous greeting: in another it might mean the beginning of a brawl.

Most people believe if they just send the message right it will be well received. They believe it is the sender's responsibility to deliver clear messages. The reality is that few people accept responsibility for anything more than their words. They have never learned that a harsh tone can deny the gentlest of words, or that forceful gestures can mask the intent of their communication.

Effective communicators know this and read behind the words, the vocal tones, the body language, so they can evaluate the real messages that are being sent. They know that as every thought is transposed to a message it is filtered through the belief system of the message sender. They also know that if they automatically react they, as receiver, will filter the message through another filter, i.e., their own belief system. The result is frequently confusion or misunderstanding. The proactive, or positive, listener, however, accepts responsibility for clearly understanding the message and facilitates the sender's efforts. The reactive listener merely reacts. He is not really listening.

A woman says huffily to her husband, "You men are all alike."

The reactive husband says, "Now what the hell do you mean by that?"

The proactive husband says, "Sounds like you think I'm like every other man in the world."

Woman: "Well, not exactly."

Proactive husband: "Could you tell me a little more about that?"

Woman: "Sometimes you're just like my dad. He'd never listen to me."

Husband: "You feel I'm not listening to you now?"

Woman: "That's right. I don't."

Husband (sitting down): "All right. What is it you want me to hear?"

Woman: "I guess I've said I needed a microwave oven ten

times in the last three months. You just say we can't afford it. Well, I can't go on running three kids around to clubs, meetings, and soccer games every day and get out a decent dinner every night. The other day Johnny said he was tired of TV dinners. And I never know what time to expect you home.''

Husband: "I guess I didn't hear how strongly you felt about it.''

Woman (shifting to proactive from reactive): "I do. I'd like to be just as good a mother as yours was, but she didn't have to run a bus service for her kids. You and your brothers came home from school and had chores to do till dark. She had time to do the cooking. I don't anymore, with the kids involved in all these activities.''

Husband: "I know that. Maybe I just don't know what microwave cooking will taste like. Let's take a look at the budget and see how we'll get it paid for.''

The husband, applying skills he had learned in management communications courses, used positive listening to move from what might have been an unpleasant argument to the point where it was possible for a rational discussion about the microwave oven.

4. Postiive Listening

Positive listening involves clearing, cooperating, and contracting.

Clearing is the prelude to changing from reactive to proactive. To clear yourself is to open up your biocomputer so that it can function free and clear of garbage—garbage generated if the message receiver lets old attitudes and old feeling habits interfere with appropriate processing of the incoming message. If we take another look at the example of microwave-oven conversation, we can clarify what garbage the husband and wife initially brought to the situation.

The woman's old attitude was: "You can't ever talk to a man. They're all alike.'' She'd heard her mother say it over and over. Her old feeling was a sense of powerlessness, the same feeling she'd had as a little girl when she wanted to talk back to her father.

The man's old attitude was: "There's never enough money to go around." He grew up in a large family on a small farm and there was literally never enough money. His old feeling habit was a feeling of frustration, something he'd sensed on his father's face on Christmas morning when everyone pretended that it wasn't just another year of "making do."

The reality for the family was that the husband was learning to use his new communications skills at home and wanted to listen to his wife. Another reality was that one $32,000 annual income his family didn't have to "make do"—they had discretionary income. Recognizing this, he "cleared" himself of his reactive tendencies, frustration, and irritation, and cooperated with his wife as she worked at expressing her feelings and the facts of her situation.

A maxim: You cannot engage in cooperative communication or positive listening without first being clear of garbage, i.e., your nonfunctional attitudes or feelings. Your communication will be biased to the extent that garbage influences your biocomputer, and the rule of "garbage in, garbage out" will apply. The wonderful payoff for those who learn to get clear is that they can deal with garbage from others without getting caught up in it.

If getting better results from communications is a desirable goal, think of ways in which your Inner Saboteur inhibits you in getting desired results from others. Check out those attitudes that may have been learned in childhood and are not functional in the present. The male executive who has a strong message that a woman's place is in the home can have great difficulty communicating with female peers in staff meetings. Ask yourself if there are any particular types of people with whom you may have difficulty communicating. One group therapist always had difficulty with forceful redheaded women in his groups until his trainer pointed out that the therapist was putting his mother's "face" on occasional group members.

The facility for getting clear in your communications will not be developed overnight. It will take thought, work, and time. And commitment. It is worth it, though. It is a great thrill to become aware that you are hearing people, *really* hearing them on a deeper level than ever before. There is a great sense of confidence and competence that comes from using that new listening skill with your children, mate, family, friends, employees, or employers. That skill can change the problems of marriage into labors of love, and work into a joy.

One-way contracts are a constant in life. The government tells you to pay taxes. Parents tell kids what to do. Husbands and wives tell each other what to do. Employers tell employees what to do. Most of these are a one-up/one-down exercise of power and give little heed to the thoughts and feelings of those who are one-down. Cooperation is very, very difficult in such situations. People cheat on their taxes. Kids rebel at their parents' dictates. Husbands and wives quarrel or divorce. Employees sabotage their employers.

Positive listening will help in clarifying communications and getting contracts for positive results.

5. The Elements of Communications Contract

It is a friendly thing to do to listen to another, to be sensitive, and also to trust that person to be sensitive to your needs. With clearing and cooperation, contracts can be made that are similar to legal contracts:

- There is a time of beginning and a time of ending.
- There is a mutual exchange of value.
- Means of accomplishment are spelled out.
- Criteria for measure performance are established.

If this seems complicated, think of the many times someone has said to you, "Why don't you come over sometime?"

Lacking in specificity, this message can be read in many different ways by a listener:

- Gosh, he really likes me.
- I wonder if he really means it.
- The hell with him. Let him come by my place.

The positive listener says, "That sounds good. Let's set a time and date now. How about Saturday around eight or Thursday next week?"

"Thursday would be better."

"OK. I'll bring the beer."

"All right. We'll have cheese and stuff. We can swim in the pool or watch the ball game."

"Whatever. See you Thursday night."

That's a simple social contract. The listener avoided playing internal guessing games and helped the sender clarify his message. He also took the risk of rejection, but people who are clear with themselves willingly do that. It often means taking risk when you have trust in yourself. *Potent people do not waste time and energy with people who are not willing to clarify their position.*

We'll come back to contracts again at the end of this chapter, but first let's examine some skills that will help you help others to clarify their messages.

6. Straight and Crooked Messages

Straight messages are specific statements of fact and/or feeling. They are honest and do not contain implications, innuendos, or hidden agendas that cloak or camouflage the intentions of the message sender. They are objective and autonomous and not influenced by your Inner Saboteur.

- I like the work you did on the Jones project.
- Will you go to dinner with me Friday night?
- I'm disappointed by your actions.

Crooked messages are those messages influenced by the voice of the Inner Saboteur. They are a reflection of the psychological structure of the message sender and are consistent with the sender's belief system, carried forward from childhood programming. While not a deliberate effort at evasion, they often result in confusion and bad feelings, or pseudo-good feelings. An example of a pseudo-good feeling is the feeling of elation that comes after winning an argument with the boss. Usually the false elation later gives way to anxiety or guilt.

An example of a crooked message might be when you tell a subordinate you are not satisfied with his job performance. Looking very sincere, he says, "Well, I did the best I could. I really tried hard." You feel frustrated, wondering how you'll ever get through to him that he is risking his employment. He feels let down and exasperated because when he was little and made a mistake his mother always complimented him for "trying hard" and said, "You get an E for effort." The grown-up reality is that he is not being paid for effort, but for performance. A straight response from him might have been, "Tell me more about your expectations."

GAMES

The practice of sending crooked messages is so prevalent that psychiatrist Eric Berne originated a system of psychotherapy, known as transactional analysis, based on it. Berne found that he could determine a great deal about individual psychological structure by observing people as they communicated in groups. He called each exchange between a sender and a receiver a transaction. A series of transactions resulting in bad feelings, the payoff, was labeled a Game. In *Games People Play* he listed 152 such Games.

You don't have to be a transactional analyst or behavioral scientist to recognize some of the more common Games o the people who play them:

Yes, But

This game is played when someone asks a question and rejects all answers with a statement prefaced by "Yes, but . . ." People who do this sometimes call themselves a devil' advocate. They don't really want an answer. They give themselves false good feelings of one-upmanship by discount ing the responder. The responder gets irritated.

If It Weren't for [You, Him, Her, Them, Politics. you name it]

This is a Game engaged in by people who never accept responsibility and can always point a finger of blame at others. They feel falsely accused. The other person feels frustrated.

Kick Me, or Stupid

These people are consistently negligent, thereby inviting others to discount them or put them down. Some of them invite attention to their mistakes by saying, "Oh, there I go again." The other party feels exasperation.

Ain't It Awful

Bitch, bitch, bitch. Such extensive complaining by two parties can lead later to feelings of guilt about wasting time. It is also a way to stifle vitality and maintain depression.

Corner

The person caught up in this Game suddenly feels power-less. It is a double bind that says, "Damned if you do and damned if you don't." The originator has a feeling or triumph of anger, saying something like "You always . . ."

Now I've Got You, You SOB

Played by people who can't feel good until they make someone else feel bad. They look for every mistake they can pounce on but never face their own faults. The receiver feels vitimized or futile.

These disruptive transactions usually occur when crooked messages are injected into what seems an apparently harmless situation. They conceal the belief systems and childhood programming of people. Take the case of a Kick Me player. They are the kind who reject praise when you say something good about them. You're not likely to hear one say, "I got so much negative attention as a child it's a habit with me. I wouldn't know what positive attention is or what to do about it." Many people in therapy learn to give up such Games, but you are probably not a therapist and it's not your job to teach people how to make such changes. Your job is to work your way through the crooked messages, to get results, and to avoid ending up with bad feelings.

Positive listening is a way to straighten out crooked messages and avoid the bad feelings and disruption brought on by Games. The first step in becoming a more potent communicator is to raise your level of awareness of crooked messages; yours and others. As you become aware of your own crooked messages, don't let your Inner Saboteur send you guilt messages for being something less than perfect. Crooked messages are a part of the human condition, and you are human.

Here's a first step in increasing awareness: Simply be aware of the times you leave a situation with any bad feelings, such as anger, irritation, disappointment, rejection, frustration, or depression. Be aware of the way these feelings interfere with the appropriate use of your time and energy. Over the course of a month or so, does any pattern emerge? Are there certain situations that consistently trigger bad feelings? Are the feelings like those in childhood when you responded to similar situations? Some people go through their entire lives getting the same scared feeling in their stomach when they talk to the boss, the same feeling they had when they talked to mother, father, or teacher.

When patterns emerge, your next step is to identify what crooked messages were involved—yours or theirs. What were the expectations of each party involved? What results were inappropriate? In answering these questions you are gathering information for clearing, for being responsible for your role in any Games.

You may find that there are some kinds of involvements, when these typically end up unsatisfactorily for you, that can be avoided. Take Morgan's story. Morgan doesn't like to stand in lines at the bank; he gets extremely irritated. His irritation precludes any clearing or objectivity. The result is he ends up in hassles that drive his blood pressure up, upset his stomach, and interfere with his effectiveness. Often he then feels guilty because he "should" do better. Now he mails his paycheck to the bank, which deposits it and sends him a receipt. This is called appropriate avoidance. If you want more time and energy to use in the important matters of managing your life, consider appropriate avoidance for some situations.

However, the chances are that you are not a recluse, and you will continue to be involved with difficult situations and people. Positive listening will help you handle crooked messages by helping your respondent to straighten out his message. Your goal is not to let communication drift into habitual patterns with negative payoffs. If you're clear with yourself, you can devote your total attention to the messages being sent and respond with messages to clarify communications:

- Tell me more about that.
- I need more information.
- I don't know what you want me to say about that.

• Sounds like you're upset.
• I really don't know what you're expecting of me.

Note that these are all statements. Never answer a question with a question; it adds to the confusion. Your goal is to help your respondent get past inappropriate feelings and get to the information you need for resolution of the situation.

In industry, business experts say that productivity could be greatly improved if management could accept constructive criticism from the workers—if more managers became communicators instead of bosses.

THREE MAGIC WORDS

The most powerful tools existing for positive listeners are three words that get magical results. They are: *Are you willing?* Are you willing to do some work on this tonight at home? Are you willing to have sex this evening? Are you willing to tell what happened on that sale you lost last week? Are you willing to tell me why I was passed over for promotion?

Sounds scary, doesn't it? Some people might say, "No, I'm not willing." Then you say, "Will you tell me why not?" They probably will, but if they don't, let it go. Their message may be:

• I need to think this over.
• I don't trust you yet.
• You let me down last time I told you.

Better to let it rest and approach the problem at some other time unless there is an urgent need such as the need to give a direct order in an emergency or a work situation.

The power of these words lies in the fact that you grant equality to your receiver. You demonstrate that you are willing to take a risk and that you are trusting the other to respond with a straight message. You disarm your Inner Saboteur by accepting responsibility for your feelings. You are setting aside old attitudes and old feeling patterns in the interest of clear communications.

Does it work? Gloria thinks so. Gloria and her husband were long-established devotees of "hinting." They rarely sent straight messages to each other, especially about going to a show. She'd hint she'd like to go to a show. He'd hint he'd rather not. They'd both go to bed angry.

She'd say, "I wonder how that new movie is."

He'd say, "Oh, you don't want to go to that junk."

One evening she came home from work and said, "Are you willing to take me to a show tonight?"

He was startled, looked at her a minute, and said, "Well . . . sure. Where did you want to go?"

Changing from crooked messages to straight messages brought life and intimacy back into their marriage.

Two managers complained to me of a serious work overload but didn't know how to bring it up with their bosses. I advised them to say something like this: "I know *my* expectations of me on his job, but I'm not sure I'm clear on *your* expectations of me. Are you willing to give me an hour sometime in the next couple of days to talk about this?" It sounded risky to them but they decided to see how it would work. The results? One man was given an assistant. The other had twenty hours of work a week cut out of his workload.

These techniques will work if you will take the risk. Positive listening will bring you many positive payoffs.

CONTRACTUAL COMMUNICATIONS

A contractual communication is a clear agreement between two people or one person and a group in order to get something done. If "contract" seems too legalistic or formidable a word, think in terms of "agreement." In some cases it might be all right to terminate a communication by saying, "That's a contract." In other cases it would be better to say, "Are we in agreement?"

The point is: Do not disengage and leave a situation still unclear. This happens every day thousands of times. Wishy-washy transactions are far more prevalent than ones that specifically call for results. When you start using the skills and knowledge of positive communications in your relationships with others you will get amazing results. You will be able to influence others. You will be potent.

You may also hear some deep feelings that you've never been exposed to before. The feeling of being listened to is tremendously moving for some people, and they will expose you to thoughts and emotions far beyond the scope of your intended communication. If that happens, just keep listening until you sense that their energy has run down. You might then gently go back to positive listening:

- Is there anything more you want to tell me?
- What would you like me to do about that?
- Is there anything we can both do to correct this?

These phrases will bring you back to negotiating for a mutual agreement. If this happens with a loved one, sometimes a hug is far more appropriate than words. If it happens with a friend, be very cautious about giving off-hand or unsolicited advice. This can arouse many bad feelings. If it happens with an employee and the information offered is something beyond the bounds of work, you might say, "This is not in my area of expertise." Increasing numbers of organizations now have psychologists and counselors to handle just such situations.

People who use straight messages often worry about hurting other people's feelings. Bear in mind that hurt feelings are generated by the Inner Saboteur of the other person. You are not responsible for the other person's feelings, although you can trigger bad feelings by your own inappropriate transmissions. Anger begets anger. Misery begets misery. And calmness and confidence beget calmness and confidence. You get back what you project. If you project and transmit your messages specifically and congruously, people will not crumble in front of you. People can handle straight messages and positive listening. Some will even welcome it.

Chapter 11

Managing Your Mind

Manage your mind or it will manage you.

You are the star of your own show. You either write your own script or play out the one that has been handed to you. You choose your fellow actors and actresses, engage the theater, and direct the action. You shoulder the responsibility for your show's success or failure. You are also the judge of the total performance. You write the reviews. You judge the applause, or lack of it.

If you brought down the curtain on your act tonight, what would the audience say? How would you feel about that? What would you change in the script? Who would you replace in the cast? What theater would you choose? Would you change the name of the play? What would you change in yourself in order to improve your performance?

In looking back over the years that you've had your show on the road, has your mind been a help or a hindrance, a benevolent or malevolent influence? Or maybe it's been indifferent, comfortable with just getting by?

In one way or another, everything already presented in this book has dealt with the management of the mind, the necessary prelude to the management of your actions. Now, if you want to capsulize the process of getting on with positive living, you can do it with three words:

1. Clearing
2. Reprogramming
3. Self-management

You might write them on the back of a business card and carry it in your wallet. When faced with doubt about an action or attitude you can ask yourself these questions:

- Am I clear on my new decisions about this matter?
- Is the reprogramming of my belief system consistent and appropriate to the matter at hand?
- How will I manage my attitudes and actions to provide a positive payoff for me?

Finding the right answers to these questions is the key to improving your life. But it is performance that counts. Peak performance has been the object of intensive study by Charles A. Garfield, a clinical psychologist, former mathematician, and computer analyst with the Apollo space mission. He says, "It can be said that you are a 'peak performer' when you perform better than other people in a given activity, perform better than you have in the past, or perform better than predicted. All of us can be considered 'peak performers' if we significantly improve our performance relative to some standard."[11]

Each of these performance categories contains the potential for negative activity generated by your Inner Saboteur. It can bar you from achieving your "wants" and has destroyed many who accomplished their "shoulds." Mind management makes the difference between poor, mediocre, and peak performance. Following are detailed descriptions of the techniques that have been used successfully by others in managing their mind.

CLEARING

Clarity of mind is a prerequisite to full use of your mental power. It represents your fullest potential for problem solving and decision making free and clear of archaic belief systems. Appropriate management of the mind requires that negative beliefs be identified and dismissed. The mind can then be reprogrammed with positive beliefs.

Internal Clearing

This process can be either contemplative, active, or both. Styles of clearing are as different as judo and American wrestling. In judo the energy of the opponent is used to his or her disadvantage. In American wrestling you use your own energy to overcome your foe. Contemplative clearing is meditative and permits the spontaneous arising of thoughts, rather than perceptual thinking. Just as water lilies beautify a quiet pond so will spontaneity and creativity bloom in a quiet mind.

To arrive at a state of not-thinking is a personal process. You can use the standardized yoga method of staring at a candle, or the individualized altered states of consciousness people undergo in biofeedback training. Some people sit quietly and repeat a mantra over and over, others use a single word or number. The repetition stops the intrusion of the constantly chattering thoughts that interfere with not-thinking. It creates a neutral atmosphere that permits thoughts to pass without the internal confusion caused by evaluative, judgmental thinking.

In his book *The Relaxation Response*, Dr. Herbert Benson identifies four basic elements for meditation: (1) a quiet environment, (2) an object to dwell upon, (3) a passive attitude, and (4) a comfortable position.[2] With these elements, it is possible to think of the mind as a movie marquee on which the words run by and disappear at the end to be replaced by other running words. Your goal is to let them run by without becoming involved with them. I once thought this was impossible. My own mind was constantly filled with chatter akin to that of marauding crows. I didn't believe that anyone could let his or her mind go blank.

Now I can do this by sitting on the couch early mornings and staring at the huge tamarisk tree rising out of the apple orchard across the way, set off against the green, gentle hills studded with pine and oak trees. Greenery brings me peace, and out of that peace I can gradually return to conscious thinking and establish my program for the day. I also find that setting aside my compulsion for rational thinking allows many creative thoughts to well up like water from a hillside spring.

Active Clearing

You can use your muscles to clear your mind. Physical exercise will slow or eliminate the rush of thoughts that go with worry, anxiety, and negative programming. Concentration on the next move of your muscles will give your mind a recess from internal hassles. If you swim, count "Stroke one, stroke two," and so on. For jogging you can say, "Step one, two," and go on from there. The same is true of any repetitive exercise; it is an excellent way to clear the mind in preparation for the reprogramming process. Progressive relaxation, which leaves both the body and mind relaxed and ready for deep learning, is covered in the next chapter.

Active clearing can be accomplished only if you learn a self-monitoring thought process that is day by day, hour by hour, minute by minute, and sometimes second by second. Awareness is the essence of mind management. In the beginning it takes a conscious effort, just as it does to learn a new dance step or to change your golf swing. And just as your muscular response becomes habitual, so will your mental response. At this stage, you have already given some attention to your belief systems, your negative messages, and the voices of your Inner Saboteur.

The first step in active clearing is to be aware of your internal dialogue and to identify a negative thought the moment it comes into your head.

The second step is to accept it as only a piece of imagination and let it drift away to be replaced by a positive thought. If you don't have a happy thought for the present or the future, recall some of the good things you've experienced in the past. The most vicious and insidious tool the Inner Saboteur has is the automatic attention the mind gives to negative memories. Its action is similar to that of the golfer who concentrates so much on figuring out what is wrong with his swing that he never gets around to "grooving" the swing that is right for him. In the early stages of active clearing it might help to write out a list of all the good things you have done in the past and all the good things you are going to do in the future. Note that I said "going to do" and not "intend to do." Doing this makes positive information available the instant you recognize that your mind has let itself surrender to fearful thoughts.

External Clearing

This refers to your programmed behaviors to anything you do with people and things that helps you perpetuate feelings of guilt, anger, regret, confusion, or other of your favorite bad feelings. If you were asked before you left the house each morning to deliberately plan all of the actions for the day that would give you bad feelings, you might mutter, "Nonsense." If you do, pay attention to the other drivers on the freeway as you drive to work. Watch for the cars that reflect the thinking of the driver—the guy who won't let someone by, the one that charges off the on-ramp as though the freeway was his, the one with her eyes on her mirror and a comb in her hand as her car weaves from lane to lane.

At lunch, watch the big wheel who comes in late and gets

huffy if a table isn't immediately available. Watch the waiter carelessly knock over a water glass and the fellow at the end of the bar who's having martini soup for lunch and will be feeling burned out by two-thirty in the afternoon.

At work, watch the office manager sweating and wringing her handkerchief because she knows she's got to go to a staff meeting and make an oral report, or the salesperson telling the boss why he or she didn't meet the call quota for the previous week.

External clearing means waking up, paying attention, being aware, giving up the belief that "the devil made me do it" and accepting the fact that "I made me do it." External clearing means getting rid of all the things you do to or with people that provide you an opportunity for a habitual negative payoff.

External clearing might also require that you reconsider the people with whom you associate and the environment in which you live. It almost smacks of martyrdom to attempt to embark on a positive-thinking/positive-action course and continue to associate with a group of people who are always complaining, "Ain't it awful that . . ." How many people do you know who are jogging for health and yet continue to smoke? It would be foolish to claim health as a high priority in life and work in a smoky, fume-filled atmosphere.

Clearing—contemplative, active, or external—can be compared to what happens when a cassette tape with a recorded song on it is put back through the tape recorder with a new song recorded. The old song is not suppressed. It is *replaced* with a new one. As you prepare yourself for the learning processes required in reprogramming, think of your mind as a cassette tape from which self-defeating messages in your old programming will be wiped off, and on which new, constructive messages will be recorded. You will create your own program geared to your "wants" instead of the old "shoulds." As you go on with your reprogramming, have faith that what you believe will come true for you, as it has for others. In time your new thinking will come as automatically as the response of a tape recorder to the push of its button.

2. REPROGRAMMING

Clearing is done in the interest of "unlearning." Reprogramming is done in the interest of "relearning," using methods that you were not taught in school. Unless you attended some very unusual schools, you were expected to learn by rote, memorizing large collections of mathematical, grammatical, historical, social, and geographical facts. Then, during a ritual known as exams, you were expected to regurgitate an appropriate number of facts. Your education was judged with the letters A, B, C, D, E, and F depending on the number of facts regurgitated.

Reprogramming is a learning process based on the principle "Think it out for yourself." Given the facts of life, as you understand them, and your experience in applying them to the management of your life, you are the only one to decide what kind of grades you want to earn. You decide what you will need in your reeducation program to give you what you want out of life. The school of life is one in which no one is barred admission. You design your own curriculum and choose your own methods of instruction, and, until demonstrated otherwise, you are your own best instructor.

Following are some reprogramming methods that have made sense to others. Some have been tested over long periods of time, some are more recent. These methods will work only if you will work. Perhaps the bset evidence for their validity is to ask someone who has changed his or her life for the better, "What worked for you?" That person will probably refer to methods similar to the following. But after that, it's up to you.

Self-Affirmation

This is a way to use words—spoken, written, or thought—to affirm yourself. To affirm yourself is to maintain the truth that you can become the person you want to be when you have made appropriate choices for yourself. It is not whistling in the dark—an affirmation program will not work if it's based on unrealistic, wishful thinking. It will work if you have made good choices, will work to carry out those choices, and gain the competency necessary to do that.

Many people have written or talked about affirmations, and they all agree that whether you are affirming yourself for the day or for the future, phrase your affirmation by saying "I am" rather than "I will," other cop-out phrases such as "I see myself doing," or—the deadliest of all—"I'm trying." Express your affirmation as a reality, as though it were already in existence.

If your goal is improved health you might say, "I am enjoying radiant good health."

If it is a better job, you can say, "I am working and doing [describe your job activity]."

If it is marriage, say, "John and I are enjoying doing [describe an activity] together," or "Mary and I are sitting on the beach watching the gulls swoop and dip over the white curling waves."

You can think, speak, or write your affirmation. You can reprogram your mind by thinking your words, hearing your words, or seeing your words in your mind. Thought is the most convenient of the three methods. You can think your affirmation before you get out of bed in the morning, while driving your car, or just before a scary experience.

Spoken affirmations may be made by yourself or with others. If you do spoken affirmation with others, be sure it is with someone you deeply trust who will be neutral and will not signal any negativity, verbally or nonverbally. When spoken affirmations are made, be highly aware of your body feelings as you speak, or of any negative thoughts that come to mind. Even though you have cleared your mind, the Inner Saboteur is a fast dancer.

In her "Creative Visualization" workshops, Shakti Gawain has the participants write an affirmation twenty times. "I am not smoking and feel wonderful" might be one. If any negative thoughts come up, people immediately turn the page over, write down the negative reaction, and then go back to rewriting the positive affirmation. This both clears the negativity from the mind and records it so that it can be dealt with later.

Some people say they feel silly going around talking to themselves. If you feel silly simply forget it. Your mind is busy all the time anyway. *Doing affirmations is a conscious and positive use of the mind when it might otherwise be unconsciously centered on negative purposes.*

Future Projection

This is another term for constructive daydreaming. It is not wishy-washy wishing, but goal-specific. You give up saying "Someday my ship will come in" in favor of seeing yourself doing whatever it means for you to have your ship come in. You want to picture achieving your goals, but if you have difficulty creating scenes in your mind, think about them. If you have sorted out your goals and planned the means by which they will be accomplished, you know what your expectations are.

Future projection is a guided fantasy—it is fantasy because it is imaginative, and it is guided because you are in control and know what you want. Suppose it is a new career that you are training for. See yourself arrive at your new job site, doing what you need to do to get to your place. See the people you will be greeting, imagine the personal exchanges that go on between you and others. Go to your bench or desk or whatever equipment it is you use to do your new work. Have a talk with your boss about your work and what you are accomplishing. Think about the praise he or she gives you for what you are doing or the response from a client or fellow worker. See yourself enjoying yourself with the people around you at coffee breaks and lunch, the conversations you will be having. Think about all the good feelings you will be getting, even about your paycheck or other financial rewards. See yourself coming home to whomever you live with and listen to the exciting conversation about the day's work. The goal of this entire fantasy is to be a constant reminder that whatever struggle it takes, there is a positive payoff out there as a reward for having successfully completed your transition.

Pictorialization

You can use pictures depicting the life you want for yourself to turn your dreams into reality, using the same process that the advertising experts use to get you to buy Whoopsy-Doodle Crackles the next time you go to the supermarket. It is called subliminal advertising. The commercial you see on television may seem totally irrelevant to you at the moment because it does not have sufficient conscious impact on you. Nevertheless, the product is being quietly imprinted in your mind and is available for automatic recall when there is an appropriate stimulus.

As mentioned in Chapter 7, you also might choose to create a futures collage around your desired self-image. After that there is no need to do any special thinking about your image. You will be aware of it each time you see it, and in time that image will become a reality in your mind. Of course, you will be doing other things in your life to move you toward your goals. But the collage, will be subliminally reinforcing your efforts. Daily and without any special effort on your part, you will be focusing your mental energies on your desires.

This is a method many athletes learned as youngsters when they cut out pictures of their heroes and heroines and put them on their bedroom walls. They created a vision of their future, and at that age, being logical did not restrict their imagination. When our son was a high jumper he put a piece of tape on the front doorframe. The tape was four inches over the top of his head. Everytime he came and went from the house it was a reminder of his goal the picture of his dreams. One day when he went to a track meet, he cleared a bar four inches over his head.

It was a technique I saw my mother use when I was a child but ignored for many years in favor of more logical and rational things. I turned back to this form of natural programming in my mid-fifties while in the middle of changing careers to become a workshop leader. On the bulletin board by our front door I put a picture from an American Management Association magazine showing a tall man standing by an easel and talking to a group of people. He was leading a workshop. Because I work from my home, I must have seen that picture twenty or thirty times a day as I moved about the house. And one day I *was* a workshop leader—my new career seemed simply to evolve out of my desires and positive actions.

3. SELF-MANAGEMENT

Whether it be called suggestology, self-hypnosis, Couéism, autosuggestion, self-suggestion, or autogenic training, self-management removes self-imposed limitations to your performance, limitations that are as terribly restrictive as a straitjacket. Coach Dean Cromwell of the University of Southern California was one of the world's greatest self-suggestion experts—though he may not have thought of himself as one. He preached a psychology of championship, instilling in his athletes the absolute belief that they were champions. Then they simply met their own expectations. Many of his young men did indeed become world and Olympic champions.

More than thirty years ago the Russians began the study of optimal human performance. They have budgeted huge amounts to research ways of encouraging their people to expand their performance potential. What they have learned they now use in training athletes, members of the Bolshoi Ballet, cosmonauts, government managers, and educators. Charles Garfield, who is a weight lifter as well as a psychologist, has studied the Russian methods extensively. His belief in those methods is reinforced by personal experience. During a visit to Europe he talked with some of the experts and, with their help, greatly exceeded the self-limiting beliefs he previously held about his maximum potential. On one occasion he actually bench-pressed 300 pounds. Then after a long preparatory process of mental rehearsal, Garfield pushed up 365 pounds of iron.

After reviewing 300 questionnaires and talking with over a hundred peak performers, Garfield found that mental rehearsal was a common practice among all of them. Peak performers visualized themselves successfully achieving their goals, and then one day the visualization simply became a reality. This practice is a fundamental process of managing the mind.

To some it may seem a paradox that clearing the mind is part of mind management—it may seem more like unmanagement. However, it takes skill and discipline to let go of the thousands of bits of information programmed into the memory bank at very early ages. Your belief systems, your logic, and your convictions are the equivalent of the software fed into a computer, and, like a computer, you will learn to respond automatically to your programming. In order to clear a computer, it is necessary to remove the tape that feeds it data. Once clearing has been accomplished the process of reprogramming can go on. And just as it takes time, thought, and effort to write new software, it takes time, thought, and effort to reprogram the mind.

Dr. Stanley Woollams, a psychiatrist, says, "You can set yourself up to feel good and be happy by what you say upon arising. The brain is like a computer—and you can choose the computer program you're going to have that day. If the message to the brain is a positive one, such as 'I feel good,' most people will feel good. When you catch yourself giving a negative message to the brain during the day, you should say, 'Cancel that.' "[3]

That's what mind management is all about.

Chapter 12

Friendly and
Unfriendly Stress

The energy generated by stress can be used positively or negatively. It all depends on individual interpretation.

To an engineer or architect, stress may mean the internal strain of a bridge or building, the ratio of force to area. To a debate coach, if may mean emphasizing a particular word. The musical composer considers stress when thinking of melody or beat. And the harried executive says to his doctor, "My God, I'm under unbelievable stress," meaning that he is feeling time and decision-making pressures.

It is this last usage of the word that requires reexamination. To many it has become synonymous with a sinister force that we must grapple with and overcome. Books, articles, and seminars are titled "How to Cope with Stress," as if to say, "In this corner we have John Doe, and in the other we have his formidable opponent, Stress." There is the overt message that we are locked in a win/lose contest with an enemy.

TAKING RESPONSIBILITY
FOR STRESS

The reality is that *we* are the enemy. The job doesn't get us down. *We* get ourselves down. The freeway traffic doesn't make us uptight. We make ourselves uptight. The kids don't drive us wild. We drive ourselves wild. We repeat learned reactions to situations arising from individual belief systems. The amount of stress generated in any circumstances is in relation to an individual's tolerance of that circumstance. Some people thrive on chaos in the office while others find it intolerable. While working in South America, I noted the Latin tolerance for tardiness created a great deal of stress on the part of American managers who were compulsively punctual and never became accustomed to the *mañana* viewpoint.

STRESS IS A LEARNED REACTION

How long a stress response lasts is also a personal matter. It can be assumed that among people in an auditorium, each one able to hear would have a rapid increase in pulse rate immediately after the sound of a loud explosion. When they realized the noise came from outside and was not a signal of impending harm, most pulse rates would return to normal. Some present, though, might dwell on the incident and take much longer to regain their physical and emotional equilibrium. Some may go home and angrily talk about the incident, regenerating the rapid heartbeat in reliving the experience.

This difference in recovery time from stress reactions can be noted in a variety of life situations: getting a job/losing a job, getting married/getting divorced, gaining a loved one/losing a loved one. Transition stages always generate stress, and how long the stress reaction is maintained determines the amount of damage the experience has done. Perhaps it would be better if we thought of stress in comparative terms—normal stress/abnormal stress, positive stress/negative stress, good stress/bad stress, or healthy stress/unhealthy stress.

A "stressful" situation, in and of itself, is neither good nor bad. But whether or not the stress energy created is then used constructively or destructively depends on the individual, and this is what people mean when they speak of being "under stress." When the stress reaction is experienced within reasonable limitations, it can be exciting and stimulating. But when that reaction is allowed to continue beyond an acceptable range, the stress energy becomes distressful. You've heard some people referred to as chronic worriers. Maybe you know someone who talks about being "wired" most of the time, or someone who is constantly charged up by situations he or she can't do anything about and wants to write a "letter to the editor" every day. These people allow their stress energy to go on indefinitely.

MODULATING YOUR STRESS RESPONSE

Hans Selye, a pioneer and leader for many years in the field of stress research, says, "Our aim shouldn't be to completely avoid stress, which at any rate would be impossible, but to learn how to recognize our typical response to stress and then try to modulate our lives in accordance with it."[1] The modulation of stress calls for the expenditure of adaptation energy: "In any case, there is just so much of it, and we must budget accordingly."[2] His research implies that mismanaging one's adaptation energy budget can lead to physical and/or emotional bankruptcy just as financial bankruptcy can result from fiscal mismanagement.

Why do some people squander their stores of adaptation energy while others manage theirs productively? Selye says, "Rather than relying on drugs or other techniques, I think there's another way to handle stress, which involves taking a different attitude toward the various events in our lives. Attitude determines whether we perceive any experience as pleasant or unpleasant, and adopting the right one can convert a negative stress into a positive one—something I call a 'eustress', employing the same Greek prefix for 'good' that occurs in such words as "euphoria' and 'euphonia.' "[3]

COPING WITH STRESS
CONSTRUCTIVELY

Unfortunately, it is easy to overlook the negative effects of unfriendly stress, because few of us have learned what stress is or how to deal with it constructively. We learn about it when the doctor says, "Well, I don't find anything really wrong with you. Have you been under any stress lately?" Doctors estimate that 80 to 85 percent of the people they see do not have any identifiable disease or illness. That seems a pretty good indication that most of us could do a great deal to enhance our physical and mental health. We can do that by giving up some of our old stress-response habits and learning new ones that will reduce the negative effects of stress on our bodies and minds.

The first step in that direction is to get new information about stress. In *Supermind* Barbara Brown writes, "The role of information to the person under stress is paramount to his relief."[4] Once a symptom of unfriendly stress is identified and connected to a cause, decisions can be made on how to avoid it, reduce it, or eliminate it—and to do it in a way that does not create another set of unfriendly stressors. Your brother-in-law may be driving you up the wall, but it may not always be possible to avoid him. Your work may be the major stressor in your life, but there may be valid reasons for not leaving it. In situational stress that doesn't seem avoidable it may be easier to change yourself than it is to change the situation. It is a matter of sorting out your values, examining your payoffs, and doing what you need to do to reduce the negative effects of self-generated stress in your life.

Learning to deal with the effects of unfriendly stress is a part of the transitional process for almost anyone who decides to be happier, make more money, improve a marriage, or enrich life in any way. In any race there is a distance between the start and the finish and a period of time to run the course. Those who finish the race learn to use their physiological and psychological stress to their own best advantage.

In order to do this effectively the mind needs to know:

1. The symptoms of stress
2. The negative messages in the belief system that cause undue stress
3. Techniques of alleviating unfriendly stress

1. Symptoms

All the possible symptoms of unfriendly stress can't be listed here, but here are some of those most easily identified:

- Body signals such as aches and pains
- Feelings of undue apprehension, anxiety and fear
- Irrational behavior caused by misplaced anger or irritation
- Excessive behavior such as overuse of tobacco, alcohol, food, drugs
- Hassle games such as preoccupation with "problems"
- Unwarranted defensiveness and avoidance of issues
- Insomnia or poor appetite

2. Causes

Once recurring symptoms of unfriendly stress have been identified, a connection to causes can be made. You are the only person who can make this connection, but some people need the help of a professional. Even the experts do not know as much as you do, but they can evaluate and help you interpret the evidence you give them. Even people who reported they are "blocked"—meaning they don't remember back beyond a certain age—can bring back early childhood memories in psychotherapy or regression therapy or with the help of a hypnotherapist.

Bob, a salesman, says, "Every time I get ready to close a sale I get the same feelings I did before I ran the quarter mile in high school. Only then I ran off all the energy and now it just sticks in my stomach." After he connected that feeling with the fear of not winnning he went back further in his memory and recalled that his father pushed him into competitive sports when he was seven, and Bob had hated having to be in "sports" when all he wanted to do was play. After realizing that his undue stress reaction was not connected with current realities, he analyzed his sales record and found he had a very good ratio of sales to prospects. He objectively accepted the fact that he was among the 20 percent of the sales team that made 80 percent of the sales. Another stressful problem for Bob was the realization that he constantly felt pressured because he had few financial reserves and no investment program for the future. He told his wife about those feelings and she willingly agreed to the establishment of a budget so that they could build a reserve account for emergencies and begin a monthly investment plan. The discipline of budgeting can be stressful, but it is a form of friendly stress. As Bob watched his net worth grow he became much more comfortable in his sales work and gradually lost his fear of failure.

It is extremely important in examining information *not* to assume that what stresses someone else will stress you. Much has been written about the evils of being a workaholic, but there is ample evidence that the adage "Hard work never killed anyone" is also valid. Dr. Selye is evidence that using stress as a friend is connected to productivity and longevity. He has written 1,600 articles and thirty books and, now in his seventies, says, "I almost always put in a ten-hour day, and often more."[5]

There are a number of stress scales developed by medical and psychological researchers that put a numerical value on the stress reaction of both "good" and "bad" happenings: a marriage, a divorce, a birth, a death. All have a stress reaction, but some are rated as more damaging than others. Again, the consensus is that the ongoing response to unfriendly stress is more damaging than the actual event which caused the stress. Connecting causes with symptoms will permit you to recognize the repetitive nature of your stress responses.

3. Techniques of Alleviating Unfriendly Stress

There are no miracles in stress reduction, but with time and effort you can use proven techniques in alleviating the negative effects of stress in your life.

Progressive Relaxation. Dr. Edmund Jacobsen differentiated between ordinary relaxation and "scientific relaxation." He felt the untrained person might feel relaxed but that residual tensions could remain. The trained person learns to achieve real and complete relaxation. Dr. Jacobsen taught people a systematic method of contracting and releasing muscles.

You can learn to do this by yourself. If you are home, it's best to lie down, but you can do many of these exercises at your desk. As a starter, rest your arm palm down on a solid object. Then draw your fingers as far up and back toward your elbow as they will move and hold till the count of three. Note the increased tension of the muscles as you do so. Then let them go. Let your hand fall loose; don't push it back to its former position. You may have to do it several times before you feel a "flush" in the muscles that is the feeling of relaxation. Typically in a workshop, about a third of those present will immediately identify the relaxed feeling in the forearm, a third will require several attempts, and the other third will simply not yet be that in touch with their bodies. However, they can heighten their awareness of body feelings by contracting and relaxing larger muscles such as the thighs or biceps.

When time and conditions are right, systematically working through all the body muscles will give great feelings of relaxation:

Toes: Curl them under as though you were picking up a marble. Hold. Relax. Raise the toes off the floor without moving the foot. Hold. Relax.

Foot: Leave your heels on the floor and elevate the foot till your calf muscles strain. Hold. Relax.

Calves: Tighten. Hold. Relax.

Continue working with every muscle system in your body that you can get to respond: thighs, groin, anus, diaphragm, pectoral, the muscles around the spine in the lower back, forearm muscles, biceps, the "angel wings" just below your shoulders, neck, jaw muscles; some can do this with the muscles of the forehead and temples. Practice and muscle awareness will gradually make it possible for you to do them all.

Warning: Do not continue with any exercise that produces pain. If any muscle consistently hurts, professional assistance is in order.

Three benefits are available for those who follow a regular program of progressive relaxation. First, you will begin to find your body sending you warning signals whenever something stressful is going on with you. When you've learned to connect your muscle reactions with stressful thinking or stressful situations, the muscles will act as signals. When you recognize these physical signals you can check out what is going on in your mind or you can immediately do a contraction-relaxation exercise with the muscle or muscles involved.

Second, you will get an immediate feeling of physical

relaxation after a few minutes of relaxation exercises, a complete work-through of the entire body on a couch or the floor at home, or as many exercises as you can handle seated at a desk. Some of these exercises can be done while walking. They will also relieve, or avoid, a host of muscular aches and pains resulting from prolonged muscle tension.

And third, as a result of increased concentration on your progessive relaxation, you will experience the clearing process discussed at length in the chapter on mind management. Your concentration will preclude your mind's involvement in the mental "hassle games" that go on with thoughts such as:

- I should have. . . .
- Why did I say that?
- I wonder what the boss thinks now?

While you are concentrating on your exercises, no garbage is being fed into your computer, and so when you have finished you can be more objective in examining the roots of your stress and deciding on the most appropriate way to deal with them.

Self-Massage. There is no greater relaxation experience than receiving a nurturing, nonsexual massage from the hands of a caring person. However, it is possible to let go of muscular tension brought on by unfriendly stress by self-massage. It can be done clothed or unclothed, at home or in the office. Undoubtedly there have been times when you have rubbed a calf or the back of your neck because of tension. That's what self-massage is—a conscious, systematic way to relax all over. It is a bit more vigorous than just rubbing. Use your thumbs and fingers to push as deeply as possible into the muscles without inflicting undue pain. Imagine your hand is like the claw of a lobster and squeeze, using your thumb and fingers like pincers on muscles in your calf, thigh, forearms, biceps, pectorals, and neck. The consequent blood flow in the body is exhilarating, and, again, occupying the mind with the self-massage process provides a few minutes of "time-out" and a quieting of the mind.

Foot Reflexology. This method presupposes that there are reflex buttons in the feet that when massaged send energizing signals to various glands and nerve centers in the body. Mildred Carter, author of *Helping Yourself with Foot Reflexology* and a practicing reflexologist for many years, says, "Reflexology is Nature's pushbutton secret for vibrant health, more dynamic living, abundant personal energy, better living without pain."[6] Her methods are clearly and simply stated in her book, which has charts for identification of the signal buttons in the foot and their connection to various parts of the body. Carter instructs the reader on how to do focused foot massage specifically applied to the "signal buttons" rather than just rubbing the feet.

Meditation. Meditative practices of various types offer both physical and mental relaxation and relief from the effects of unfriendly stress. We are more concerned with its physical benefits. In his research concerning physiological changes during transcendantal meditation, Dr. Robert Keith Wallace noted marked decreases in oxygen consumption and heart rate and an increase in skin resistance.[7] (Skin resistance decreases during stress or anxiety.) Some meditators reported a reduction in hypertension.

There are a variety of meditative methods, but here are some suggestions that draw upon a number of methods or techniques.

1. Seat yourself comfortably in a quiet place and shut your eyes.
2. Relax. After some practice with progressive relaxation you will be able to relax sufficiently for your purpose without going through the entire series of relaxation exercises.

3. Breathe down in your abdomen rather than from your chest. If you have difficulty with this, put your hand on your stomach below your sternum and feel the movement as you breathe in and out.

4. Repeat a number or word while breathing out. Use a word that has a peaceful meaning to you.

5. Continue for ten to twenty minutes.

6. If distracting or negative thoughts creep in, let them go and keep repeating your word or number.

7 . Do your meditative practice twice a day but not until two hours after eating. The digestion process interferes with meditation.

If you make this a regular practice, your mind and body will appreciate it.

Stop—Think. Use this technique when your body or mind sends signals that it is reacting to unfriendly stress and circumstances are too public for you to use the techniques just mentioned. Pay attention to signals like a back pain, clenching your jaws, tightness in your temples, or a tight diaphragm. In time those signals will become as evident as the bell and flashing red light of a railroad crossing that warn you to "stop, look, and listen." What's behind those body signals—anger, irritation, anxiety, or other stressors? Stop—Think is a triggering mechanism alerting you to the need for objective thinking and evaluating the influence of your Inner Saboteur. Stop—Think is the moment of opportunity when you can terminate a negative stress response.

All of us regularly face situations that contain elements of both friendly and unfriendly stress. They are a part of the process of life and, if avoided, lead to diminished potency. Learning to convert unfriendly stress to friendly stress is a big part in becoming an autonomous individual. A very common example is the job performance appraisal interview.

Sam is an example of a person who more or less stumbled on a Stop—Think process and used it to turn an unpleasant situation to his advantage. He was a very competent account executive at a successful advertising agency. When it came time for his annual job performance appraisal he suffered pains in his stomach and complained at home. Sometimes he talked about the possibility of an ulcer with his wife, but each year the pains went away after he received his usual high rating. One evening, obviously irritated, his wife said, "Why don't you stop doing this to yourself? You do a good job. You know it. Harry knows it. And I bet he doesn't like those interviews any more than you do."

Sam did a lot of thinking about that. Something he hadn't realized came through to him. He told his wife, "You know, the feeling I get in those interviews is like when I had to show Dad my report card."

Without realizing it, Sam developed a Stop—Think technique. Just before his next appraisal interview he reviewed these thoughts:

- I do a good job, and I have much evidence of that.
- This might be just as scary for Harry as it is for me.
- I am not being grilled by my father about my report card.

In the interview the first thing he said to Harry was, "I really feel uptight. How do you feel?"

Harry said, "I do too. I hate these damn things. Worst part of my job."

That took the tension out of the situation, and Sam's unfriendly stress was converted to friendly stress when they agreed on the necessary steps Sam needed to take to win a coveted promotion. As time went on, Sam learned to use this Stop—Think technique in other situations that had once been troublesome.

Stop—Think will not only ease the strain on your body, it will also enrich your problem-solving and decision-making skills. Disconnecting from the kind of thoughts that provoke distress, you can begin the positive thinking appropriate to the situation at hand. You can sort out the hard questions:

- Is this stress warranted or is it something from my child-hood programming?
- How can I use my stress response in my own best interest?
- Do I have the competence needed to handle this situation? If not, what do I need to do to acquire it?

Competence is the keystone of confidence, and the more competent you are, the less you will need the Stop—Think technique. Competence is fundamental to self-esteem and promotes good body feelings. Feeling less than competent can take a constant physical toll because of the resultant ongoing negative stress.

Unwarranted or unrealistic ambitions can also be powerful generators of unfriendly stress and can be the pathway to psychosomatic illness. Unfortunately, when ambition is thwarted, our American mythology dictates that harder work will bring success in the traditional sense and that ill health is considered a merit badge for performance.

UTILIZING UNFRIENDLY STRESS FOR POSITIVE RESULTS

Converting unfriendly stress is a matter of changing negatives to positives. A salesperson, needing to earn money for herself and child, may convert her anxiety energy into accomplishment energy by maintaining a tight schedule or telephone calls on prospects while her cohorts take a coffee break, gripe about slow business, and foster increased levels of their anxiety.

In nearly every situation that generates unfriendly stress the effects can be reduced by the decision to take positive action and to follow through on that decision. Just thinking back about the successful outcome of a constructive action can serve as a placebo that will relieve unfriendly stress. The decision to *do something* unblocks the immobilizing effects of negative stress. Writers present a dramatic example of this. Some complain of "writer's block" as though their minds or bodies had in some way been crippled and they couldn't think or write. Writer's block is nothing more than self-immobilization, the work of the Inner Saboteur, and a demonstration of a terrible power contained in a negative belief system.

In his article "How to Cope with the Stress of Writing," Tom Mach states, "As writers, we need to have our creative juices going for us. That small surge of adrenaline we experience when we know an article must be completed on schedule, or the intense emotion we sustain in the scene of our story helps us immediately. John Steinbeck, outraged at discovering the deplorable plight of the migrant workers in California, had stress working for him when he wrote *The Grapes of Wrath*."[8] Steinbeck wrote out his rage. But instead of letting the anger fester, he took positive action. He used his distress for the benefit of others—and benefited himself handsomely.

Whatever your lifework or life-style, you can use stress productively. Taking positive action earns positive payoffs.

Chapter 13

How to Be Up
On a Down Day

*A life without ups and downs would be
dull. Accept your mood swings as a
part of the exciting challenge of life.
Competently handling your mood swings
will add to your joy of living.*

Life is not all a bowl of cherries, but neither is it all lemons
and sour cream. Your appreciation of life's joys is heightened
by the bad experiences. Reveries about a trouble-free life
grant a welcome respite from the stress of daily living, but
reveries are not reality. For a moment, fantasize you have just
been handed a computer printout that describes every day of
your life from now on, and every day is rosy. What happens
to the challenge of life and the zest for living? The jet set
don't get to be jet-setters by accident. They are in search of
excitement to fill the void of absent challenge.

Life is a constant swing from up to down and back again.
The secret of good living is to be in charge of those swings,
to prevent the Inner Saboteur from tricking you in times of
either exuberance or despondency. With the exception of
medically identifiable mood swings, you can be in charge of

most ups and downs. You can learn how to be responsible for your moods just as others have.

This is a startling statement to some. In my twelve years of teaching personal development in classes and workshops I've found this concept has always produced the most discussion. I did not agree with it when it was first proposed to me. Now, my belief is based on my own personal experience of learning how to be in charge of my moods. The list of People-helping experts that follows shows that others have found this too.

Eric Berne, M.D., defines depression in *What Do You Say After You Say Hello?* as, "the failure of a dialogue between the Child and the Parent."[1] This refers to the internal struggle between childlike "wants" and parentlike "shoulds." The expression of "wants" may result in feelings of guilt for having defied the "shoulds." The suppression of "wants" and surrender to "shoulds" may result in feelings of hopelessness and helplessness, and thus produce depression. Once a person becomes aware of this, he has the ability to control his depression.

Aaron T. Beck, M.D., wrote in *Cognitive Therapy and the Emotional Disorders*, "Man has the key to understanding and solving his psychological disturbance within the scope of his own awareness."[2] He suggests that individual problems are distortions of reality based on erroneous premises and assumptions. Once a person has uncovered the erroneous thought, problem-solving faculties can be used to correct erroneous thinking.

David D. Burns, M.D., wrote *Feeling Good* as a consequence of his work with Dr. Beck at the University of Pennsylvania School of Medicine. Their viewpoint is well expressed by the title of an article about cognitive therapy that appeared in *Reader's Digest*, "*Think* Your Way Out of Depression."[3]

Roger L. Gould, M.D., is the author of *Transformations* and says that his book "is about the evolution of adult consciousness as we release ourselves from the constraint of childhood consciousness."[4] In it he outlines "The Seven-

Step Inner Dialogue for Mastering Childhood Demons.'' It is a process of thought and action that opens the way to autonomy.

Mary McClure Goulding, M.S.W.; and *Robert L. Goulding, M.D.*, wrote *Changing Lives Through Redecision Therapy*. Their conclusions are derived from long experience in clinical practice. They teach their methods to psychotherapists from all over the world who come to train at the Western Institute for Group and Family Therapy. In the first two sentences of their book they state: "This book was written to teach psychotherapists how to cure people. *It is also written to help people cure themselves*"[5] (italics added).

Many professional and nonprofessional people have learned, and are learning, to get more out of life by the management of their minds and the powerful mastery of their Inner Saboteurs. Folk Wisdom says that the proof of the pudding is in the eating. My own convictions are based on the experience of transformations and transition as I trained with the Gouldings and observed dozens of others who have successfully changed.

While doing research and writing a master's thesis in my early fifties, I became aware that my mood swings were terribly disruptive of calm progression toward my goals. My past life had been like that of a high hurdler: up and down, up and down, up and down. Sometimes my ups had been more disruptive than my downs. In exuberant enthusiasm I would commit myself to a new task or new direction. I'd go through a period of frantic achievement laced with periods of despair and self-doubt. Once the goal had been attained, something else would attract me and I'd charge off again like Don Quixote, alive with excitement and hiding my doubts under a coat of armor. By age fifty I began wondering what life would be like for me at sixty, sixty-five, seventy. My question was: Am I doomed to do this forever?

LIFE SCRIPTS

As I began my study of group psychotherapy, the idea of life scripts clicked with me the first time I heard about it. Having a memory bank that fed old messages into my computer made sense. It fit my life. I could look back over my life and identify the messages about ups and downs that had ruled my decisions.

The "up" messages were:

- You can be (or do) anything you want to be (or do).
- Someday your ship will come in.
- Don't just stand there. Do something.
- Don't give up the ship. (Don't quit.)
- If at first you don't succeed, try, try, again.

The "down" messages were:

- Life's a struggle.
- You crazy kid. You did it again.
- You always bite off more than you can chew.
- He who dances pays the piper.
- Sing before breakfast and cry before dinner.

To the best of my memory those specific words were stated over and over to me, even though they now appear condensed and a little distorted by time. Those messages were modeled for me by my mother and stepfather. They lived a life of rapid ups and downs.

The decision made at fifty-two to get a master's degree and to train in psychotherapy was the first decision I'd ever made with rational thought in advance. I didn't know exactly what my direction would be, but I had enjoyed the experience of teaching an adult class and wanted to get on with being the writer I had dreamed of being for so many years. My master's degree was a part of my plan, and though I didn't think in those terms at that time, the best way to sabotage my future was to not complete my thesis.

Once I realized that my life problems were of my own making it was fairly easy for me to make new, constructive decisions. It took some time, though, for me to understand that my feelings, as tools of my Inner Saboteur, often sabotaged my logic. My permanent change began as I modified the old "up" messages to become more consistent with the reality of my experience:

- You can be anything you want to be when you are adequately prepared and take constructive action.
- Someday your ship will come in—after you've learned to navigate it, chosen your direction, and become master of your destiny.
- Don't just stand there. Do something appropriate.
- Don't give up the ship? Baloney. There are appropriate times to let go and redirect your efforts.
- "If at first you don't succeed, try, try, again" won't cut the buck. The big payoffs are for achievement, not for effort.

Thinking this way facilitated my progress. The feelings that I associated with negativity empowered my Inner Saboteur in its efforts to thwart my plan: feelings of guilt, anxiety, depression, or futility.

Dealing with the "downs" took more time and effort. The first step was to make positive thoughts out of negative ones—thoughts I chose for myself rather than those I'd incorporated in my belief systems as a child. The new messages were:

- Life's not a struggle. I am aware of many people who enjoy their work and life.
  - "You crazy kid. You did it again."—not true. I'd successfully fulfilled many ventures in the past but I didn't give myself credit for them.

- "You always bite off more than you can chew." Still partially true, but greatly diminished. I've learned to say "No," to myself and to others. I've adopted a more rational assessment of my abilities, energies, and time allocations.
- "He who dances pays the piper." I've quit feeling guilty for having fun and learned to predict just how long it takes for depression to strike after spending time or money "foolishly."
- "Sing before breakfast and cry before dinner." False. Being joyful is a matter of choice, and I can choose to be joyful all day long.

WHAT TO DO WHEN NEGATIVE THOUGHTS INTERFERE

Gradually this thinking brought into my consciousness an awareness of the whirling dialogue my mind harbored. As I connected my feelings with my thoughts I was able to change my thoughts from negative to positive. I didn't suppress the negative thoughts—I acknowledged them, identified them and their source, and let them go, replacing them with positive ones. When negative feelings interfered with work on my master's thesis, this is the process I followed:

Body Awareness

In my training I had learned to recognize which parts of my body responded to which messages. Anxiety produces a queasy feeling in the stomach. Depression produces a slackening or slumping of posture. Grim determination or anger results in muscle tension that could reach the point of painful spasms. My goal in doing my thesis was to write four pages a day while also working as a group counselor and teaching some classes. When I got the funny feeling in my stomach I knew I was reacting to anxiety that could diminish my productivity.

Thought Awareness

When the burden seemed too much, the little boy in me would daydream about all the wonderful things there'd be in my life *after* I completed my thesis. Then my Inner Saboteur would shyly whisper, "There you go again, you crazy kid. You're just dreaming." Then came: "What if you don't get your Master's degree? Besides, who's going to employ a fifty-four-year-old just because he has a master's?" If I pushed ahead with grim determination I'd soon have pains in my back that made typing a torture.

Behavior Modification

This is a learning process based on the idea that people learn—or relearn—behavior as a result of the consequences of that behavior. It implies that people will make a habit of behavior that produces positive results. The behavior I wanted to change was thinking about the future, because it took time away from the work at hand and because it led to anxiety and depression. Using a golf-stroke counter, I recorded each time I caught myself thinking about the future. I kept a record and at the end of the week gave myself a reward, some small luxury I might not otherwise have given myself. The reward was for paying attention to my thinking. A gimmick perhaps, but it worked for me.

In the beginning I'd click my stroke counter six or seven times during the time I spent working on my thesis. My score gradually came down as I paid more attention to the dialogue in my head. In a few weeks I had almost given up the tendency to cross my bridges before I came to them. When I did catch myself I immediately put my mind back to work on the thesis. By taking the positive action of recording my thought processes I aborted the nonproductive thinking about the future, quit having the painful muscle spasms that worry inflicted on my back, and finished my thesis on time. The other rewards? That master's degree opened the way for me to enter the most enjoyable and productive period of my life at an age at which I once would have been considered over the hill.

This may sound simple to you, but the reality was that I stumbled around many different fields of psychological thought until I found what worked for me. At that time none of the books mentioned earlier in this chapter had been published. I've now seen hundreds use this process to become positive-thinking/positive-action types.

ATTITUDE MODIFICATION

You might be one of those who feel down moods are something to fight. It is important to accept the naturalness of mood swings and recognize that there are many theories about their causes, ranging from astrology to sugar consumption. Possibly the most popular theory is that of biorhythms.

The biorhythm theory proposes that everyone's life is influenced by predictable patterns. There is a physical cycle of twenty-three days, an emotional cycle of twenty-eight days, and an intellectual cycle of thirty-three days. Each cycle is 50 percent up and 50 percent down. Thousands of people who hold to the biorhythm theory run their lives according to their biorhythm charts. Awareness of these cycles has helped reduce accidents in some large transportation companies, and there are executives who plan their work schedules by them. Whether you run your life by a chart or not is for you to decide. The point is that mood swings are a fact of life and can be handled better when they are accepted as natural and not suppressed. They certainly do not indicate a weakness of character.

How to Keep Up on a Down Day

Here are the elements of keeping up on a down day:
Awareness   Connection   Release
Acceptance   Decision   Action

Awareness. Knowing you feel down may seem pointless, but many people have built up a wall over the years to protect themselves from emotions or from hearing their internal dialogue. When this defensiveness is blocked from awareness, physical pain can be the result. For now, pay attention to any body pain that cannot be related to a cause, especially if a doctor cannot identify the source of pain.

Acceptance. Accept that down feelings are a part of the human condition. To fight those feelings is to increase mental stress and physical tension. To suppress the feeling is to invite the Inner Saboteur to break out at some future time or place in a fashion disruptive to a tranquil existence.

Connection. Can you connect this situation and feeling to previous situations? Has this happened over and over? What triggered it? Is there a pattern of similarity? Is the feeling you have in mind one you experienced in college? In high school? In grade school? In your family?

What is the connection between the feeling and negative messages in your programming? How did you feel when criticized as a child, and what was the message connected with that? Do you get the same feeling today? When you weren't listened to as a child, how did you feel, and what is the message about that? The more you track down the history of your feelings and messages, the more information you will have to make new choices of positive action.

Decision. The moment you connect a current situation and feeling with a childhood experience and accept the fact that you have the power to change your feelings, you are faced with a decision. Are you going to hold on to the bad feeling five minutes, five hours, five days, or five weeks? Forever?

This decision is the turning point. Will you rule your life or just go along with your Inner Saboteur? Once you realize that many feelings and emotions are a part of your childhood programming, you can decide whether or not to continue them or learn the process of managing them constructively.

Release. Releasing is the prelude to taking positive action. But the potential benefit of that action is diminished to the degree that you are unclear regarding the desired results. *Lack of clarity is the welcome mat for the Inner Saboteur.*

There are many techniques for clearing, releasing, or letting go. Meditation, deep breathing, and deep relaxation are among them and have been discussed in the chapter on stress. Some other techniques will follow.

Action. Once you decide that five or, at most, ten minutes of self-induced bad feelings is enough, it is time to get on with positive living, and that calls for positive action. What is appropriate for you is a personal matter, but it is possible to learn from steps others have taken.

Self-Defeating Feelings—the Substance of Sabotage

Guilt from Procrastination. Some people suffer a constant mild depression from feeling guilty about procrastination. For some it is a form of rebellion, a reaction against authority, a childlike message that says, "You can tell me to do it but you can't tell me when." Another prime cause of procrastination is a fear of failure and the imagined consequences of such failure.

The first positive action to be taken with the down feelings connected to procrastination is to sort out the "shoulds" or the "have-tos" of the situation from the "want tos" and the "need tos." For some there is a continued feeling of resistance to having to arrive at work at a certain time—so much so that the use of time cards by management has become an issue of labor negotiations.

Unless you are a very unusual person, you are at work voluntarily. You asked for the job; you weren't drafted for it. Accepting that, it is then possible to say: "I want this job, and in order to keep it, I want to get to work on time." It is a subtle but powerful change in attitude, and it has worked for others. Whether you want to stop smoking, go on a diet, or make other desirable change, the foundation must be a decision to "want" and to give up the feeling of "should." That makes it easier to take positive steps and avoid procrastination.

Procrastination is a time-management problem. George was a rebellious procrastinator. When George was living with an authoritarian father as a child, his only way to have any sense of individuality came in his rebellion against his father's demands. He did his required chores, but never on time. As an adult he felt rebellious every time he received any communication from management, verbal or written, that appeared to be an order.

After his procrastination had brought several reprimands from his supervisor he began to realize that procrastination might block his career progress. He made up a little game for himself. Every time he felt rebellious he said, "Oh, what the hell." A touch of humor helped him resist the voice of his Inner Saboteur and get on with the work required.

The fear of failure is common among beginning salespeople, and many then give in to procrastination. They postpone the bad feelings that come from rejection, from being cut off on the telephone or when making a cold call on a stranger. Mingling with a group of sales survivors, ones who have become successful, you will hear many say they once had the same feelings.

How did they get over it? By doing it, by making calls until the old fear feelings dissipated, by recognizing the law of averages. Sales managers are fond of saying, "Hey, .300

makes a star hitter in baseball. You can't hit 'em if you don't step up to bat.'' The successful survivors in sales get over their procrastination by risking failure until they've made a habit of success.

Habitual procrastination may not be easy to overcome, but the solution is simple. The rule is *do it*, if it is approrpriate to your goals in life.

Disappointment. When he is not around others, Jack slumps in his chair and lets himself feel the disappointment. Then, like a parent, he says to himself. ''Poor little boy. Ain't it awful? What will you do now?'' About two or three minutes of that and Jack laughs. His mind is clear and he goes on to the next call feeling up. When a sales slump gets him down, he looks at last month's or last year's performance record, or even his tax return. His objective mind tells him, ''You did it once, you can do it again.''

Anger. For Patrick there is no better cure than the old folk saying ''Count to ten.'' This gives him time to recognize that his anger is not with the people he is with now, but with those he left behind. He is very much aware of his anger messages and his Inner Saboteur, and he recognizes how many of his anger reactions are only habits he learned from his father.

If you find that anger is a difficult habit for you, think back to childhood. One woman said, ''The only emotion I ever saw in my home was anger. There was neither joy nor sadness. In response to whatever happens to me now, my only option is anger.'' That woman later added, ''I don't get angry much anymore. It doesn't change anything and it diminishes my potency.''

Anger was Bill's operational procedure for years until his doctor finally had to put him on medication for essential hypertension. The doctor, who was also one of Bill's golfing companions warned: ''You might do yourself a real favor if you'd give up that terrible-temper routine of yours.'' Bill has never completely gotten over his anger habits, but he has now alleviated them a great deal. One positive action was to identify the situations and people that seem to trigger his anger. Now he avoids them whenever possible. When that isn't possible he says to himself, "Is anger worth a ten-point jump in my blood pressure?" Most of the time he decides that it isn't. He's a better boss and husband for it.

Rebellion and Resentment. Ronald reacted to his father's authoritarian manner with the habit of rebellious thinking and feeling. He knows he must be very careful of "black moods," especially when he talks to the boss or senses resistance from one of his peers. At such times, just before making contact, he takes a deep breath and says, "This is not my father."

In so doing, he is reminding himself that he does not have to carry his childhood feelings into his current working situation. "It may sound silly," Ronald says, "but it works."

Low Self-Esteem. Stewart has a stroke board. On the door of his home office he has pinned a number of letters from clients or friends who have enjoyed his services. Stewart also has a testimonial book with letters from satisfied clients mounted between plastic sheets. He put it together originally to show prospective clients, but when he is feeling down he reviews the letters to bolster his personal esteem.

Sometimes Margaret gets to thinking of herself as "only a housewife." She knows that doesn't make sense, but her mother had worked as well as raising a family, and Margaret sometimes feels that being a housewife is not enough. She is not in economic need and enjoys all aspects of her family connection. When she's feeling down, she goes to her "memory drawer" where she has stored many cards and notes her husband and children have given her over the years. Ten minutes of memories restore her usually pleasant mood and sense of being worthwhile.

Anxiety. Louise is also a housewife, but her bad feelings come in the form of anxiety attacks. She has spells when she worries excessively that her husband is disappointed in her as a housekeeper or cook despite his frequent reassurance otherwise. Louise's mother was a perfectionist and Louise had many "be perfect" messages in her belief system.

At a weekend church retreat Louise learned something about belief systems. She learned that her need for reassurance from her husband was a crooked transaction. She didn't like that about herself and began to talk straight to her husband. He gave his cooperation, and they were able to work out a contract about housework. He said: "You don't have to be perfect for me. I think you're damn competent. Would being competent be enough for you?" That was OK for Louise. Now when she begins to get the old anxiety feeling she reminds herself that she is competent. The few times she lets her Inner Saboteur get her down, she sends specific messages to her husband. "I'm feeling down. I need some reassurance." He likes that. He says, "It sures beats hearing you sigh and having to guess what's going on with you."

Loneliness. Harriet is retired and widowed. When loneliness creeps into her mind to the extent of interfering with her life she recognizes she is responsible for the choice between aloneness and loneliness. She then decides that she is alone but not lonely. She thinks about all the privileges of being alone: setting her own pace, no phones ringing, puttering around the house, or just reading a book. When loneliness gets to her she goes to the Senior Center Friendship Group or takes a volunteer assignment to go visit a homebound person who cannot get out for companionship.

MASTERING YOUR MOOD SWINGS

There are many moods that are the work of the Inner Saboteur and that interfere with happy, effective living. There are many ways of overcoming mood swings. The key is recognizing personal responsibility for such swings and doing something appropriate about them, rather than following past habits that result in inappropriate thoughts and feelings. It is unlikely that anyone will completely let go of the old negative beliefs, but such beliefs can be weakened and rapidly dealt with using the process outlined in this chapter. A workshop participant brought in a simple diagram to illustrate her goals.

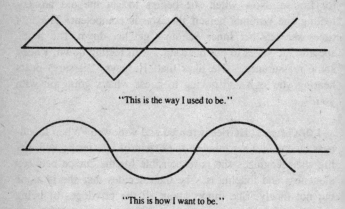

"This is the way I used to be."

"This is how I want to be."

She followed with, "See? This diagram shows I'm aware of moods. I know I'll always have to work on my mood swings, but I sure like life a lot more now that I'm in charge of them."

On those days when it just seems impossible to manage your moods, play a little game of "as if." Act "as if" you were happy and enthusiastic. Pretend everything is right in your world. Do it for an hour, a day. Smile at the next person you pass on the street. Somebody will give you a smile back. Whatever you do, don't put off those things you feel need doing today—to do so is to invite more depression tomorrow.

Joe was a negative-thinking/positive-action type who learned this the hard way. When he felt negative, talked negative, and projected negativism, he didn't make sales. One day his sales manager said to him, "Get out. Go somewhere else. I don't want you dripping gloom over everybody else around here." Joe was upset about that but soon realized he's been done a favor. He's long since learned that to make the income he wanted all he had to do was tell fifteen people about his product every day. He decided that if negativism was reducing his ratio of sales to calls he wanted to do something about that, so on his down days he "faked it," acted as if he was happy. In time Joe learned he could make many sales when he felt down but acted up. Of course, a few sales put him back in an up mood. He learned that his positive attitude, despite negative feelings, increased his sales, made him feel better, and eventually led to his becoming a positive-thinking/positive-action type.

Becoming the master of your moods is the beginning of becoming the person you want to be and getting the rewards that go with being that kind of person. Accepting the reality that "they" don't make you happy or sad, that *you* make yourself happy or sad, is a giant step forward in the direction of positive living.

Chapter 14

Permission to Prosper

Permission is in the mind of the possessor. Giving yourself permission to prosper is an antidote to negative messages about prosperity. Whether or not to exercise permission is a matter of choice.

Prosperity, as a word, is only as meaningful as your definition of it. To measure your prosperity by the definition of others is to put yourself at the service of a multitude of the "shoulds" and "ought tos" proclaimed by your culture, your family, your religion, and your education.

How you define prosperity has a great deal to do with your self-image. Without a clear definition, it's difficult to answer such questions as: Am I prosperous? If not, what am I doing wrong? What price am I willing to pay to achieve my definition of prosperity? Not being clear on what prosperity means to you is an open invitation to your Inner Saboteur to plague your life with worries and problems.

If you will pause a moment and write out your definition of prosperity it will help you as you consider your future.

Simply write out the rest of this sentence: "My idea of prosperity is . . ." Put down the first things that come to mind. Don't try to evaluate or be logical. You can sort out what you've written after you've finished this chapter, and go about sorting out the prices and priorities inherent in the search for the prosperity you envision.

While growing up we adopt many beliefs that emanate from others about prosperity. Possibly we measure ourselves as poor in relation to our school friends. Some of us grow up in environments where there is never a scarcity of things. But it isn't until we begin to earn a living that we begin to test the reality and practicality of our belief systems. We then realize that what went on with us as children is not necessarily related to our grown-up world. A young lady raised in a doctor's family moves away and finds out what it means to get by on a minimum-wage job. A young man whose father paid for everything with credit cards gets in a financial mess because he accepted and used all the credit cards offered in television commercials.

Prosperity has traditionally meant the acquisition and display of "things." The implied message is: "I have all these things because I am smarter, slicker, stronger, or work harder than the rest of you." How many big cars, fancy homes, and trips to Europe have been bought for show rather than need or interest? How many millions have been spent on advertising to convince people they can "be somebody" only if they have—and display—Brand A? How much credit has been extended so that people could buy their identity on the time plan?

Now an increasing number of pioneers are emerging who reject the belief that life's a struggle, that all rewards will be had in heaven; who reject the Puritan work ethic as a binding code; who want identity for themselves rather than for their possessions; and who know both intellectually and intuitively that the world is changing so quickly that traditional economic, political, and social beliefs are losing their validity, baffling experts and ordinary folks alike.

There is a search for what's called a New Prosperity. What brought about this cultural phonemenon is difficult to pinpoint: maybe the Vietnam war, maybe the drug scene, maybe the explosive growth of the human potential movement in the late 1960s and most of the 1970s. Maybe more people are seeing the world with their own eyes, and what they see is the reality of a crumbling mythology. Traditional prosperity is not guranteed by virtue of "going to college." The automobile assembly line no longer offers security. Teaching, once the haven of so many job seekers, has become, to many, a boring pastime stifled in the blanket of bureaucracy and the indifference of student and parents. So many jobs are so far removed from the end product that workers, even managers, see no meaning in their work. Many of us are disillusioned by our leaders who sit in Washington and cry "sacrifice" while they refuse to give up any of the comforts of power.

Now, in the 1980s, there is a turn toward a New Prosperity that makes sense to many people. Marching to one's own drum has become socially acceptable and economically feasible. Long hair, beards, and granny dresses are no longer the marks of only "hippies" or "drop-outs." In a few companies, executives can refuse to uproot their families by moving to strange territory and no longer fear being forevermore banished from consideration for a promotion. A lawyer trades the courtroom for a massage table and teaches acupressure. A dentist becomes a Gestalt therapist. A teacher tunes cars to finance his life as a sculptor. A family earns its way making dog collars treated with eucalyptus oil. A former high-powered salesman owns and operates two eateries. A doctor bakes bread in his own bakery to relax from the stress of his practice.

People are doing "their thing" in a balanced style somewhere between the demand for conformity and the rebelliousness that went on for a while during the Vietnam war. Many accomplish this by living simpler lives, no matter how much money they have. Those who share in the New Prosperity seek something more than money, interpreting success in their own way. Some of the components of the New Prosperity are discussed below.

MEANINGFUL LIVING

Most people want to be creative and expressive in their work and see the connection between their life and the lives of others through the product of their efforts. A maker of custom picture frames connects with customers who come into the shop, admire his work, and give him their personal treasures to be framed. He derives pleasure not only from his work but also from the connection with his customers. A berry farmer no longer crates and ships his berries off to market. People come to his farm and pick their own berries. He knows he is helping them reduce the cost of living as well as making possible a return to the simpler life-style by producing their own jams and jellies. At the gate where he weighs out what they have garnered there is a camaraderie and talk of family life. A hairdresser gives up her swank salon and her society customers in the city to run a little shop in her home on the outskirts of a country town. Her husband, a former executive, does custom carpentry and home renovation because he likes working with his hands.

Few people will completely escape the need to rely on the production-distribution-marketing chain that has marked the American business style. Nevertheless, they are reducing their dependence on that system while increasing the meaning of their daily lives, both through the choice of their jobs and through their direct relationships with those who buy, or barter, for their products. At flea markets, at craft fairs, and through cooperative markets, they are bypassing the middleman while enhancing the meaning in their working lives.

POWER AND CONTROL AT WORK

Most of us who grew up during the Depression had only one rule in life: "Get a job. Any job. Get a job and keep it." Those of us who followed that rule gave away the power to be in control of our lives. We did what we were told to do. We went where they told us to go. We suffered terrible indignities in the pursuit of economic security and the dream that someday retirement would bring us freedom. In 1940, 300,000 men took the federal Civil Service examination for the United States Border Patrol. The pay was $2,000 a year, little more than $38 a week. I was one of them. There was nothing in my belief system that said the pursuit of my own goals was anything more than foolish daydreaming. My messages were:

- Life's a struggle.
- A man makes a living.
- A man supports his family.

People seeking the New Prosperity either do not have or have discarded much of the misinformation that arises out of this work ethic. They want to work and are willing to work, but they want a greater say in *how* they work. Usually they go to work at something they trained for or feel is right for them and do not discover what they do or don't want until they have had a few years of experience. The process begins after graduation from high school or college. Some women marry and, fifteen or twenty years later, go back to work knowing very much what they want out of their work. Those "wants" are often in conflict with the traditional male/female system in the work place.

A consequence is that both men and women are seeking more power and control of their lives at their work place. When they don't get that, their effectiveness and productivity decline, so much so that many corporations are moving away from authoritarianism toward democracy to increase productivity and retain creative workers who might otherwise leave. There are job-enrichment programs that put a worker in closer contact with the total job process, or that give a working team more power in determining how their work will be performed. Of course, this is rarely altruistic on the part of the corporation. It is done in the interest of bottom-line figures.

If you think your job could be more interesting with some changes in your required manner of performance, start thinking in terms of bottom-line figures. The question is: How can you make your work more meaningful to you and increase your effectiveness and productivity? One positive step in that direction would be to read a few books and magazines on management. This will enable you to understand more of the management viewpoint and discover more about the innovative job practices that are going on all over the country. When you know a way you can add to the bottom-line figures of your unit or organization, take a risk. Make an appointment with your boss to talk to him or her about your expanded job classification. Use your new communications style in doing that. You might say something like: "Boss, I'd like to talk with you about my job. I think I know what you expect of me and I know what I expect of me, but I'd just like to be sure I'm on the right track."

Sound scary? You wouldn't want to admit to the boss you don't know *exactly* what is wanted? Well, how many times in your working life have you walked away from a conversation saying to yourself, "I wonder what in hell he or she really wants of me"? Remind yourself that people wouldn't still be saying "Nothing ventured, nothing gained" if there weren't more than a grain of truth in it.

A secretary trapped in a position she felt to be a meaningless dead end tried this approach. She told her boss how she could perform better with some changes in her work routine, along with her hopes about the future. "I want to help people and help my organization by doing so," she said. He was fascinated. No worker had ever approached him in this fashion before. He gave her permission to make some changes in her work and suggested some books for her to read. He helped her outline a course of her adult extension study at a community college. When she had demonstrated her conviction by continued positive action, he approved her attendance at company-sponsored supervisory and management seminars that had been previously reserved for top management. In time she became an administrative assistant and is now a personnel manager. She knew what she wanted and asked for it.

TIME AND THE NEW PROSPERITY

Time is becoming an increasingly precious possession to those who feel their personal lives are as valuable as their working lives. A working mother is tired of meaningless and arbitary nine-to-five rules and demands to come in from ten to six so that she can get the kids off to school without a maelstrom of emotions every morning. A valued research and development man says, "This is silly. I can think better at home, so I'm going to do that two days a week and come in here only three days." A young girl says, "I only work half-time so I can learn to cook and garden, see my friends, and practice my guitar." The list goes on and on.

The new values placed on time have led to organizational responses from corporations, including the concept of flextime. Flextime means that within the limits of a time core when the full working team is most needed, employees can set the time of arrival and departure. If that core is ten to three, some workers might be in from seven to three, some from eight to four, and some from ten to six.

Another possibility is shared jobs. This is something for two people who only want to work part-time and can find an employment situation that accommodates their need. Each might work four hours a day, or each might work every other day. Some professional married couples work a shared job so that they can also share the job of raising children.

Permanent part-time work is particularly popular with two-worker families and retirees. There is a need for thousands of part-time workers, exclusive of seasonal needs like those of a ski resort or a department store at Christmas. Many large companies and small businesses have need for part-time workers on a regular basis. This simplest way to explore the possibilities of part-time work is to register with one of the many agencies listed in the newspaper classified section.

Some people want more time for themselves yet also want the life that economic prosperity provides. They become free lances so that they can control their own hours. Harriet was a public relations person with a corporation in a large city, but then found a small town she loved and wanted to live in. She moved and now has time for her new life-style. She advertises her services, but most of her work comes from referrals. A businessman wanted to get on with the writing he had abandoned early in life to support a family. He took some training in group leadership skills, taught a few courses in supervision and management, and then became a free lance running training courses sponsored by training centers, colleges, and the Chamber of Commerce. Now he is a writer four days a week and a trainer three days a week. He's getting everything he wants out of life because he changed his belief system. For years he believed he had to have a ''job,'' meaning a salary earned by conforming to the expectations of others. Now he has the freedom to be his own man.

Jay Levinson says, ''I have earned considerably more money without a job than I did with a job, yet I rarely work more than three days a week.'' Jay, author of *Earning Money Without a Job: The Economics of Freedom*, differentiates between work and having a job. For years he had a job but no freedom. He says, ''Sure, I only work three days a week, but I work. I bust my tail off those three days, but that leaves four days for my family, or skiing, or teaching other people how to earn money without a job.''[1]

If you want more control over your time to use it in the way you choose, you can do that. Remember: What people have done, people can do.

HEALTH

In recent years there has been a rapidly increasing awareness that money and things are rotten substitutes for good health. The evidence comes from everywhere. For quite a few years now, executive health has been a concern of large corporations. In the 1970s large numbers of people believed that if preventive health measures were good for executives they were good for everybody. In the 1960s, President Kennedy created a national fitness program. Ever since, jogging and tennis have remained popular and are not in danger of dying out as a fad. You've undoubtedly seen someone go through a hotel lobby in a running suit and jogging shoes, or perhaps while boarding a plane you've been poked in the ribs by the handle of a tennis racquet jutting out of someone's bag. Exercise is a priority, even when traveling. In short, people have decided that health is fundamental to their store of prosperity.

Meaningful living, personal time, personal power, health— these factors of New Prosperity really don't look so new at all. They seem common to the dreams of many who have been trapped in the tentacles of an industrialized age. Yet there are always a few in our midst who manage to get these things for themselves, who rise beyond the circumstances of average living and find a balanced abundance in life. It is as if they have been given some special permission to be different from the rest of us. But it is up to each individual to give himself that permission. To have that self-permission to prosper is to be free of the self-defeating attitudes and actions of the Inner Saboteur.

SELF-DEFEATING PROGRAMS

Some self-limiting messages in belief systems are:

- Be happy with what you've got.
- Don't be pushy.
- A woman's place is in the home.
- Money doesn't grow on trees.
- You can't have everything.

Think back over your childhood and recall the times you felt put-down or discounted by older people about your talents and abilities. If you do not find any such times, you may be one of the fortunate few who have a seemingly natural permission to prosper. In *Victims of Success*, Dr. Benjamin B. Wolman tells of a young man whose life was crippled by the fear of outstripping his father, a man who was brilliant but had not graduated from college. The son had sought the help of a psychoanalyst after having stayed in college ten years and accumulating between 400 and 550 units of credit. He kept himself from graduating by changing majors.[2]

Programmed into my early belief systems was an impression that making money was motivated by greed. My stepfather, a very intelligent but bellicose man, was always telling the boss where to head in. When the Depression hit, his job-jumping record caught up with him and he ended up digging ditches with the Works Progress Administration. He became a Technocrat and constantly belittled the capitalists. Eventually I too felt there was something wrong with making money. I wanted it; I strived for it. But when selling, often felt guilty because I hadn't really "earned" it. After recovering from that attitude I had to learn how to enjoy myself as a part of my New Prosperity.

Permission is in the mind of the possessor. It is a property of the psyche, and ownership lies with the individual. For many, prosperity is like a fence separating the land of money and the land of self. Uncomfortable with straddling the either/or fence that separates the two, they opt either for the pursuit of either one or the other. Permission to prosper means getting rid of the fence and enjoying the best of two worlds: the tangibles of financial success and the intangibles of self-actualization.

Suzy was a preacher's kid and was raised in genteel poverty, meaning just a shade above dirt-poor. All her little girlfriends received store-bought dresses from J.C. Penney or the Montgomery Ward catalog. Suzy's came from the donation barrel behind the church door, and she felt terrible humiliation whenever she sensed one of the other girls recognized a discarded dress on her. In middle age, Suzy got tired of all the meekness, humility, and penny-pinching that she had been programmed for. She says, "I just got tired, totally tired, of all that stuff. I decided to live and enjoy life."

That decision led her back to school and a degree in psychology. In learning theory she recognized how much she had been the victim of her programming. During an intensive training session she made a decision to ignore her Inner Saboteur and please herself. Now she has the richness of self-knowledge, a good income, and, though she is not extravagant, two closets full of the kinds of clothes she dreamed of as a child. Suzy gave up the fantasy of Cinderella and took responsibility for transforming that fantasy into a reality.

Maybe the simplest way to describe the New Prosperity is through the example of Seth and Marilyn Manning, a couple who knew the rules of traditional success but discovered for themselves what total prosperity is all about. Both were programmed to work and to believe in work as the means to acquire important material things. Their beautiful Spanish-style adobe home is testimony of their ability to get ahead in the traditional way—Marilyn as a communications specialist, and Seth as president of his own insurance and financial-planning firm. Somehow, though, the accomplishment of their financial dreams did not bring with it the happiness they had assumed automatically went with financial prosperity.

"What we found out was that money in the bank doesn't guarantee happiness. We had to discover how to find happiness for ourselves."

That discovery came about more by chance than by design. In order to meet some requirements for her degree, Marilyn took a graduate course in psychology. Without having planned it that way, she found a key to a better way of life. In the class she found people interacting and sharing their lives with each other in a way alien to her relationship with Seth. She talked to Seth about it, but he was apprehensive. He said, "I figured, why stir up trouble? Leave well enough alone."

Marilyn gently persisted, and then a crisis in the life of each stimulated their mutual pursuit of a New Prosperity. Marilyn had had two children in two years and suffered a lingering depression. She loved her children but had been so indoctrinated in the work ethic that dropping her career confronted her with an identity crisis. During that period Seth underwent a painful experience in the breakup of a business partnership.

For a while they were "groupies," attending every kind of self-discovery workshop they thought might help them in answering the call to "know thyself." They realigned their goals in life and established new priorities. "We spent a lot of time, energy, and money to get where we are, but we see that as an exchange. Money that used to go for parties was redirected to the costs of learning. Time that went for social activities was channeled into attending classes. Energies that had gone to socializing were directed to personal development and new ways to communicate with each other."

As they went along, they became increasingly aware that the more they contributed to the well-being of each other, and of others around them, the more their environment contributed to them. In their development process it seemed their financial rewards increased in direct ratio to their personal growth. An added richness to their life is the joy they get in sharing their experience and knowledge with others in their "Expanding Your Prosperity" seminars.

Marilyn believes very strongly that communication is the keystone for enjoyable relationships and teaches people how to be open and honest with each other without having anyone suffer in the process. One of Seth's strongest beliefs is that money is a by-product of service and that increased competency increases prosperity. They are also both strong believers in the process of clearing, aware that hanging on to guilt, anxiety, frustration, anger, timidity, or other bad feelings depletes the human reservoir of positive energy and diverts it to negative channels.

Seth and Marilyn are positive thinkers who take positive action. The joy and pleasure they get out of life is available to others willing to invest the time, energy, and effort in the pursuit of the New Prosperity and to learn how to give themselves permission to prosper.

Chapter 15

Being Your Own Boss

The gold medals go to those who be-lieve they will make possible what oth-ers consider impossible. Possibility and impossibility are only concepts in an individual's belief system. Faith is the most common characteristic of champions.

The American dream of independence is a part of our national belief system—an inheritance from the colonists, pioneers, and individualists of our earlier years. Our parents, teachers, and school books planted many positive messages of indepen-dence in our childhood programs. Paradoxically, we also received substantial negative input that often makes the pur-suit of personal and economic freedom a playing field for the Inner Saboteur.

Dreams do not become reality until plans have been made, goals set, desires established, priorities decided on, and a commitment to transition made—all followed by positive action. To dream fervently and not make those dreams come true is to foster frustration and dis-ease with life. *Yet there*

*are many who go on trudging along in a rut and never break
out because they are more comfortable with getting by than
with the process of getting more.*

There is nothing wrong with getting by; some people are
happy getting by and live a rich life in many ways. This
chapter does not necessarily apply to them. It is for those
restless, dissatisfied people who *want* to run their own show,
make as little or as much money as they want, and work the
hours and days of their choosing.

If you have ever dreamed of independence, believe that
what others have done, you can do too. Tempering your
dream with a realistic evaluation of your competencies, and
the understanding that persistence and determination are abso-
lutely essential, will enable you to pursue independence
successfully. Few people who make it on their own just
"luck out." A lot is heard of the dazzling success stories of
a Pet Rock or a book like *The Lazy Man's Way to Riches*, and
the money that suddenly poured in, but little is heard of the
years of struggle that preceded the successful event.

Never mind the scintillating stories. Recognize that thousands of people in this country, most of them as ordinary as
you and I, are living out their dreams by being self-employed.
Government statistics back this up. For example, in 1979,
excluding agriculture, there were 6.7 million self-employed.
In 1977, 702,000 women owned their own businesses. About
47 percent of them worked from their home, and 157 of the
in-the-house businesses grossed $1 million or more annually.
The numbers of younger people in business for themselves is
increasing. In 1972 about 40 percent of the self-employed
were sixteen to forty-four years of age. In 1979 that figure
had grown to 51 percent.

All of these figures are bound to increase as we move
further into the new world of technology. Computers and
word processors offer a tremendous potential for those who
want to control their life-styles by choosing to live where they
want to and work the hours they work.

Bill and Helen

When Bill and Helen married, Bill was a salaried electronic data processing manager and Carol a salaried secretary. When Bill became a consultant and seminar leader, Carol became his partner, handling public relations and writing manuals needed for their clients. Now they have their own computer and word processor in their home. They are putting out two newsletters and see a big market for the sale of information. Most important is the realization that they can give up the rush and smog of the big city and move to a quiet country setting where the trees are green, the sky is blue, and there is no violence in the schools.

THE THREE CLASSES OF SELF-EMPLOYMENT

Sales People

Although there is no theoretical limit to the number of ways a person can be self-employed, it is possible to fit all the ways into three categories: salespeople, independents, and entrepreneurs. I've excluded retail salespeople or those who are paid salaries; rather, I am speaking now of those who work completely on a commission basis. They do not buy and resell. They sell a product and are paid a percentage of the amount received. They might sell life insurance or be a regional representative for a manufacturer. They set their own hours. There is no start-up investment required for inventory. Most of them do their own paperwork and do not have to pay for secretarial work.

Independents

These are the free lances who sell only their own services or products. In some cases they make those products themselves, and sometimes they have a spouse, friend, or relative as partner. They do not have any employees, nor a guaranteed income. Some deal only with retailers, some only with the public, and some with both.

Examples of those who make and sell their own products include cabinet-makers, potters, painters, dressmakers, jewelers, candlemakers, and tile makers. There's really an endless list of people making products. Some producers augment their income by these activities, while others make producing and selling a full-time occupation. They enjoy a sense of meaningfulness that comes from their creativity, from seeing a finished product, and from meeting the person who is going to take that product home. There is a feeling of participation rather than the feeling of being a mere cog in a machine that delivers the end product never seen by the worker who contributes to its production.

In fact, many craftspeople have burned out in the traditional ways of "making a living." There are thousands who, like Byron, spent their days dreaming of someday being on their own. Since he was a kid, he'd been a whittler and could carve beautiful miniature animals even while carrying on a conversation. But as an adult, he found himself divorced and alone (his kids were grown) and completely bored with his job. At the time he said: "It was now or never. I knew I did good work. I knew people would buy my work. The only way was up. Every day I stayed in that job I hated myself for being chicken." Byron doesn't hate himself now. He's proud of having made the break and enjoys working in his own little shop doing things his way. He receives added enjoyment from the high school adult classes he teaches in woodcarving.

Ironically, it was his boss who put Byron on the road to independence. There had been an ongoing personality conflict between them. On day the boss threw a brochure down on Byron's desk describing a management workshop on interpersonal communications. Byron attended once and was interested enough to go to several more. Over a three-year period, his awareness and personal responsibility for his attitudes and actions brought a reversal of his outlook. He gave up his reoccupation with being a victim and instead became a manager of his life. He coupled his new positive thinking with positive action and opened the way for getting more, much more, out of life.

Another group of independents are those who sell their services. These people have spent years training and working to develop their expertise in a particular area. Some get tired of organizational bureaucracy. Some have a strong desire to be in control of their lives, on and off the job. They want to set their own hours, choose the people they do business with, and live in an area of their choice. Some of them were phased out by a plant closure, a business failure, or a corporate merger. There are also those who have a larger goal in life than making a living. They might be artists, sculptors, or writers who have a marketable skill that they use to pay the bills so they can give more attention to the primary goal in their life. If you'll look in the Yellow Pages, the classified ads, or the advertising of the small, free weekly newspapers in your area you'll find scores of independents listed who sell their services. If you use their services, you'll usually find them a happy group.

Don has a degree in environmental studies but couldn't find a job where he wanted to live. Now he's in the business of maintaining and servicing mobile homes in a coastal area that attracts many retirees who need Don's services. He says, "I love it. I'm helping people, I love the area, I make a good living, and I have time to enjoy the beach and forest with my wife and kids." Laughing, he adds, "And I don't have to go to all those damned meetings of the planners and the public."

Yet another group, the mail-order specialists, falls in between the independents and our third category, entrepreneurs. Some stay one-person operations, or, at most, mom-and-pop operations. Others expand, become merchandisers, and may get into the-money-management areas of entrepreneurship. Usually they buy products and resell them by mail. Some create and sell information by mail. Others do the same by means of tape cassettes. Some eventually become big operators and advertise their goods or services in full-page ads in newspapers and magazines. Some make it. Some don't. All agree, "Nothing ventured, nothing gained."

Jerry Buchanan says he was a "chicken to feathers" salesman for twenty years doing full-commission work for educational institutions. Sometimes he did well, and sometimes there was too much month left at the end of the money. At age forty-five he took a look at where he'd been and where he was going.

That year he gave up direct selling and started a small information-selling mail-order business, which slowly bloomed into a very successful publishing house. He tells how he did it in his mail-order book *The Writer's Utopia Formula Report*. When the checks started pouring in from all over the world he realized he'd hit on a winning subject and started a newsletter for writers, *Towers Club, USA Newsletter*.

That venture has been so successful that in just ten short years he has gone from "chicken to feathers" selling to being one of the wealthiest mail-order kings in America. His huge mansion on a hill overlooking Vancouver, Washington, is far removed from the days when he sometimes stood in unemployment or food-stamp lines.

Entrepreneurs

The difference between entrepreneurs and independents is that the former win or lose in direct relationship to their ability to manage money or people or both. They must also know how, or learn how, to research the market for their products, to distribute them, and to raise capital when required.

The time has long passed when the budding entrepreneur can go in to his friendly banker and sell a hunch about making and selling a new product—so much so that designing and writing a business plan is a major subject at some schools, as it is at the Center for Innovation and Entrepreneurial Development at the University of California, Santa Cruz, where students set up mock businesses in workshops. Some of these businesses later become full-functioning enterprises.

This book is not meant to urge you to become self-employed. It is meant to help those of you who have dreamed of being your own boss examine, and understand, how your Inner Saboteur can lead you to abandon your vision of getting more out of life. It is also meant to encourage you to consider having an ace in the hole that might be called your contingency plan. Security is one thought that the Inner Saboteur always presents to people who consider striking out on their own. The reality is that economic security is a personal possession. Relegating it to others is only an illusion. Consider all of the hundreds of thousands of people who sweat out years of stagnation in boring jobs, doping themselves with dreams of "someday," only to have inflation make a nightmare out of retirement. Security is only as good as the budget behind it, whether it be government or private. Companies fail or sell out and pension plans evaporate.

MYTHOLOGICAL BLOCKS TO SELF-EMPLOYMENT

Many of the blocks to becoming self-employed are based in myth, a lack of understanding of the real attitudes and actions of those who are their own bosses. Some elements which make up that myth are:

Goals. It is commonly felt that to make more money or become wealthy is a major motivation of entrepreneurial types. Not so. Researchers consistently report that becoming wealthy is a by-product of "doing your own thing." Because you like it, you devote time and energy to it, become good at it, and consequently do well financially.

Gamblers. To think of going on your own as a gamble is to buy into a myth and trigger many negative beliefs about gambling. If you are debating going on your own, think of it as an investment in your future. When Mac was considering self-publishing a book, he had many reservations about spending part of his savings. Although he was quite sure he had enough buyers for his book to at least break even, he spoke of it as a gamble to his banker, who said, "Look, Mac, it's an investment." Mac netted about $10,000 from the book and earned another $30,000 to $40,000 through public appearances—all the result of giving himself permission to invest in himself.

Loners. Some people think of the self-employed as though they lived the life of trappers walking the solitary forest in the winter. Nothing could be further from the truth. Sure, the entrepreneurs, the independents, and the salespeople may drop out of the car pool or miss the coffee-break gang, but they soon find their place in a new network of people. Support from others is essential for the enjoyment of the independent life-style, and it can come from family, friends, peers, and customers. There is also great empathy and rapport among those who pioneer the territory of personal independence.

THE AMWAY EXAMPLE OF SUPPORT AND FRIENDSHIP

It is highly unlikely that anyone could ever generate the "get up and go" needed to pursue his or her dreams without the friendship and support of others, without the synergy created by encouragement above one's own psychological resources. Consider, for example, Jay Van Andel and Rich DeVos of Amway fame. They were youngsters in high school when fate brought them together in 1940. Friendship kept them together. After school they became business partners because they liked and respected each other. As they went along, additional support came from their wives. In 1949 they became distributors for Nutrilite Products. In 1959 they launched the Amway Corporation from the basements of their homes in Michigan. In fiscal 1981, Amway's sales at estimated retail were $1.4 billion. Because of the constructive benefits they received from the support of their wives, both men place great emphasis on marital teamwork, and about 75 percent of Amway's one million independent distributors are couples working together to get more out of life—psychologically and economically.

BEING YOUR OWN BOSS

The reasons why people successfully become their own bosses are almost as varied as the number who have done so. Motivation is a personal matter. Some simply want to do things their own way. Some feel they are making a contribution to others. Some feel they have built the "better mousetrap." Some seek power. And there are those who want to slip through life with as little resistance as possible. The young lady who sells bagels from a pushcart in a West Coast resort town speaks for them: "It's a nice life. I sleep late. I'm out in God's clean air and can smell the ocean. In the evening I play my guitar with my friends, and two nights a week I study music at the community college. For right now, it's wonderful."

For many, "right now" means that they understand the story about the straw that broke the camel's back. They've suffered their last put-down from a boss; maybe they've been fired. They got tired of just getting by on an average income. The idea of financial independence burned so strongly within that they just couldn't listen to the excuses of their Inner Saboteur. They looked ahead five, ten, fifteen years and said, "Is this all there is?"

Don Dible is one of those who had the burning desire to be his own man. With a solid background in electronics and an outstanding reputation in sales, he felt it was time to "stand on his own two feet." He went into business for himself. When he encountered adversity, Don demonstrated that most precious of all attitudes of independents and entrepreneurs: There is no such thing as bad experience; there is only experience.

Don realized that although he had found an abundance of books on managing an existing business, there were few to guide the fledging entrepreneur in the establishment of a new business. To fill that gap, Don wrote, edited, published, and distributed *Up Your Own Organization*. He then learned how to develop and deliver seminars and went on the road talking about his book and about entrepreneurship. The book became a best-seller, and Don is now a highly regarded platform speaker and seminar leader.

In his book, Don stresses the importance of competence and says, "The single greatest underlying cause of business failures, or bankruptcy, is incompetence, which accounts for about 45 percent of the failures."[1]

That's a high percentage of incompetence, yet every one of those who ended up in the failure statistics probably thought he or she was competent to make it to the top. The tragedy is that most of them *were* competent—but only in the narrow field of their expertise. They lacked competence in the broader sense of being an independent or an entrepreneur. An outstanding example of this is the mistake made in so many organizations when they promote an outstanding salesperson to sales manager only to find that the competence of selling may not carry forward to the competence of training others to sell.

Talking to people who have failed quickly reveals that they just didn't "see" the narrowness of their competence. When the postmortem is rendered on their failure they say, "Sure. I see it now. But I sure didn't see it then." That is one of the most insidious activities of the Inner Saboteur: It clouds our psychological vision so that sometimes we "just don't see it."

WATCH OUT FOR THE INNER SABOTEUR

Here are some messages from childhood programming that make sense on their own but that can be distorted by contaminated thinking:

- You can be (do) anything you want to be (do).
- Hard work solves all problems.
- You're just as good as the next person.

These are all valid messages when tempered by rational thinking, but the Inner Saboteur is not rational. It contaminates these messages with impulsiveness. Making crucial life decisions can be an agonizing transition, and at times it is overwhelmingly tempting to escape that agony by taking precipitate action. One way to avoid such action is to ask yourself, "Who'll say 'I told you so if I fail?' "

Failing to consider the voices of the past easily leads many people into the either/or trap: I must either stay in this dull and boring job, or quit and go all out in my new venture. They become so overwhelmed with the desire to get going they become impatient and fail to train themselves in the additional competencies necessary to their hoped-for accomplishment. They also overlook the fact that thousands of people who simply couldn't afford to quit a job to explore new fields have built new businesses during nights and weekends, frequently working from their homes. Many in mail-order businesses made their transition that way.

How people manage to sabotage their potential for success would make a never-ending list, but here are a handful of ways I've noted during more than fifty years of awareness and investigation.

Some people are easily taken in when they buy an existing business. Anyone buying a business is foolish not to retain a neutral professional to examine the books. People who have never been in a small business find it hard to believe that anyone would resort to fraudulent bookkeeping when selling out. Sally and Henry bought a launderette and never thought to observe the business a day or two or count the daily customer flow to check against the purported cash flow. Because of their naiveté, they went broke.

Concerned about initial start-up costs, people sometimes set up a new business in an offbeat location, ignoring the reality that location is everything to some businesses. They mistakenly believe the world will beat a path to their door once their business is known. Harry set up a rapid-print shop in a low-rent residential neighborhood, but all the competition was located in the business district, where convenience counts. Harry didn't make it.

Gil felt burned out in his engineering job and let a smooth-talking life insurance sales manager convince him he would be just great as an estate planner. Gil wanted to change careers so badly he never thought of asking to go on a sales call or even to ask a few friends if they would let him be their financial planner. When he called on his first few prospects he was astounded at the physical reactions he had: His stomach churned, he was soaked in perspiration, his palms felt clammy. The manager reassured him, telling him that this would disappear in a few weeks. The feelings didn't go away; in fact, they heightened when Gil found that he had to make enough sales to justify his drawing account.

When Gil's Inner Saboteur began whispering, "See, stupid, you really blew it," Gil suffered a period of severe depression. He felt he'd have to admit to himself he was a failure, which was in conflict with much of his belief system. Finally, desperately struggling with his pride, Gil went in to see the personnel manager of his former employer, who said, "Good Lord, Gil, why didn't you come and talk with me in the first place? We're always looking for good engineers in the sales department." Gil didn't have an answer, but he rejoined the company and became a sales engineer, doing very well at it

ıd enjoying the freedom of movement, the increased respon-
bility for creativity, and his client contact.

Then there are those who got through the hard days at the
art and began to look like winners, only to let psychological
ıuirks trip them up. Ralph had two dreams: owning his small
ıpermarket, and being a scratch golfer. After a few years of
reat effort, with golf only on Sunday, he was out of debt and
ɛeling comfortable. He gave his manager a raise and said,
'It's your turn now. I'm going to play golf three times a
ɛeek.'' By the time Ralph worked his handicap down to
ıree, the manager had the business almost in shambles. It
ɔok some tough talk from his accountant even then to get
ƙalph to give up his dream of being a scratch handicapper.
ɪe did it, though, letting the manager go and getting back
nto the store again on a seven-day-a-week basis. Eventually
ıe restored his former good business position, played golf
•nly on Wednesday and Saturday afternoons, and settled for a
ɛven handicap.

When obstinacy and stubbornness are confused with determination they can become the weapons of the Inner Saboteur.
)ld Charley was a working stiff whose dream was a little
ɔlace in the country where he could raise chickens without
ınybody telling him what to do. When he was granted a small
ɪisability pension he figured that it would be enough, along
ʋith his veteran's pension, to see him through the start-up
ɔeriod. He found some run-down chicken houses on a coun-
ry piece of land with a small house trailer. Then he went to
ɪe big feed warehouse in the county center and got a contract
ɔ raise pullets which they would buy back from him. They
ɔaid him by the weight and specified the maximum allowable
n pounds and ounces. At first Charley did fine—he was
ɛalizing his dream. But with his programming for being a
ʋictim, he just didn't know how to enjoy his small success.

Charley's Inner Saboteur kept hinting. ''The more they
ʋeigh, the more they should pay.'' That made sense to
Charley, even if it didn't make sense to the poultry producer.
At first Charley tried to let a few overweight pullets slip

through. When he was warned he eased off for a bit, but the
began his shenanigans again. Eventually his contract wa
canceled and Charley was back where he'd always bee
broke, embittered, and blaming the big guys that never gav
the little guys a chance.

I hope these case histories will not be taken as demonstra
tions of negativism. They are warnings that optimism can b
a heady stimulant that needs to be tempered with practicality
It is not prudent to embark on a new life direction withou
acknowledging that your new future will have both ups an
downs. It is wise to be prepared for the downs and t
reprogram your belief system appropriately. NASA didn
land a space shot on the moon by ignoring the possibilities fe
failure.

Ask anyone who has failed in his or her new directions
"How did you arrange to fail?" You'll probably get a startle
stare and a response like: "What are you talking about? That'
a ridiculous question." Maybe it is. Maybe the questio
should be: "How did your Inner Saboteur arrange for you t
fail?" Austin M. Elliot publishes a newsletter for the Sma
Businessman's Clinic and has been a consultant to small
business owners for nineteen years. He says, "The ways o
failing seem almost infinite."

The same might be said of marriage, friendships, life
fulfillment, or any other human endeavor.

The number of reasons for success is also almost infinite
because they vary according to the individual involved. If yo
want to be in charge of your destiny the best source o
information is someone who is doing what you want to do
Look one of them up and tell him or her what you have i
mind. Ask what is good about this occupation. Also, asl
what is bad. You will get valuable information in response t
either question. Don't be shy about approaching such people
Most successful people (remember, we include something
more than money in the definition of success) are willing to be
helpful to others. They enjoy it. You are not taking from
them. You are adding to their enjoyment of success. They

may give back to you some great encouragement for the support you need to get started.

The rule for getting started is: *Do it*. A dream becomes a goal the moment positive action is taken and the risk of action is accepted. A race doesn't begin until somebody leaves the starting blocks. From that point on, competence, commitment, and determination are the factors contributing to the quality of success. In the sales field there is a firm, and long-held, belief that 20 percent of the salespeople make 80 percent of the sales. That's probably as good a rule as any to apply to getting more out of life by being your own boss. Decide now you will be one of the top 20 percent. You will be if you want to, choose to, and go about doing the right things for yourself the right way. Failure is only an illusion of the Inner Saboteur. Setbacks are an opportunity for learning, they are only detours on the road to your goals in life.

Chapter 16

Growing Up as You Grow Older

There are only two choices: stagnate or grow. Stagnation is dreary and boring. Growth is exciting, joyful, and a safeguard against burnout.

Chronological aging is not a sign of growing up. It is only a sign of growing older, a day at a time. Growing up is the process of maturation. Maturation is synonymous with wisdom—it is learning tested by experience. The opportunity for further growth lies ahead, and to avoid or deny it leaves only the option of growing older.

STAGNATION AND BURNOUT

Growing older without growing up results in stagnation. To turn away the world's reality and harbor the illusions of childhood is the prologue to stagnation. Psychic energy is stifled by stagnation, just as a pool without a flow of fresh water stagnates and loses its life-giving energy. Unless psychic energy is restored, the will to take positive action dies. Burnout is the result. Burned-out people lock away their learning, experience, and wisdom behind a steel door of listlessness.

Somewhere along the line those who only grow older have been deceived by their Inner Saboteurs and their belief systems. In part, that is because so many people's belief systems include illusory chronological indicators of growth. Our cultural mythology contains many pseudo rites of passage as proclaimed by custom or law. Some of us cling to the magical belief that at a certain point in life we will be mature and live happily ever after. Someday we can smoke, drink, vote, have sex, get married, get promoted, be our own boss, or retire. We suffer along from milepost to milepost with our eyes glassy, staring at "someday" and missing the thrill of growing, changing, and experiencing life one day at a time.

THE IFD DISEASE

There are illusory measurements of growth that lead to frustration and disappointment. Back in 1946, Wendell Johnson wrote in *People in Quandaries:* "We may call it the IFD disease: from idealism to frustration to disappointment. Probably no one of us entirely escapes it. It is of epidemic proportions."[1] The frustration phase is stagnation; deep disappointment is the mark of burnout. Unfortunately, *stagnation results in years of diminished personal productivity and effectivness before the burnout crisis point is identified.*

To be rationally idealistic is to have an internal balance of hopes and dreams that are consistent with your abilities. No amount of persistence will deliver anyone to a mirage centered in a desert of irrational dreams. If this seems limiting, think of Don Quixote and his battle with the windmill. His heart was pure but his mind wasn't clear. In contrast, Albert Schweitzer pursued idealistic goals all his life, goals considered irrational by some of his friends. But he achieved those goals only because he tempered the idealism of his heart with the rationality of his mind. He went about things in the right way. He suffered frustration but knew how to cope with it. He suffered disappontment but did not let it discourage him. He never burned out. He termed himself "a man of individual action," and the results of his actions have lived long after his death. His goals were born in idealism, but "doing the right thing the right way" kept him from the IFD disease. Also bear in mind that Schweitzer changed goals in his lifetime when it was necessary to follow his heart. His careers in music and the ministry ran concurrently for some time before he became a doctor.

PERSONAL PERFORMANCE APPRAISAL

One sign of maturing, of growing up, is to move consistently in the direction of your chosen goals without surrendering to the frustration that arises out of inappropriate self-management. Another mark of maturity is to examine original goals and evaluate your experience as you pursue them. From time to time a personal performance appraisal of life-effectiveness evaluation is in order. The questions to ask yourself are:

- How am I doing in the pursuit of my goals?
- How do I feel about that?
- What can I do, beginning today, to accelerate my progress?
- Am I still on the right path and am I doing the right things in the right way?
- What are the environmental signs of my progress? (Such signs include promotions, professional recognition, income, relationships, independence, and other measurements, consistent with your life's directions.)

- Is my world still supportive of my goals, economically, technically, politically, socially?
- Have I increased my level of competence as needed for the attainment of my goals?
- How do I feel now about my potency in getting what I want out of my career or my life in general? On a scale of 1 (powerless) to 10 (very powerful), how would I rate myself on potency?

Bill

Bill always said, "I'm a hell of a good assistant and I don't care to be a boss." In high school he always won second or third place in the mile, but never first. In college he was assistant manager of the track team. In his work he made it to his position as executive assistant to the department manager. Bill liked it. He took a lot of positive action and became the indispensable assistant. When his boss suddenly succumbed to a heart attack, Bill's corporation thrust him into the manager's position, even though he had not been tested for his problem-solving or decision-making abilities.

Bill survived by working long, hard hours. He became a "firefighter"—spending so much time putting out "fires" that there was no time for the art of planning. In time he found a competent assistant himself but was unable to delegate responsibility for fear of revealing his weaknesses. He lived in constant dread of being fired. His Inner Saboteur told him over and over, "You're really not good enough for the top spot." His dread of responsibility was so strong that he discounted any evidence he was a good manager, even when he was given raises for his performance. As his stagnation intensified there were moments of panic when he felt like running away from the office. Ironically, Bill felt it was fortunate that he developed an ulcer. With his doctor's blessing he asked for a less stressful position and was granted transfer to a staff position where decision-making was not required. Once again he's an "almost winner." He professes no regrets but has been heard to say, "If it weren't for my ulcer I could be a vice-president."

Bill's negative belief system included limitations he would not let himself exceed. His body cooperated and helped him get out of an intolerable situation before he burned out. But he is still in a limbo of stagnation, ruled by his Inner Saboteur.

Steve

Steve was the opposite of Bill. He'd gone to work in the industrial shop of a big corporation while a teenager. He worked up the hard way, becoming a machinist, then foreman, and eventually manager of the shop. He loved his work, loved managing people, and loved the way chunks of metal were transformed into usable goods. But as supervisor, he grew further and further away from people and products. His time was taken up doing cost-effectiveness studies to satisfy the people in the front office. He had to do government paperwork by the ream in order to justify the shop's program for the Occupational Safety and Health Administration; there were Affirmative Action people to talk to, a special training program for minorities to administer, and an increasingly militant union to deal with. "Hell," he'd say, "I'm just a damn clerk around here."

As time went on, Steve felt less capable of supervising. He felt he'd lost the power to get work done in the way that had once been his greatest thrill. Eventually he lost interest, burned out, and went through the necessary motions to get him through to retirement. At home he'd say, "Two more years; that's it. I've got the years in and I'll be fifty-five."

Both Steve and Bill let their work stop them in the growing-up process. Bill stymied himself with his internal convictions. Steve let external conditions block his growth. Either might have avoided burnout—Bill by learning how to deal with his Inner Saboteur, and Steve by taking some management courses to help with his paperwork and management problems. Both let stagnation freeze their level of competence well below their potential.

POWERLESSNESS

One of the basic elements of stagnation and burnout is the feeling of having lost the power to relate satisfactorily an expenditure of energy and effort to a desired result. This is particularly true of people who can measure their effectiveness only by the performance of other people. Managers, police, psychotherapists, minister, teachers, and parole officers are examples of professionals who are considered agents of human change, and who often find themselves in conflict with human nature. People cannot change until they are willing to change. We are resistant to unilateral contracts of change, even when the changer is "supposed" to influence the changee by virtue of power emanating from an organization or society. Most of those in the people-changing business start out with some idealism concerning their goals. Gradually individual, societal, and organizational resistance leads to frustration for many of them. As the frustration intensifies, the helpless feelings increase. Some reexamine their goals in the light of reality and cope with their new situations. The same applies to people in almost any walk of life, from retail clerks to college professors.

In the 1950s, Donald B. Miller began studying the human factors involved in engineering obsolescence. In his book *Personal Vitality* he writes: "In the sense that life provides the space for reaching and satisfying higher need-levels, continued learning is a part of life. Learning is precursor to need-satisfaction."[2]

CONTINUING EDUCATION

The explosive growth in the adult education field in the past decade is evidence that growing numbers of adults are no longer willing to stagnate, to grow older without growing up.

Hundreds of thousands are trooping into classrooms evenings and weekends to keep up with the outpouring of new information deluging the world. In 1973, Wilbur Cross wrote an article for the *Chicago Tribune* titled "Weekends to Stretch Your Mind." Within a few days the Office of Publications in Continuing Education at Syracuse University was swamped with 1,500 letters. At the end of two years, the school and *Reader's Digest* (which had reprinted the article) had received over 6,000 queries.

CREATIVE EXPRESSION

Creative expression is another way to avoid stagnation and burnout. It is fortunate when creative expression also satisfies an individual's economic needs, but a creative hobby has provided a joyful life for many by helping them overcome the ennui of a dull job or a lackluster life. Creativity might even mean sanity for some. Sidney M. Jourard, writing in *The Transparent Self*, states: "I have little doubt but that we therapists have lost the chance to make some professional fees because a prospective patient came to achieve catharsis, insight into and compassion for him/herself, through writing a poem, a novel or play. Disclosure of one's being can be therapeutic."[3]

I believe this observation also applies to the potter, the composer, the painter, the cabinetmaker, the sculptor, or anyone else whose creative thought is translated into visual or oral form through physical action. Singers and musicians hear their product; writers and painters see theirs. They possess tangible evidence of their creativity that can inspire them to a greater performance and to advance learning. Equally important is the availability of positive, or even negative, feedback from others.

"Burnout. Gosh, I never thought of it." This is Jules Archer speaking, author of sixty published books. "I guess I just have such a tremendous curiosity about people and I like to write about them. It's like a self-generating battery. I just keep regenerating myself." Now, in his retirement years, Jules regenerates himself by teaching others better ways to write, by teaching alternative views of American history, by rollerskating, and by writing an occasional television script. Certainly Jules is growing older, but his continual learning keeps him growing up.

MAKING CONSTRUCTIVE CHANGE

If you accept the fact that learning is the key to personal and/or professional growth, then the next question becomes: What should you learn? To help guide you, here are four areas where learning is often needed for change:

1. Changing you
2. Changing them
3. Changing it
4. Changing methodology

1. Changing You

Sometimes people find themselves in periods of frustration or disappointment in marriage or employment. They have rational reasons for continuing the situation and resign themselves to martyrdom, hoping to suffer in silence, but more often boring their friends with their complaints. They cut themselves off from joy as they struggle under the load. Acceptance is different from resignation. Acceptance is to say. "Well, this is the way it is. I really can't do anything about [him, her, or it]. It's time to get on with my life." Realizing the need to change ourselves, we find new means of life satisfaction that keep us growing up.

College campuses are dotted with older adults preparing

themselves for a second career while at the same time maintaining their vitality and vigor in their current work. I've talked with dozens of government workers stuck in the bog of frustration that is the trademark of bureaucracy. They accept it as a reality yet cater to their own needs for life satisfaction by learning a hobby or training for a second career.

One police sergeant became an expert in the making of Western jewelry and opened his own shop after he retired. One supervisor set out to learn to be a better manager by studying the psychology of human behavior. He learned, in the process, to understand himself, which not only improved his managerial performance but went a long way in revitalizing him personally. "Changing you" by new learning is sometimes the only means of dealing with stagnation.

2. Changing Them

Changing others is difficult but not impossible. The keynote is willingness. Willingness is only obtainable from others when they feel your objectives make sense in their own minds. Better to leave well enough alone than to frustrate yourself through authoritarian efforts. You cannot change anyone—in marriage, family, relationships, or organizations—unless you can provide a spark of desire and a supportive climate for change. One of the myths of management is that we can motivate others. Not so. Manipulate, yes; motivate, no. Motivation comes from within, as a response to the urge for certain payoffs to the candidate for change.

Every other week the *Behavioral Sciences Newsletter* reports on the application of behavioral theories to management. Each issue recommends several new strategies to "change" employees and improve productivity. There are many such newsletters and reports producing a torrent of words about changing people at work. Adding to this confusing mass of information is the flood of theses and dissertations piling up in graduate schools of business administration. In the meantime, managers go on stagnating and burning out.

The same condition exists in the ranks of the psychotherapists and marital counselors—stagnation and burnout continue to afflict them. The ones who escape are the ones who go on learning, who continue with their own therapy from time to time to get rid of their accumulated garbage.

Pat desperately wanted his wife to change. In middle age, he saw himself burning out and changed his career to become a marital counselor. For ten years he tried to counsel his wife, hoping she would make some changes that matched his in the interest of marital harmony. They got along in the usual way, but he kept wanting just a little more in their relationship. He was logical and persuasive. She'd say, "I agree." She listened but she didn't hear.

One week was particularly bad: three arguments in three days. "You didn't fix the bookshelf as you said you would." "You burned the dinner again." "Why didn't you say what was on your mind?" After the third spat his wife became very upset. She asked herself: "Don't I want to be happy? I could do some of the things Pat suggests. Maybe I'm just as responsible as he is for these quarrels."

At that moment she was ready for change. Change became something she wanted rather than something she felt Pat was thrusting upon her in a win/lose way. She began reading one of the books he had suggested to her and felt much clearer, as though cataracts of resistance had once blurred her vision and had now miraculously disappeared. From that point on the two have been enjoying their life together on a win/win basis.

People change when they are ready to change. One way to facilitate that change is to offer a win/win climate. Find out what people want and what they are willing to do to get it. If you have carefully evaluated the potential for change in a person or group, communicate your need for change by sending "I" messages that are not evaluative nor judgmental. For example: "I have need of cooperation because the production quota is not being met," rather than "You guys are goofing off again and making me look bad upstairs."

Ask the involved parties what their needs are and then

listen to them. Hear them. Ask them what they are willing to give to get their needs met. Listen to the answers. Hear them. Use the communications skills outlined in Chapters 10 and 11. Then, and only then, can you begin to develop a mutual agreement—a contract for solutions.

If you are not as successful in "changing them" as you'd like, consider the use of a neutral, skilled arbitrator, if the others are willing to accept such assistance.

The president of a small electronics firm knew he had a good product and a good market for that product, but his firm skittered along the edge of solvency. People in the plant just weren't getting along together. No one talked straight; there were many crooked messages floating around.

With the agreement of the executive staff an outside consultant was brought in who taught the president and his managers to talk straight to one another. During the last session he asked all of the twelve present to finish this statement: "My biggest problem with this company is . . ." With that information out in the open, agreements were made that turned the group into a team. A year later the sales and productivity trends were up and the president, who had once thought of selling out to end his frustration, was enjoying life, running a successful company, doing what he wanted to do.

Warning: To attempt an intervention of this sort in either personal or organizational problems requires a high degree of mutual trust. Without trust, you invite crooked responses. Also, do not use this technique with another unless you are willing to negotiate some change for yourself. If someone says, "My biggest problem with you is you," be prepared to listen. It might be time to "change you."

Another thing to keep in mind is that there are no panaceas for changing others. If you are working with, or living with, a manipulative, cranky, uncompromising, dull, arrogant clod, recall that you are in that relationship by choice. When others won't change, you have two options. You can accept and adjust—change you. Or you can get away. Both are difficult decisions but life is filled with difficult decisions. Recognizing the need for change is only half the battle. Changing is the other half.

3. Changing It

Changing "it" means dealing with your environment. If your negative belief system hampers your willingness to influence external factors in your life, you may need to go back and do some more work on "changing you." You probably have far more power to alter or change your environment than you give yourself credit for, but the first step usually entails the risk of change.

The simplest example of "changing it" would be that of a race driver who modifies his car's engine to get more power. A more complex example would be redesigning one's office or worksite. Every housewife knows what it means to revitalize herself by hanging some new curtains or changing work environment.

Your first step is to realistically evaluate your power to alter your surroundings. You won't know your power until you test it. Don't let your Inner Saboteur put you off by hinting, "Nobody's ever done that around here before." A group of women once brightened up a gloomy, gray social welfare office by simply putting flowers on their desks. It had never been done before because no one had wanted to take the risk.

One way to test your power is to ask your boss or mate about the dream you want to translate into reality. Use questions like these:

- I'm really feeling desperate about this struggle to make ends meet. I think I'd feel better if we set up a budget and stuck to it. How do you feel about that?
- I'm just about exhausted with the struggle of getting two kids off to school, catching a bus and getting here by eight-thirty in the morning. I've been keeping a record of

my incoming calls, and nothing important ever starts to happen until after nine-thirty. I could actually do a better job here if I could come in at nine-thirty and stay an hour later. In that time I could sort out the important information you need and would have it on your desk for you when you come in mornings. How do you feel about that?

• If we had a videotape recorder in the training department I'm sure I could cut out a lot of lost time when workers are off the job. Would you be willing to include the cost in the training budget?

Note that all of these proposed changes are based in reality and followed up by the risk of rejection. It is the fear of rejection that keeps many people stuck in frustrating situations. To grow entails risk, dealing with risk, and then accepting some changes.

Max is a free-lance electronic data processing consultant. He doesn't like to wear a suit, even though his fee is $1,000 a day. In his contract he stipulates that he will not wear a suit and tie during his assignments. His clients don't object, but Max admits to having been a little nervous the first time he offered that contract to a prospective customer.

Max might not be able to get away with that stipulation if he did not have an excellent reputation. He religiously devotes at least six hours a week to learning more about his business. When you test your power to change "it" and someone else has the power to veto, be certain that you are competent. To ask for change and be anything less than competent is to invite disaster.

A life insurance agent asked his manager for a half-time secretary. The manager said: "No problem. Just write enough additional policies to pay her salary." After thinking it over the agent was afraid to take the risk and went back to feeling frustrated, blaming his average performance on a lack of support.

If you find you do not have the power to change "it" and feel compelled to stay in a frustrating situation, a second job may be a means of revitalization. Marianne tends bar and makes leaded glass panes to sell at the flea market on weekends. Morgan makes $20,000 a year waiting tables at a swank café evenings. During the daytime he is rebuilding two houses and will eventually sell them to buy his own café. Guy is an electronics engineer and would like to work only half-time for his multinational firm. The firm won't permit it, but he feels his retirement benefits are too good to walk away from. So he avoids burnout by playing guitar professionally in cofeehouses at night. All three of these people keep themselves growing with their off-the-job activities. All are growing older, but also growing up.

Another way to change "it" is to change jobs, but this is not constructive unless done judiciously. Many people say, "I don't know what I want to do." There are two ways to find out. One is to do it. Find something you think you'd like to do and explore the possibility of moonlighting. Find out at first hand the advantages and disadvantages of that work. Selling easily lends itself to this approach. Real estate, life insurance, general insurance, home-care products, and mutual funds are among the many products that can be sold part-time.

The other way to find out what you want to do is to call upon professional assistance. Community colleges offer classes and workshops designed to help you find the right career. There are reputable individuals and centers who can help; in the appendix you'll find some information on where to contact them.

4. Changing Methodology

To change methodology is to change the way you feel about living your life. It is akin to "changing you" but relies more on changing actions than on changing belief systems. Someone with a mild case of procrastination can obtain a book on time management and put its advice into practice. A willing person with family problems can take a course in parent effectiveness training and put that training into practice. A manager who had difficulty keeping up in his field can buy a cassette player for his car and listen to informative tapes while commuting.

To go about changing methodology, ask yourself:

- What is the problem that needs correcting?
- What is the bad feeling connected with my performance?
- What do I need to do to change?
- What method is best suited to my needs?
- What kind of good feelings do I expect by making my change?

The goal is positive payoffs, and they are available to anyone willing to grow and learn.

One of the fringe benefits of growing up instead of just getting older is that you are getting set for sixty, sixty-five, seventy, or longer. There is no magic age that sees the end of life's developmental tasks. To disregard preparation for the future is to stagnate and enter the golden years at a disadvantage. Historically the presumption has been that everyone retires at sixty-five and lives happily ever after. This myth is rapidly giving ground in the face of inflation, failures in Social Security and pension systems, and a growing body of information about emotional upheaval brought on by that state of unemployment known as retirement.

The decision to continue personal growth is a decision for the management of your future, a future that is rushing at us so frighteningly fast that some people fight desperately to bring back the past, hoping for a stabilization that never existed. The past, in my life time, has seen two world wars, Korea, Vietnam, and scores of lesser battles. It has seen the Depression, numerous recessions, civil war in the ghettos, and the advancement of Fourth of July rockets into nuclear missiles. There is no stability to be recaptured from the past except the illusions fostered by avoidance. This country was founded on change, thrived on change, and will grow on change.

How you handle yourself in the future is your responsibility. The capacity for coping with change is based on the willingness to learn and grow—up, as well as older. It is a process of self-renewal that offers meaning and joy in the years ahead. For those who feel self-concern is selfish, consider how every constructive change in an individual affects others and adds a speck of increased positive energy to the world.

Chapter 17

Handy Hints
for Positive Action

*The time to start taking positive action
is today. And tomorrow, and tomorrow,
and every day thereafter. Action is the
catalyst that turns a dream into reality.*

In school you are educated to pass examinations on what
you've learned. Education for living, however, is something
acquired only by testing yourself, your skills, your knowledge,
and your competence against the world. For some it is exclusively a process in trial and error. Others combine this process with information acquired from those who have already
learned by trial and error and are willing to share their
wisdom. "Street smarts" is a phrase that comes from the
big-city environment to describe those who gain their education by surviving in that environment. "Life smarts" is a
phrase to describe the learning about living that comes from
years of getting more, getting something extra out of life.

Resourcefulness is the essence of "life smarts," and it
isn't taught in school. "Resourceful" is defined as being
"able to deal skillfully and promptly with new situations,
difficulties." People whose parents were patient and didn't

238

consider an error a sin were encouraged to be resourceful. The child who is fortunate enough to start part-time work early in life has the opportunity to witness adult experience and test it out in his or her "real world." They get to learn by trial and error early and usually have the support of their elders as they do so. Unfortunately, hundreds of thousands of people never know what it is to work and live in the real world until after they have left college and the shelter of home. They've never had the chance to learn "life smarts." It's like learning to paddle your own canoe down a gentle stream until it reaches the ocean, then being suddenly confronted with the turbulent surf of a violent sea.

To deal skillfully and promptly with new situations and difficulties requires competence. Competence in the working/living situation is the difference between positive action, indifferent action, and negative action—no action is a form of negative action. Taking positive action by learning from the experience of others saves time in the process of gaining "life smarts." The huge market for seminars and workshops in this country demonstrates the almost universal search for the means of taking positive action and applying new knowledge and skills to the process of positive living.

The following sections will give you some handy hints on "life smarts."

STRUCTURING TIME

How time is used determines the quality of your life. Your use of time, and how you feel about that use, marks the difference between happiness, ennui, and unhappiness. There was a time when a man and woman awakened to a hostile world and spent all their waking hours in a struggle for one more day of survival. There was no optional time.

Now there is abundance of optional time. Instead of thinking in terms of a 40-hour work week it would be better to think of a 168-hour "life week." That's right—168 hours to allocate as you choose for work, sleep, leisure, or indolence. The difficulty for many is that choices lead to decisions, and decisions carry the weight of responsibility and the risk of bad feelings if a poor choice is made. The other side of the paradox is that *not* making decisions about the use of time is itself a decision to drift, to wander aimlessly through life surrendering the quality of life to others.

Setting goals is imperative to the constructive use of time. Another imperative is to know that what you are doing is what you *want* to do, that *you* are the one who decided to do it. Only then can you decide what you need to do. With a future goal in mind the only question then becomes: What do you need to do today to reach tomorrow's goal?

Time management is as simple as that. When you reduce your time allocations to "wants" and "needs" you thwart the Inner Saboteur's rebellious reaction against "have tos" and "ought tos." Then, even though it is hard work and requires self-discipline, there is joy in the use of time.

It is rather astounding that otherwise competent people traipse off to one- and two-day seminars and spend sizable amounts of money hoping someone will teach them how to manage their time. Once a goal is set and needs determined, priorities for use of time can be established. Every Sunday afternoon or early Monday morning, regularly set aside fifteen minutes to list the things you need to do, the ones that will give you a sense of accomplishment or well-being. These should include family, hobbies, recreation, or other needs that when fulfilled will add to the quality of your life. Number the items on your list in the order of priority. Put that list where it is visible to you at least once an hour. (Mine is paper-clipped to the calendar right over my typewriter.) The next step is—*do it*.

Maybe you'd like to try Susan Bagby's idea. Susan is a free-lance writer and editor with a basic goal of making a living, and a broader goal of becoming an established writer. Editing is an enjoyable way for her to make a living while she strives for her longer-range goals. Susan draws a target with a bull's-eye rated 1 at the center. Around that center are numbered concentric circles, with 10 being the outer circle. In the bull's-eye she lists her major goal, and then labels the others in the outer circles in the order of importance. Thus, at any time she can glance at her target and check out how the day's or the hour's activity is meeting her needs. When she sees she is aiming off-center, she brings herself back into focus.

Other handy hints which might appeal to you can be found in Alan Lakein's book *How to Get Control of Your Time and Your Life.* Then—*do it*. Don't let your Inner Saboteur con you with the myth that discipline is tantamount to cheerlessness. Discipline is the gateway to freedom and will provide you with the time to get everything you want out of life.

INVESTING IN YOURSELF

The management of both time and money calls for budgeting. To deny yourself the opportunity of achieving your goals for lack of money is usually a self-deception. Of course, there are times when true poverty delays the achievement of goals, but the American dream is filled with stories of poor people who saved pennies to buy books for night school. In contrast are the two fellows I overheard at an introductory lecture for a self-improvement seminar. As they were leaving one said to his friend, "I guess that all makes sense, but who can afford the cost?" The reality was that both golfed, bowled, hunted, and fished. Both had nice homes with all the amenities. They were socially active, and the money they spent for liquor every month would support a family for a year in some underdeveloped countries.

In this society most people who are getting by do have the money for self-investment *if* they rearrange their priorities. Sometimes this calls for family decisions, and it is appropriate to look at family goals as well as individual goals when setting priorities. During any reevaluation period the use of contracting skills mentioned earlier in this book will be helpful so that each family member can contribute. Sometimes this may cause stress, but the chances are that the stress is already there, and it might as well be out in the open.

"You Have to Spend Money to Make Money" is emblazoned in foot-high gold letters above the entryway to a successful management consulting firm in New York. It is what they tell their clients. This same maxim also applies in the field of life management. If you have any doubt about this, ask yourself, "What would I have given in time and money five, ten, fifteen years ago to have avoided some of the problems I've had in my life?" Careful planning and self-investment *now* will give payoffs five, ten, fifteen years in the future.

Career counselors and workshop leaders regularly hear statements like "I know I don't like what I'm doing, but I don't know what else to do. I guess I don't really know what I want to do."

Sometimes this is legitimate. But sometimes it is only a means of forestalling responsibility and positive action. People pay a lot of money to go to classes, workshops, and counseling to provide themselves with the illusion they are "doing something," when in reality they are only marking time. They say things like:

- Well, I'm really trying.
- At least I'm making progress.
- One of these days . . .

When they are given constructive advice, they say, "Yes, but . . ." and reel off all of the reasons why they can't take immediate action to correct their situation in life. What they get out of all this evasion of responsibility is a temporary good feeling from talking about their wishes and substituting conversation for action. Sooner or later the good feelings give way to feelings of guilt or hopelessness as the Inner Saboteur reminds them of all the things they "should" be doing.

CHOOSING MODELS

One way to dispel the uncertainty of life directions is to find someone who is a model, doing the things you think you'd like to do, living the way you think you'd like to live. To pick a model is one way of bringing your wishes into consciousness in terms of reality. That's why success books are so popular. The problem is that too many of the readers get vicarious feelings of action rather than actually emulating their heroes. If you read such books, study the personal qualities of the people they are written about.

If you are fortunate to have someone in your community who has a career or life-style you would like for yourself, find a way to meet this person. Get acquainted. Find out what his or her motivation is—you may or may not be motivated the same way. Ask such people what they don't like about their lives as well as what they do like. You will be fortunate if you find out you are on the wrong track before the expenditure of substantial amounts of time and money.

You are also fortunate if you had a good model as a child and have found it a productive one to follow. Some professions and life-styles run in families for several generations because the older generation is a model for the younger one.

You are most fortunate if you find a model willing to become a mentor. If that should happen, remember that the day will come when you will feel you've learned all you can from that person, and unless you've become fast friends, let go of the relationship gracefully.

Let your model become a part of your visual imagery

program. Some people paste a small photo of themselves over the face of their model's picture. It helps them see themselves in the new role they are assuming in life.

CREATIVE PROBLEM SOLVING

Your success in life is directly related to your ability to solve life problems. Life problems do not lead themselves to mathematical solutions and are strongly resistant to logic. In fact, they often arise out of the failure of logic when applied to humans. When people try to figure out "why" they act as they do and "why" things don't go right for them, the result is frequently frustration, a block that seems impassable. Logic calls for either/or solutions and for trying to make sense by using old information and methods.

What is called for in breaking through an impasse is new thinking in tune with the present and the future: intuitive and creative thinking freed from the straitjacket of logic. This does not mean all past learning must be discarded; it means that all you are can be expanded by using your imagination in connection with your learning. One way to do that is with "what if" exercises, imagining what would happen "if" you did this or they did that. Visualize what would happen "if" you resolved a problem in an unexpected way. Brainstorm it. Think of all the crazy solutions you can and write them down. Disregard all the negative thoughts that might arise. Let the part of you that is still a child run free. When you have written down all your ideas, put your list away for a day or two.

When you go back to it, don't let your Inner Saboteur tell you it's a silly game. Don't pooh-pooh it. The method has been successfully used many times by many people. When you look at your list objectively you may be surprised how your responses make sense if considered in the light of new ideas. Given normal health and diet, children are bright, intuitive, and imaginative little creatures, but those qualities tend to be stifled by the regimentation inflicted on them during the process of childhood programming. Using the imagination helps break the impasse that occurs when the subconscious and the conscious are locked in conflict.

One man asked his therapist for help with a problem that was hurting his business and upsetting his family relationships. He and some partners had invented a little black electronic box and were trying to market it. Because of his Inner Saboteur, the businessman was trying to "do everything" and rescue all involved from failure. In the meantime, he was losing many hours that the family felt belonged to them. The therapist suggested, "Imagine that black box is on the desk. Tell it what you think of it. Then give it a voice and let it talk back to you." The man felt a little self-conscious, but went along with the experiment. In rather coarse language he told the black box what he thought of it, how he worried, and how it was affecting his family.

Then he thought for a moment and gave the box a voice. That voice brought to the surface many thoughts that had been suppressed by the businessman. It said, "Hey, I didn't invent me. You did it. Those guys aren't my partners. It's your business if you want to carry them. I didn't ask you to stay down here at the office when you could have been home with the kids."

It took about a half hour to get all the subconscious thinking out in the open once the man's mind was "clear" regarding the little black box. Facing up to his own reasponsibility for the impulse he had reached, he sold his interest in the box to his partners within a week, got back on the right track with his major business endeavor, and began revitalizing his family life.

You can do the same thing with your problems. Give them a voice. If your problem involves others, put a picture of some people on a desk, or a table, or propped in a chair; use photos of the parties involved if you can. Then tell them all your thoughts about the situation. Don't be polite. Don't be surprised if some unexpected anger breaks out—the other party isn't hearing it, so there'll be no harm done, and it may help you avoid bursting out angrily at the real them at some later date.

Now think a few minutes about that other person or group of people. You know a lot about them. Give a voice to the other side. When everything's been said from that side of the aisle, go back to yourself. Let the exchanges go on as long as there are conflicting issues. When you feel it is all out of your system, let it go for a while. It is very likely that later, while you are not thinking about it, fresh ideas will flash on in your mind.

You can do the same with "thing" problems. Get a little cardboard box and write the name of the "thing" on it. Give a voice to it. Have a conversation back and forth with it. You have nothing to lose, so test it. Don't let your Inner Saboteur put you off by telling you "Don't be childish, "because that's exactly what you are trying to do—reawaken your childlike intuition and creativity.

If you have a few trusted friends you can use the brainstorming method popular in business and organizational management. Get together once in a while, or call an emergency meeting if necessary, to generate synergy, a collective energy arising from a cooperative group. Have a moderator who does not contribute ideas, but instead stops any input that goes like:

- You should . . .
- You ought to . . .
- My advice to you is . . .

Evaluative and judgmental statements are not appropriate. It is agreed that no one argues for his or her investment in a viewpoint. The purpose is to keep the ideas flowing. If you hear something that sounds right for you, you can say, "Tell me more of about that." Do not try to solve the problem in this group. If you get an idea you'd like to pursue, call the individual who gave it to you later—maybe invite him or her to lunch—and talk it over. And never say, "Yes, but . . ." while in the group. To voice objections invites arguments or dissension and is a waste of time and energy.

Whatever you do when faced with problems, don't let a negative belief about your ability to solve problems block your efforts for improvement. Some people have a "Don't think" message in their programming because they were put down constantly every time they tried to reason anything out as a child. If those thoughts come up, remember they are just thoughts. Creative problem-solving methods are worth learning and will get you past many barricades that might otherwise block your positive living.

LEARNING HOW TO LEARN

Learning, as defined here, does not mean education. It means acquiring new information and methods for translating that information into constructive experience. You are the one who determines what you want to learn, and, barring the absolute need for a degree of some sort, you design your own curriculum in the University of Life. You will have full responsibility for what you learn and how you use that learning. Even if you find it imperative to get a formal degree for a promotion or a license to be in business, it is up to you to control as much as possible what you will study.

Whatever learning program you choose, whether it be assertiveness training or a master's degree in business administration, it is your choice and you are in it because you want to be. You have determined your motivation, and knowing this you will find it easier to delegate the time required to reach your goal. Knowing you are doing what you want to do will be important when you are tempted to stay home and watch TV or buy some new gadgets rather than spend money for attendance at a workshop.

Choose with great care those people from whom you want to learn. Academic status and/or licenses to practice have no relationship to quality of instruction; sometimes they camouflage incompetence. The best reference for a course or teacher is a reference for someone who has learned from that teacher and demonstrates that it was worthwhile. Good teachers do not tell you what to do, they show you how to do it.

Having the encouragement and support of family, friends, and associates is tremendously important. Loners can make it, but the way seems faster and easier when camaraderie is available. If you do not have that kind of support, you will find in the appendix of this book the name of an organization that will provide information about self-help groups throughout the country.

HOT DOG, ATTABOY, HOT DOG, ATTAGIRL

Stroking is not flattery. It is showing appreciation and recognition to another human being; it is an understanding of the universal need for acceptance. Unconditional stroking is to say, "It's nice to work around you." It is done with no expectation of payoff other than what you might get out of brightening another's day. Conditional stroking is to say, "You did a good job yesterday. And I hope you will keep it up." Some might consider this manipulation, but manipulation isn't necessarily bad. Conditional stroking is an ethical manipulation when it is done to let people know where they stand.

Some people find it hard to give strokes. They were raised in families that said, "You know when you've done a good job. We don't need to tell you." Nonstroking or negative-stroking parents simply don't understand the need for strokes or why anyone should want them.

One of the most positive actions you can take to enhance

all of your human relationships is to be aware of your stroking patterns. A simple way to do that is to ask yourself, "If I were this person, what recognition would I like at this time?" Then follow your intuition.

THAT FIRST PROMOTION

No matter how high you may rise in life, there is never any change that will so much influence your way of being with others as your first management promotion. Suddenly, and usually with little preparation for it, your peers are no longer friends but employees. That is an uncontrovertible fact. You can call them friendly employees or whatever you wish, but once you have the power of management, you are seen differently. You are no longer one of the gang, you are one of "them." This change is so powerful that some people quit supervisory jobs, or avoid promotion.

Another separating factor in the relationship between the new supervisor and former friends is the sometimes dramatic change in interests. While the old gang reads the sports page the new boss is reading about the introduction of the Japanese management style to the American business scene. The woman who used to attend PTA meetings after work gives up her old friends to attend business school two nights a week while she is working toward her master's in business administration. These changes are inevitable. Accept them as part of your transition. The members of the old gang who feel good about themselves will wish you well. The ones who don't will project their faults on you, and there is no sense giving yourself bad feelings in letting go of relationships with such people.

The next rocky point for the fledgling manager or business owner comes with the awareness of becoming a judge of others' attitudes and actions. Performance appraisal, formal or informal, is an absolute necessity for those with the responsibility for getting the job done. This judgmental task is so distasteful, and so frequently neglected, one national corporation tells its employees to *demand* performance appraisals. The trick is to be a boss without being bossy. It is not a time to be listening to messages out of your childhood programming that say:

- Don't be critical. Who do you think you are?
- If you can't speak well of someone, don't speak at all.
- Don't be uppity.

When you are faced for the first time with the often stressful task of evaluating a fellow human being, think of yourself as a coach and concentrate on a constructive approach. You cannot motivate anyone, but you can inspire them and facilitate their self-motivation.

Whatever you do, when you get that first promotion or hire your first employee take it upon yourself to learn more about human behavior in the work situation. In using that information it is important for you to know which leadership style is appropriate for you. In *The OK Boss*, Muriel James lists seven such styles: critic, coach, shadow, analyst, pacifier, fighter, and inventor. She also says, "Each behavior style has its not-OK side and OK side."[1] You can greatly increase your effectiveness as a leader in your organization or business by examining your belief systems and changing your attitude from "Do what I say because I said it" to "Let's see how we can work this out together."

The positive fringe benefit is that the techniques that are helpful in business are also helpful in the encouragement of family teamwork.

THE MARITAL TEAM

Fortunate is the pair that can work together in harmony. Harmony is the consequence of mutual respect and a win/win ambiance. It is based on a contract, implied or explicit, as to who does what, and who is responsible for what. An unharmonious arrangement was clearly expressed by a woman selling Mexican pottery at a flea market. Rather sadly she said, "How come I'm doing this and keeping books when he and his partner go to Mexico and do the buying?" That's one-up/one-down situation.

When married couples engage in joint ventures it is very easy to fall into the "Me Tarzan, you Jane" relationship unless there has been an explicit contract agreed upon. Despite all the advances of the feminists in recent years, the programming of many women leads them to accept the myth that the male is the boss. It also leads some men to shouldering heavier burdens of responsibility than they prefer. The ideal arrangement is found by an open exchange of views and honest communication. When that happens the friction arising from constant togetherness, on the job and off, can be alleviated. One of the greatest problems in partnerships occurs when both partners want the same job, mainly to be the top dog, the one out front who meets the public. That leaves no one to do the administrative and clerical work. When that happens, dissension is automatic. However, if those issues are negotiated, nontraditional roles may be the result. In one very successful real estate firm the wife does the selling and the husband stays in the back office to handle the paperwork.

Contracts are essential to harmony in the dual-career team with the wife and husband pursuing separate careers. All the goodies two incomes will buy are not worth it if one member of the team is feeling put-upon. You've read about contractual communications earlier in this book, but here's a special, and very positive, action that will be helpful to the dual-career team. Write out a list of your hopes and expectations.

Do your lists separately without consulting each other. The purpose is to reveal the facts and eliminate assumptions. Take your time doing this. When the lists are complete, arrange a time when you can discuss them without interruption. Don't let the discussion be an argument—no judgments and no evaluations—just clarification to each other's position. Then leave it at that for a week or two, making additions or deletions from your lists.

The next session will be one for mediation and negotiation. It is a time for exploring old messages that might interfere with a harmonious relationship. One liberated male wanted his wife to be his equal in their business of promoting and presenting seminars. One day she said, "I don't want to be equal. I'm not comfortable in public. Just let me stay home and answer the phone, do the mail, write the letters, and pay the bills." He realized he'd been pushing her in order to enhance his image as a "modern man." Now they have a comfortable and successful marriage and business.

One strong motivation for many men and women who decide on joint ventureship is the desire to enrich the quality of their family life. Having more control of their time, they can arrange for one or the other to be with the kids. For many women this means they can have the self-esteem they need by being workers and also the good feelings that come from motherhood. Children learn from parents who work for themselves, and can earn their spending money helping out. Ideally, they will find that work can be fun, one of the greatest gifts a child can receive.

EXAMINE YOUR MYTHS

Taking positive action to manage your life directions requires the examination of many myths that were perhaps once true, but that now are still around only because of the power of repetition. Here are some myths you might consider reject-ing because they are tempting material for the Inner Saboteur to work with:

Over the Hill

Forget it. The only people who are over the hill because of age are those who have chosen to be that way. There are thousands of the "over forties" enrolled in college courses throughout the nation. Some seek self-understanding, some want higher degrees of competence in their current careers, some are training for change or second careers, some are simply fulfilling a long-suppressed curiosity about the world and the people in it. They are exploding the myth of sociogenic programming about aging: "You can't teach an old dog new tricks." Not only can an "old dog" learn new tricks, infla-tion and changes in pension and Social Security laws demand the learning of new tricks!

Anyone who is forty and neglects thinking ahead is not looking out for his or her own best interests. Of course, the forties can be a busy time: Turning points are passed so rapidly they easily can be ignored, children leave home, marriages are disrupted, promotions slip by, and the hills get a little steeper. Anyone who reaches age fifty and is not doing serious thinking about planning for the Golden Years runs a high risk that those years will turn to dross.

Certainly when you were young it was true that the race goes to the swift, but remember that only applies to the short distances. Over the long haul, stamina and faith can keep you among the front runners. Get the word "old" out of your vocabulary. Don't dwell on little aches and pains. Recognize that your body needs a little more attention and maintenance, but don't be morbid about it.

Set new goals and get excited about achieving them. Excite-ment generates energy and is fundamental to revitalization. What have you been doing so long and so regularly that it bores you? Give it up. Get into some new activities that

excite you, maybe some long-disregarded dream like being a
painter, writer, poet or carpenter. Besides energizing your life
you might find a road to a new career and life-style. You
might also be developing an ace in the hole against the
always threatening possibility that you will be the victim of
the business culture's myth about old dogs and new tricks.

The years after fifty can be a wonderful and beautiful time
for those who take and accept responsibility for seeing to it
that their "ship comes in."

The Peter Principle

Remember that one? "In a hierarchy every employee tends
to rise to his or her level of incompetence." The fallacy in
that statement in that it assumes it applies to everyone. Some
employees continue increasing their competence to the day of
retirement. Maybe the key word in this myth is "hierarchy."
People who want to go on growing in the sense of personal
development tend to get out of the hierarchy and find a
structure that is supportive of their needs.

Competence is a matter of choice. It is also a matter of
interest. There is little incentive to seek additional competence when work is dull and boring. The motivation for competence can be taken for granted when work is interesting and
fun. If the Peter Principle applies to you, maybe you are in
the wrong job. Only you are responsible for that. Dreaming
about pie in the sky after retirement is a scary substitute for
having work without meaning.

CREDIT CARDS

Tear them up. Throw them away. The only appropriate
need for a credit card is for those who drive a lot and need it
for gasoline, or those who have business expenses they need

to keep listed separately from personal ones. Use cash, checks or charge accounts when necessary.

This is not an argument against credit. Credit is an appropriate means of doing business when buying a house, a car, or a "big ticket" item like a refrigerator, or paying off a hospital bill. Credit is not appropriate when it simply satisfies the impulse or massages the ego. One young lad, watching his father pay for an expensive dinner with a credit card and sign the charge slip with a grandiose flourish, said, "Dad, don't you even look at the amount?" Not considering the amount is the reason that so many people earning between $25,000 and $45,000 annually are forced into bankruptcy each year. Many literally worry themselves sick. If you are one, stop it. Operating on a cash basis will hurt for a while, but you'll soon get used to it and even feel good about your ability to handle money. Happiness is more important than a big-screen TV set.

Managing your life constructively includes the prudent management of money. Don't confuse the word "prudent" with "stingy." They are not the same. Keep in mind that incompetence in handling financing probably brings on as many illnesses and family problems as it does business failures. Your health and your family are just as much your business as your career. Eliminating money-related stress is good business in all departments of your life.

GIVING YOURSELF AWAY

Smile at a stranger. Help an old lady across the street. Be an active member of a community agency. Make gadgets and give them to agencies for rummage sales. Be a part-time people helper.

Make a contribution to your world. That world will give it back and a little extra to boot. This may sound old-fashioned, but it is really a part of childhood programming and buried in the belief systems of many of us who were taught, "You are your brother's keeper." To give yourself away, within reason, makes you a harbor open to all the good things going on in your world.

Dottie Walters is one of the most successful, and busiest, women in the world. She has never forgotten what it's meant to her to become responsible for her own life and bring herself out of the bog of adversity. She always makes time for an encouraging word to another.

Dottie speaks internationally, publishes *Anthologies of Inspiration*, and publishes *Sharing Ideas*, a newsletter to help people in the public speaking business. Helping others is a part of her policy for positive living. She says, "As part of a psychological round table one day, the leader asked each of us to compose our own epitaph. Mine was: 'She inspired us.' What greater reward is there in life than to see other people's visions, and to help them pile idea on idea until their dream castles take form and shape? To help others is such fun and so rewarding. I do it because I love to. No game or sport ever invented is half so thrilling."

WRITE A PERSONAL POLICY FOR YOUR LIFE

There is magic in the written word when it applies to you. A personal policy for your life is a statement of purpose, philosophy, and ethics. It forces you to think out in specific terms what your life is all about, the meaning you want it to have for you. It also commits you to taking positive action. Somehow the act of writing out a personal policy for life has a power that is often dissipated when expressed orally. The spoken word drifts away and is often lost to memory. The written word is a lasting testament of your decision and choice of destiny.

Here's an example of having a personal policy for successful living. At age twenty-six, Mark Victor Hansen was bankrupt, and the only way for him was up. Mark says, "It may be uncomfortable to be down, but there's nothing bad about it. The only bad is staying down." In seven years Mark has gone from scratch to six figures a year. He's in constant demand as an inspirational-motivational speaker and averages $1,500 an appearance. That's a big change in only seven years for a young man who once parked his beat-up old Volkswagon two blocks from a prospect's office for fear he'd been seen in it.

Here's Mark's policy for work and life. "My purpose is to entertain, enliven, enlighten, encourage, and enrich as many lives as possible without sacrificing my personal integrity or personal freedom." And he means that. He refuses to be involved in business transactions that might diminish his integrity. He constantly strives to improve the effectiveness of his time management so he may have the personal freedom he demands for himself. Mark has written a book called *Future Diary*, which sold over 20,000 copies in its first year. In it the reader lists the things he or she wants to do and what to do to get them. His own *Future Diary* has 371 pages of goals. When he accomplishes one he writes next to it, "Victory," thereby moving from success to success.

Life is wonderful for those who know where they are going. An important step for everyone who would like to know a little more about their destination is to write a policy for personal living. Make it short. Make it specific. Make it fit your need for economic reward, your desire for rich human relationships, and the way in which you connect with your community. Make it compatible with your principles and ethics. Whatever you do, make it. Nothing will help you more in clarifying your mission, your calling, or your role in life.

Appendix

Which Way Next?

The only way to get where you're going is to take the next step. No one can take it for you. Others have been your way before you. When you stumble don't shy away from seeking a guide.

Winners do what they need to do to get the job done. If, after three months, six months, a year, you are not moving forward toward your goals, don't hesitate to seek help from others who have been the way before you or who have special training to help others make constructive change. There are many people who have difficulty translating book learning into action but who, with the help of a teacher, are able to use their new knowledge. It's like the fellow who said, "I understand the book. My problem is, I don't *do it*."

Here are the names of some sources that can assist in finding people who can help in learning how to *do it:*

The Association of Humanistic Psychology
325 Ninth Street
San Francisco, CA 94103

The AHP membership is composed of people interested in expanding human potential. They can provide you with the names and addresses of centers in your area where a variety of programs may be offered to facilitate personal growth.

Impact
Box 1094
San Luis Obispo, CA 93406

You can write Impact for information about assertiveness training.

International Transactional Analysis Association
1772 Vallejo Street
San Francisco, CA 94123

The ITAA has rigorous standards for accredited practitioners of transactional analysis. It will provide you with the names of people, institutes, or centers where basic training in TA is offered. Special Interest Members teach applications of TA to education, business, and interpersonal communications. Clinical Members are therapists.

Career Planning and Adult Development Network
1190 South Bascom Avenue, Suite 211
San José, CA 95128

This is a national group of people who may one day be classified as "life organizers," offering assistance in an area that lies between formal education and psychotherapy. Some are exclusively career counselors; others facilitate personal growth. Though they are too new for a formal philosophy or policy, their general goal is to help people get a grip on their career directions, because such people are more effective in management, both on and off the job, than those who do not know their directions.

National YMCA
Program Resources
6400 Shafer Court
Rosemount, IL 60018

The YMCA has a family Communication Skills Center. It offers training programs in marital communications and parenting. You may obtain information on these programs from your local YMCA or YWCA.

Western Institute for Group and Family Therapy
262 Gaffey Road
Watsonville, CA 95076

Hundreds of therapists in the United States have been trained at this institute in redecision therapy. The goal is to show people how to help themselves by discovering their life scripts (childhood programming), understanding the negative aspects of those scripts, and effectively making new decisions. If you write WIGFT it will provide you with the name of a redecision therapist in your area.

Wherever you expect to receive help from another human being, whether mate, friend, mentor, teacher, counselor, or therapist. keep one absolute rule in mind: Unless you have specifically asked for advice, carefully avoid those who talk in terms of "you should" or "you ought to." Tolerate it if you wish from someone close to you, but make your own decisions. Put up with it from a teacher if you must to earn credits for a class. Even go along with it from a mentor if you can keep your sense of autonomy intact. However, it is inappropriate for a counselor or therapist to lay his or her trip upon you. After all, your goal is to live your life the way you "want," not to exchange one set of "shoulds" for another.

Glossary

Words can be unreliable as a tool for communication, because meanings vary from mind to mind. In order to transfer the meaning in *my* mind to *your* mind, I want you to know what I mean by certain words used in this book. They may or may not conform to the meanings others have placed upon them.

belief system the perceptions one has of self, others, and the world, and his/her personal rules of life

biocomputer the mental mechanism that processes information and has the capacity to solve problems and make decisions

childhood programming the development in childhood of a belief system that is based on external influences and internal decisions concerning those influences

crooked language unspecific statements or questions that begin with words like "I think I might," "Don't you think that," "What do you think of," or "What do you think about." Crooked language is a cloak for hidden agendas.

Games with a capital G, as in Eric Berne's *Games People Play*. My definition: any dialogue or action that results in bad feelings or inappropriate good feelings such as "winning" an argument. Inappropriate good feelings usually lead to later bad feelings such as anxiety, guilt, or depression.

garbage as in "garbage in, garbage out"; negative information that diminishes the capacity of the human computer to solve problems and make decisions appropriately.

growth increase in one's competence in life and career skills

Inner Saboteur the internal demon that feeds garbage into the human computer

life script a plan for life decided on in childhood that positively or negatively influences attitudes, feelings, and behaviors in adulthood. Such influences are usually outside of current awareness.

prosperity an abundance of physical, psychological, spiritual, communal, familial, and economic resources.

specificity semantic responsibility: saying clearly, directly, and consistently what your needs are, rather than using language as a tool to avoid intimacy or cover over your own fears

straight language specific statements or questions that begin with words like "I want," "I will," "I need," or "I won't"

strokes physical or psychological recognition. Strokes can be self-administered or other-administered

transformation the consequence of constructive change in a belief system

unconscious childhood learning that has been integrated into a belief system but has been forgotten and is outside of current awareness

Your World your personal world, the people environment with which you interact

Notes

Chapter 1

1. Joe Graedon, *The People's Pharmacy—2* (New York: Avon, 1980).
2. David D. Burns, M.D., *Feeling Good: The New Mood Therapy* (New York: Morrow, 1980).
3. Thomas A. Harris, M.D. *I'm OK—You're OK* (New York: Harper & Row, 1969).

Chapter 2

1. Wendell Johnson, *People in Quandaries* (New York: Harper & Brothers, 1945), p. 15.
2. Ibid., p. 11.
3. Ibid., p. 7.

Chapter 3

1. Eric Berne, *Principles of Group Treatment* (New York: Oxford University Press, 1966)

Chapter 6

1. Eric Berne, *Games People Play* (New York: Grove Press, 1964).
2. Roberto Assagioli, *The Act of Will* (New York: Viking, 1973), p. 10.
3. Franklin H. Ernest, Jr., "The OK Corall: The Grid for Get on With," *Transactional Analysis Journal*, Vol. 1, No. 4 (October, 1971), p. 33.

4. Mary McClure Goulding and Robert L. Goulding, *Changing Lives Through Redecision Therapy* (New York: Brunner/Mazel, 1979), p. 6.

Chapter 8

1. Abraham H. Maslow, *Motivation and Personality* (New York: Harper & Row, 1954).

Chapter 9

1. Albert Mehrabian, "Communications Without Words," *Psychology Today*, September 1968.

Chapter 11

1. Charles Garfield, "How to Achieve Peak Performance," handout for a Peak Performance Workshop, May 30, 1981, First Unitarian Church, San Francisco, California.
2. Herbert Benson, *The Relaxation Response* (New York: Morrow, 1975).
3. Stanley Woollams, M.D., personal correspondence, October 15, 1981.

Chapter 12

1. Hans Selye, interview with Laurence Cherry, "On the Real Benefits of Eustress," *Psychology Today*, March 1978, p. 60.
2. Hans Selye, *The Stress of Life* (New York: McGraw-Hill, 1956), p. 66.
3. Selye interview with Cherry, p. 63.
4. Barbara Brown, *Supermind: The Ultimate Energy* (New York: Harper & Row, 1980), p. 269.
5. Selye interview with Cherry, p. 60.
6. Mildred Carter, *Helping Yourself with Foot Reflexology* (West Nyack, NY: Parker, 1969).
7. Robert Keith Wallace, "Physiological Effects of Transcendental Meditation," *Science*, Vol 167 (March 1970), pp. 1751–54.
8. Tom Mach, "How to Cope with the Stress of Writing," *Writer's Digest*, July 1981, p. 22.

Chapter 13

1. Eric Berne, *What Do You Say After You say Hello?* (New York: Grove Press, 1972), p. 443.

2. Aaron T. Beck, *Cognitive Therapy and the Emotional Disorders* (New York: International Universities Press, 1976), p. 3.
3. Edward Ziegler, "*Think* Your Way Out of Depression" *Reader's Digest*, December 1980.
4. Roger Gould, *Transformations: Growth and Change in Adult Life* (New York: Simon & Schuster, 1978), p. 15.
5. Mary McClure Goulding and Robert L. Goulding, *Changing Lives Through Redecision Therapy* (New York: Brunner/Mazel, 1979) p. 3.

Chapter 14

1. Jay Levinson, personal correspondence, July 30, 1980.
2. Benjamin B. Wolman, *Victims of Success: Emotional Problems of Executives* (New York: Quadrangle/New York Times Book Co., 1973), p. 68.

Chapter 15

1. Don M. Dible, *Up Your Own Organization* (Santa Clara, Calif.: Entrepreneur Press, 1971), p. 41.

Chapter 16

1. Wendell Johnson, *People in Quandaries* (New York: Harper & Brothers, 1945), pp. 14–15.
2. Donald B. Miller, *Personal Vitality* (Reading, Mass.: Addison-Wesley, 1977), p. 179.
3. Sidney M. Jourard, *The Transparent Self* (Princeton, N.J.: Van Nostrand, 1964), p. 42.

Chapter 17

1. Muriel James, *The OK Boss* (Reading, Mass.: Addison-Wesley, 1975), p. 8.

Bibliography

Adams, Ramona S., Ott, Herbert A., and Cowley, Audeane S.
Letting Go: Uncomplicating Your Life. New York: Macmillan, 1980.

Alberti, Robert E., and Emmons, Michael L. *Your Perfect Right*.
San Luis Obispo, Calif.: Impact, 1970.

Assagioli, Robert. *The Act of Will*. New York: Viking, 1973.

Beck, Aaron T. *Cognitive Therapy and the Emotional Disorders*.
New York: International Universities, Press, 1975.

Benson, Herbert. *The Relaxation Response*. New York: Morrow,
1975.

Berne, Eric. *Games People Play*. New York: Grove, 1964.

——. *Principles of Group Treatment*. New York: Oxford University Press, 1966.

——. *What Do You Say After You Say Hello?* New York: Grove,
1972.

Bolles, Richard N. *The Three Boxes of Life*. Berkeley, Calif.:
Ten Speed Press, 1978.

Brown, Barbara. *Supermind: The Ultimate Energy*. New York:
Harper & Row, 1980.

Coudert, Jo. *Advice from a Failure*, New York: Stein & Day,
1965.

Dible, Donald M. *Up Your Own Organization*. Santa Clara,
Calif.: Entrepreneur, 1971.

Fast, Julius. *Body Language*. New York: Evans, 1970.

Gawain, Shakti. *Creative Visualization*. Mill Valley, Calif.: Whatever Publishing, 1978.

Glasser, William. *Reality Therapy*. New York: Harper & Row,
1965.

Goble, Frank. *The Third Force*. New York: Grossman, 1970.

Gordon, Thomas. *Leadership Effectiveness Training*. New York: Peter H. Wyden, 1977.

Gould, Roger L. *Transformations: Growth and Change in Adult Life*. New York: Simon & Schuster, 1978.

Goulding, Mary McClure, and Goulding, Robert L. *Changing Lives Through Redecision Therapy*. New York: Brunner/ Mazel, 1979.

Hanxen, Mark Victor. *How to Achieve Total Prosperity*. Newport Beach, Calif.: M. V. Hansen Associates, 1981.

Harris, Thomas A. *I'm OK—You're OK*. New York: Harper & Row, 1969.

Hill, Napoleon. *Think and Grow Rich*, rev. ed. New York: Fawcett, 1960.

Hooper, Doug. *You Are What You Think*. Danville, Calif.: Hooper, 1980.

Humphreys, Christmas. *Walk On*. Wheaton, Ill.: Theosophical Publishing House, 1947.

James, Muriel. *The OK Boss*. Reading, Mass.: Addison-Wesley, 1975.

Jacobsen, Edmund. *You Must Relax*. New York: McGraw-Hill, 1934.

Johnson, Wendell. *People in Quandaries*. New York: Harper & Brothers, 1946.

Jongeward, Dorothy, and James, Muriel. *Born to Win*. Reading. Mass.: Addison-Wesley, 1971.

Jongeward, Dorothy, and Scott, Dru. *Women as Winners*. Reading, Mass.: Addison-Wesley, 1976.

Jourard, Sidney. *The Transparent Self*. Princeton, N.J.: Van Nostrand, 1964.

Lakein, Alan. *How to Get Control of Your Time and Your Life*. New York: Peter H. Wyden, 1973.

Levinson, Daniel J., Darrow, Charlotte N., Klein, Edward B., Levinson, Maria H., and McKee, Braxton. *Seasons of a Man's life*. New York: Knopf, 1978.

Levinson, Jay Conrad. *Earning Money Without a Job: The Economics of Freedom*. New York: Holt, Rinehart & Winston, 1979.

Lozanov, Georgi. *Suggestology and Outlines of Suggestopedy*. New York: Gordon and Breach, 1978.

Lynch, James. J. *The Broken Heart: The Medical Consequences of Loneliness*. New York: Basic Books, 1977.

Maltz, Maxwell. *Psycho-Cybernetics*, Englewood Cliffs, N.J.: Prentice-Hall, 1960.

Maslow, Abraham H. *Motivation and Personality*. New York: Harper & Row, 1954.

Meininger, Jut. *Success Through Transactional Analysis*. New York: Grosset & Dunlap, 1973.

Miller, Donald. *Personal Vitality*. Reading, Mass.: Addison-Wesley, 1977.

Nirenberg, Jesse S. *Getting Through to People*. Englewood Cliffs, N.J.: Prentice-Hall, 1963.

Oyle, Irving. *The Healing Mind*. Milbrae, Calif.: Celestial Arts, 1975.

Peale, Normal Vincent. *The Power of Positive Thinking*. Englewood Cliffs, N.J.: Prentice-Hall, 1952.

Perls, Frederick S. *Ego, Hunger and Aggression*. New York: Random House, 1969.

———. *Gestalt Therapy Verbatim*. Lafayette, Calif.: Real People Press, 1969.

Potter, Beverly A. *Beating Job Burnout*. San Francisco, Calif.: Harbor Publishing, 1980.

Satir, Virginia, *Peoplemaking*. Palo Alto, Calif.: Science and Behavior Books, 1972.

Schiffman, Muriel. *Self Therapy: Techniques for Personal Growth*. Menlo Park, Calif.: Self-published, 1967.

Selye, Hans. *The Stress of Life*. New York: McGraw-Hill, 1956.

Steiner, Claude M. *Scripts People Live*. New York: Grove, 1974.

Stevens, Barry. *Don't Push the River (It Flows by Itself)*. Lafayette, Calif.: Real People Press, 1970.

Rogers, Carl. *On Becoming a Person*. Boston, Mass.: Houghton Mifflin, 1951.

Toffler, Alvin. *Future Shock*, New York: Random House, 1970.

———. *The Third Wave*. New York: Morrow, 1980.

White, Earl. *Nourishing Self Esteem*. Capitola, Calif.: Whitenwife, 1981.

Wolman, Benjamin B. *Victims of Success: Emotional Problems of Executives*. New York: Quadrangle/New York Times Book Co., 1973.

Yankelovich, Daniel. *New Rules: Searching for Self-Fulfillment in a World Turned Upside Down*. New York: Random House, 1981.

Index

Action, 78, 98–99
    see also Positive action
Act of Will, The (Assagioli),
    82
Adaptors, 104–05, 114
Affirmations, 158–59
Aggressiveness, 61
Amway Corporation, 214–15
Archer, Jules, 228–29
"Are you willing?", 147–48
"As if" principle, 30–31
Assagioli, Robert, 82
Assertiveness, 61
Attentiveness, 59–60
Attitude modification,
    185–91

Beck, Dr. Aaron T., 179
Behavior modification,
    184–85
Belief systems, 83, 137–39
Benson, Dr. Herbert, 153–54
Berne, Eric, 35, 143, 179
Blaming others, 4, 19–21
Body awareness, 183
Body language, 122–123, 126,
    138–39
Brown, Barbara, 167
Burns, Dr. David D., 4, 179

Campbell, Dr. Coyne, 29
Career Script questionnaire,
    37–50
Carter, Mildred, 173
Change, constructive, 229–37

*Changing Lives Through
    Redecision Therapy*
    (Goulding and Goulding),
    87, 180
Childhood programming,
    13–14, 19, 20, 35,
    37–50, 85–86, 97, 128
    see also Life scripts
Clarification, 136, 139
Clearing your mind, 153–157
Communications, positive, 61,
    117–50
    positive listening, 132–50
Constructive change,
    229–237
Continuing education,
    227–28
Contracts, 89, 90, 96,
    134–37, 141–42, 148–49
Corner game, 144–45
Crooked messages, 142–47,
    148
Coué, Emile, 65
Conditioned response, 27
Cousins, Norman, 8
Creative expression, 228–29
Credit cards, 254–55
Criticism, handling, 19–23,
    40–41
Cromwell, Dean, 161
Cross, Wilbur, 228

Decisions, 6–9, 77, 95–96
Defensiveness, 19–21
Depression, 4, 22–23

Destiny, self-determination of your, 3–15, 25–26, 82
"Destiny and Script Choices," 36–37
DeVos, Rich, 214–15
Dible, Don, 215–16
Doubt and action, 98–99

Earning Money Without a Job: The Economics of Freedom (Levinson), 201
Either/or syndrome, 30
Elliot, Austin M., 220
Entrepreneurs, 211–13

Facts, separating feelings from, 136–37
Feeling Good (Burns), 179
Feelings:
 Career Script questionnaire, 38–50
 choosing to change, 87–88
 recognizing patterns, 14–15, 37–40
 self-defeating, 187–91
 separating facts from, 136–37
First promotion, 249–50
First step, taking the, 99
Foot reflexology, 173
Frustration/irritation pattern, 36
Frying-Pan types, 104, 108–11
Future Diary (Hansen), 256–57
Future projects, 159–60

Games, 143–47
Games People Play (Berne), 36, 143
Garbage in—garbage out, 24–25, 140
Garfield, Charles, 52, 152, 162
Gawain, Shakti, 159
Geller, Uri, 64

Getting started, taking responsibility for, 94–96
Glossary, 261
Gould, Dr. Roger L., 179–80
Goulding, Mary and Bob, 87, 180

Haiberg, Dr. Gordon, 36–37
Hansen, Mark Victor, 257
Harris, Dr. Thomas A., 7
Health, 202
Helping others, 255–57
 organizations devoted to, 258–60
Helping Yourself with Foot Reflexology (Carter), 173
High intensity level of internal conflict, 71–72
How to Get Control of Your Time and Your Life (Lakein), 241
Human programming, 5, 24–25
 reprogramming, 5, 6–9, 157–61

IFD disease, 223–24
If It Weren't For . . . . game, 144
I'm OK—You're OK (Harris), 7
Independents, 209–12
Inner Saboteur, 16–34, 49, 65, 96–97, 217–21
Interpretation of stimulus, 6–7
Investing in yourself, 241–43
"I will" and "I won't," 33, 93–94

Jacobsen, Dr. Edmund, 170
Johnson, Wendell, 32, 92–93, 223
Jourad, Sidney, M., 228

Kennedy, John F., 202
Kick Me, or Stupid game, 144

Lakein, Alan, 241
Learning how to learn,
    247–48
Levinson, Jay, 201
Life scripts, 13, 36–37, 181–83
    questionnaire, 37–50
    see also Childhood
    programming
Listening, positive, 132–50
Looking back to see ahead,
    35–50
Low intensity level of
    internal conflict, 68–69

Mach, Tom, 177
Marital team, 251–52
Maturity and growth, 222–37
Meditation, 173
Medium intensity level of
    internal conflict, 69–70
Mehrabian, Albert, 123
Miller, Donald B., 227
Mind management, 151–63
Models for change, 102–14,
    243
Mood swings, mastering,
    178–93
Motivation, 77, 79–88
Myths, examining your, 252–54

Natural response, 6
Negative action, 68
Negative thinking, 66–67, 68,
    84, 99, 119–20, 183–84
Now I've Got You, You SOB
    game, 145–47

Only-Road-Is-Up types, 104,
    105–108
Open-mindedness, 54–55
Organization, 77, 89–101
Over the Hill myth, 253–54

Parents, *see* Childhood
    programming; Life scripts
Payoffs, examining your,
    83–84

Peale, Norman Vincent, 65
People in Quandaries
    (Johnson), 32, 92, 223
Performance appraisal,
    personal, 224–226
Permission to prosper, 194–206
Persecutor role, 48
Persistence, 59, 101
Personality, model of, 9–12
Personal policy for your life,
    256–57
Personal Vitality (Miller), 227
Peter Principle, 254
Pictorialization, 160–61
Positive action, 64–78,
    238–57
Positive communications,
    61–62, 117–50
Positive listening, 132–50
Positive self-imagery, 56–57
Positive thinking, 58, 66,
    67–68, 76
Potent person, how to be a,
    51–63
Powerlessness, 227
Power of Positive Thinking
    (Peale), 65
Praise, 40, 81, 248
Predictions, 45–48
Problem(s):
    clear statement of, 92–93
    -solving, 42–43, 244–47
Programmed response, 27–29
Programming, *see* Human
    programming
Progressive relaxation, 170–72
Projection of blame on
    others, 19–20
Promotion, first, 249–50
Prosperity, New, 194–206
Public speaking, fear of, 41

Qubein, Nido, 15

Relaxation, 101, 170–72
Relaxation Response, The
    (Benson), 153

Reprogramming, 5, 6–9, 36, 157
Rescuer role, 48
Resourcefulness, 58–59, 238
Response, 6
Responsibility, self-, 33, 94–96
Roosevelt, Franklin D., 62

Sabotage, see Inner Saboteur
Sales people, 209
Sefness, W. R., 36
Self-affirmation, 158–59
Self-awareness, 53–54
Self-defeating programs, 203–06
Self-determination of your destiny, 25–26
Self-direction, 55–56
Self-employment, 207–221
Self-esteem, low, 190
Self-imagery, 56–57, 121, 160–61
Self-massage, 172–73
Self-motivation, 77, 79–88, 95
Self-responsibility, 33–34, 94–96
Self-truth, 9
Selye, Hans, 166–67
Semantics, 32–33, 80, 127
Specificity in communication, 124, 127, 134, 135
Stagnation and burnout, 222–23
Stein, Gertrude, 29–30
Steinbeck, John, 177
Stimulus, 5
Stop-Think technique, 174–76
Storage, 6
Straight messages, 142, 148
Stress, 164–77
Stroking, 23, 248
Supermind (Brown), 167

Thackeray, William, 101
Theme of your life, 48

Thought awareness, 184
Time:
 and the New Prosperity, 200–02
 structuring, 239–41
Transformations (Gould), 179–80
Transition, 78, 102–14
Transparent Self (Jourad), 228

Up Your Own Organization (Dible), 216

Van Andel, Jay, 214–15
Victim role, 48–49
Victims of Success (Wolman), 203
Videotape training, 130
Visualizing your future, 91–92
Vitality, 62–63
Vocal tone, 124–26, 137–39

Wallace, Dr. Robert Keith, 173
Walters, Dottie, 256
Wanderers, 104, 111–12
Wanting, 80–81
Western Institute for Group and Family Therapy, 87
What Do You Say After You Say Hello? (Berne), 179
Will, exercising your, 81–82
Willingness, 80–81, 84–85
Wishing, 80–81
Wolman, Dr. Benjamin B., 203
Woollams, Dr. Stanley, 162–63
Words, see Communications, positive
Work, attitudes towards, 43–45, 198–200

Yes, But game, 144

From the MENTOR Executive Library

(0451)

Buy them at your local

bookstore or use coupon

on next page for ordering.

MENTOR Titles of Interest

YOU CAN MAKE YOUR FUTURE
BETTER THAN YOUR PAST

HOW TO BE A POTENT PERSON

3 STEPS TO SELF-RESPONSIBILITY

WORDS THAT CAN MAKE OR BREAK YOU

14 KEY POINTS TO
BUILDING A POSITIVE LIFE SCRIPT

MANAGING YOUR MIND
TO IMPROVE YOUR HEALTH

INCREASING COMPETENCE
AND SELF-CONFIDENCE

AND COUNTLESS OTHER WAYS TO REPROGRAM
YOURSELF FOR THE SUCCESS YOU WANT

DARE TO CHANGE

"CLEAR, USEFUL, TIMELY…
A BOOK WORTH READING."
—MURIEL JAMES
CO-AUTHOR OF *BORN TO WIN*

"PRACTICAL, WORKABLE…GOES BEHIND
THE USUAL PLATITUDES TO
THE HEART OF SELF-IMPROVEMENT."
—PAUL J. MEYER, PRESIDENT,
SUCCESS MOTIVATION INSTITUTE

ISBN 0-451-13523-7